Dalit Literature:
Journey from Repression to Resistance

Dalit Literature:
Journey from Repression to Resistance

Edited by
Dr S. Chelliah
Dr Bijender Singh

KALPAZ

First Published, 2019

Published by

Kalpaz Publications
C-30, Satyawati Nagar,
Delhi – 110052
Ph.: 011-47034999, 9811692060
www.kalpazpublications.com
E-mail: kalpaz@hotmail.com

Printed at: G. Print Process, Delhi

Cataloging in Publication Data—DK
Courtesy: D.K. Agencies (P) Ltd. <docinfo@dkagencies.com>

Dalit literature : journey from repression to resistance / edited by Dr S. Chelliah, Dr Bijender SIngh.
pages cm
Contributed articles.
ISBN 9789353240523

1. Indic literature—20th century—History and criticism.
2. Dalits in literature. I. Chelliah, S., editor. II. Singh, Bijender, editor.

LCC PK5410.D35C44 2019 | DDC 891.4 23

Contents

Foreword

> A Dalit history of caste politics brings into view a wider set of relationships – those between state, caste and community, between nation and minority, and ultimately, between the religious and the political. The history of how untouchables became Dalits is the story of how alterations in the social relations of caste became central to debates about equality and discrimination.
>
> (Rao, *The Caste Question* 7)

Dalit Literature is the literature of the marginalised classes in India. Basically, Dalit means a person who hails from the lowest stratum of the society. Dalits have been beleaguered since ages and they have been deprived of the basic human rights. Dalits were erstwhile known from different names in different ages and in the modern time also, they are living their life much segregated and demurred from the mainstream society. The Indian Constitution has safeguarded their rights but there is no any so-called becoming rule in the society to give them back their lost prestige and the status of equality. Even today Dalits are "Bahiskrit Bharat".

In South Africa, the policy of the Apartheid also segregated white people from the blacks. Even their demesnes were separated. Nelson Mandela put a check on this abominable policy which divided the human beings into classes and deprived the other human beings of their basic rights. In India also, most of Dalits living in the rural areas are still deprived of the equal rights. They live in the separate places from the upper caste people and their main occupation is labour. Their children have to go to the government schools for education and they have to march towards the government hospitals for the medical facilities. Most of the Dalits, in the 21th century also don't have the basic amenities in their houses.

Dr Bhimrao Ambedkar's contribution played a pivotal role in improving their status, providing them equal status and giving them equal opportunities in the government services. Many social reformers like Dr B.R. Ambedkar, Swami Achhutanand, Jyotiba Phule, Savitribai Phule etc. worked for Dalit upliftment and left no stone unturned in providing them equal status.

Swami Achhutanand 'Harihar' was a major Dalit social reformer and Dalit awakener. His real name was Heeralal. He removed the darkness from the eyes of Dalits because he could get equal education because his father was in the British Army before the Independence of India. He got a good knowledge of English and Urdu. He joined Arya Samaj under the influence of Swami Sachchidanand in 1905 and deeply studied the Vedas and Satyarth Prakash by Swami Dayanand but he realised in 1912 that even the leaders of Arya Samaj had the Brahminic tendencies and he found them hypocrite. After that he started criticising Arya Samaj from 1912 to 1917. He started Aadi Hindu Revolution in 1922 for the upliftment of Dalits through his newspaper *Adi Hindu*. He organised around two hundred conferences all over India. The purpose of these conferences was to provide equal rights to Dalits.

Dalits have to contend with many problems in their lives. Dalit suppression, humiliation and atrocity are main problems in India. The upper caste people pressurise them and exploit them. Dr C.D. Naik comments:

> How atrocities are augmented under reform regime? There were no atrocities of the kind Dalits experienced during this saner globalisation period. They are in the form of physical punishment as Dalit minds are enlightened enough to thwart dominant's subjugation....Thus atrocities are dependent on the factors of dependence on middle castes powered further by reform boost to caste system of inequality reinforced by reduction in jobs, deteriorating health care, expensive education and biased income distribution and so on. Has the new reform given Dalits land in rural setting?
>
> (Naik, *Buddhism and Dalits Social Philosophy and Traditions* 50)

The background of Dalit writing is very important to understand present writing and assuming future of Dalits. Raidas declared himself an 'untouchable' in his poems which deeply inspired Dr B.R. Ambedkar because Raidas had fought against untouchability using poetry as a tool. After being immensely inspired by him, Ambedkar wrote an important book called *The Untouchable* and dedicated it to Raidas, Nandnar and Chokhamela.

Ambedkar believed that untouchability is more severe and inhuman than black slavery, because the owners pay a certain amount in order to "buy" a slave whereas an untouchable is compelled to carry services for free. Dalit Literature is born to spring the feelings of self-respect amongst Dalits and Adivasis and it inspires them at the same time to improve their quality of life.

Indian caste system is like a thunderclap for the rights and esteem of the Dalits and laws alone cannot enable people to become better beings. Hence the need of Dalit Literature arises. Indians often idealise the American model but how they have fought from slavery and segregation is conveniently ignored. The United States officially apologised for Jim Crow Laws that marked African-Americans as second-class citizens. In order to give equal opportunities to the Blacks, they issued "affirmative action" in the United States in "executive order number 10925" signed by the President John F. Kennedy on 6 March 1961 which included a provision that government contractors "take affirmative action to ensure that applicants are employed and employees are treated during employment, without regard to their race, creed, colour or national origin."

Black Literature teaches us a lesson that if slavery problem can be resolved in South Africa, the problems of Dalits also can be sorted out. In Indian universities and publishing houses, most of the people at the top positions are from upper castes. Thus, the need of Dalit representation is also being felt in every walk of social life. Many Dalit people are working to enrich Dalit Literature these days and the contribution of non-Dalit writers, who understand the agonies of this marginalised class, is really commendable.

Dr S. Chelliah and Dr Bijender Singh's anthology, a collection of twenty-six papers, is a wonderful addendum in the present warehouse of Dalit Literature. Dalit Literature has been written originally in English, in the local languages and then Dalit Writings in English. This anthology contains those works which have been published in English. All the papers have been beautifully written and their language is simple to complex according to requirements.

The first paper has been written by the editors encompassing a brief introduction on Dalit consciousness in Indian Writing in English. Dr Pallavi Saxena, Dr Suruchi Sharma, Dr V. Nagarajan, Dr F. Vincent Rajasekar, S. Divya and Dr Sakunthala A.I. have shed light on different works on Dalit themes in Indian Writing in English. Dr C. Ramya, Neha Raina, N. Kaushi Reddy and Dr Prachi have also focused on different aspects of Dalit Literature.

Harish Mangalam, Dr V. Nagarajan, Dr S. Pushpalatha, Dr Ishrat Jahan, Guni Vats, A.P. Pavithra Bhuvaneshwari and Dr Jayashree Hazarika have focused on the general themes on Dalit Literature while Dr Shalini Saxena, Dr M. Richard Enrico, Dr V. Nagarajan, K.M. Keerthika, Sanjay Kumar, Disha Sharma, S.F. Filomine White Sheela, Dr Kusum Kanger, Dr Sumitra Singh and Dr Sadhana Agrawal have analysed different Dalit autobiographies from various perspectives. Thus, all the papers yield this book a very ingenious look.

Last but not the least; I must not forget to owe my deep-seated gratitude to Dr Bijender Singh who invited me to write the foreword for this anthology. I am grateful to Dr S. Chelliah and Dr Bijender Singh for their munificent invitation for giving me an opportunity to write few words about Dalit Literature. This book is a must read anthology and a significant contribution in the existing Dalit Literature. I extend my warmest congratulations and best wishes to both the editors for bringing out this anthology so exquisitely and judiciously.

Dr Sheoraj Singh 'Bechain'
Writer: *My Childhood on My Shoulders*
Professor, Department of Hindi,
University of Delhi

Introduction

Indian English Literature is a Pan-Indian Literature, the readership of which has got spread all over the country and abroad, with a sustainable body of writing in genres such as poetry, novel, short-story and drama in Indian English Literature. Truly speaking, Indian English Literature has a dual identity, for it is both Indian Literature and Postcolonial Literature simultaneously. Indian Writing in English is at its Himalayan heights in the current literary scenario because our writers are supposed to have set milestones in the field of fiction and drama. At present, Indian authors in English are no longer dependent on their British counterparts; rather they are flourishing by leaps and bounds by dint of their own calibre and competency.

Writers like Salman Rushdie, Ruth Prawer Jhabvala, Arundhati Roy, Kiran Desai, Anita Desai and Aravind Adiga have tried their level best to dwell upon the theme of social criticism, social realism, societal issues etc and especially the cause of women, their constant search for identity, gender discrimination and some other unexplored aspects of social realism like subaltern consciousness and Dalit sensibility, diasporic experience, which are all found to be both profound and analytical. The publication of novels in 1930's by Mulk Raj Anand, R.K. Narayan and Raja Rao did significantly herald rather triumphantly the arrival of Indian English fiction on Indian English literary scene. Anand's *Untouchable* (1935) and *Coolie* (1936), Narayan's *Swami and Friends* (1935) and Rao's *Kanthapura* (1938) are considered out and out the marvellous landmarks in the history of pre-independent Indian English literature, followed by such partition novelists such as Manohar Malgonkar, Attia Hossain, and Khushwant Singh who all depicted their literary art and skill in picturising the horror of partition and communal violence in their works. After that attention was drawn towards depiction of diasporic experience, subaltern theme, eco-critical perspective, Dalit consciousness and many such related issues by many Indian notable authors.

Indian English Literature has, no doubt, taken an interesting departure from traditional literature to a study of Dalits and Adivasis literature. As is well-known to all, literature is an important component that not only drives us towards some superb realisation but also enriches our lives. It is nothing but a very stark reflection of our lives and culture. It is commonly held and eventually understood that the growing impact of social media and information technology life Facebook, Twitter, Instagram etc apparently has not exerted any significant influence on the lives of Adivasis and Dalits. However, New Literature which has emerged from these two neglected communities, actually being eluded from mainstream literature, is undergoing faster metamorphosis. In future course of time, literature may not be restricted to any given genre. It will surely cross the daunting boundaries to reach all the people.

This book is a humble attempt to make Dalit consciousness deep rooted in the literary minds of all readers and writers who are dealing with new expressions and experiences, continuously struggling with different social issues and problems pertaining to Dalit identity and consciousness. The very word 'Dalit,' derived from Sanskrit, means 'ground,' 'suppressed,' 'crushed,' or 'broken to pieces,' is used to describe the people or communities that have remained downtrodden and who are historically and structurally suppressed and excluded from the mainstream of society. After the Govt. Act passed in 1935, the word 'Dalit' got its English translation as 'Depressed Classes' to refer to downtrodden people of India hitherto referred as 'Harijan' by Mahatma Gandhi. Dr Babasaheb Ambedkar used Gandhi's term so as to give a new, respectful and empowering identity to the so-called untouchable castes in preference to the term 'Harijan' which means 'people of God'.

Dalit Literature was primarily written to voice to the Dalits. During 1960's, Dalit Literature emerged in the beginning in Marathi language and later, it gradually started to show its growth in Gujarati, Hindi, Kannada, Telugu, Bengali and Tamil languages. Quite obviously, bringing out the agony and experience in the lives of Dalits, Dalit Literature portrays the caste humiliation, injustice and discrimination suffered under the hands of upper caste people. Study of Dalit Literature is considered as a healing medicine to cure the traumas of the past. So Dalit Literature is considered as an attempt to bring to the forefront the experiences of discrimination, violence, social disability, economic inequality, issue of identity, experience of pain and communal bias. During 1960's, a few writers like Baburao Bagul, Bandhu Madhav, Shankarrao Kharat, Narayan Surve and Anna Bhau Sathe gave vent to Dalit concerns and issues in their works, among whom Baburao Bagul is considered as a pioneer of Marathi Dalit Writings in Marathi and his collection of short-stories entitled *Jevha Mi Jaat Chorali* published in 1963 shook the traditional foundations of Marathi literature with its radical depictions of social exploitation.

Later on, Dalit writers started to explore both in Indian and English languages. Bama's *Karukku* and *Sangati*, Dr Narendra Jadhav's *Untouchables: My Family's Triumphant Journey Out of the Caste System in Modern India*, Sharankumar Limbale's *Akkarmashi*: *The Outcaste*, Joseph Macwan's *The Stepchild*, Om Prakash Valmiki's *Joothan: A Dalit's Life*, Baby Kamble's *The Prison We Broke*, Urmila Pawar's *The Weave of My Life* etc are worth mentioning here for profound expression of Dalit consciousness in literature. Daya Pawar, Arjun Dangle, Sheoraj Singh Bechain, Laxman Gaikwad, Balbir Madhopuri, Rabi Singh, Namdeo Dhasal, Dutta Bhagat, Lakshman Mane, Palamalai, Sudhakar, Mahasweta Devi, Sara Joseph, Kumaran Asan, and Premchand are some of the notable writers writing in diverse Indian languages with the sole intention of bringing about social change rather than recreation or mere intellectual sophistry.

Falling in line with the thinking and writing of the above-mentioned writers, an attempt has been made in the form of a book with a good collect of papers entitled as *Dalit Literature: Journey from Repression to Resistance* so as to help the readers not only under the Dalits' way of life but also to frame a new outlook purely intended to form 'a new society' and 'a new literature' with fresh concerns. Disintegration, social curse, loss of valuation, social inequality and psychological suppression are the terms often applied for defining the experience of the Dalits who are struggling to achieve their economic self-reliance, political stability and a national self-esteem which are yet beyond their reach. No doubt, the condition of Dalits has become more miserable in the recent whirlwind of globalisation and the throes of marginalisation, disintegration and nowhereness have become more painful and unbearable than ever. This book has been designed in such a way to help the readers develop a deep concern and genuine pain for the suppressed and oppressed people. It is nothing but a modest attempt to examine the societal concerns with a focus on Dalit consciousness felt and experienced rooted deep in the current society struggling for roots in value and culture. No doubt, this book will knock the hearts of the readers helping them to identify and understand the real problems / issues of Dalits existing in the society. Truly speaking, this book is an anthology of twenty-six scholarly research papers contributed by some different teachers, scholars and reputed writers.

In this anthology, the first paper entitled "Dalit and Subaltern Consciousness as Projected by Select Indian Novelists in Their Fictional World: A Critical Appraisal" is a joint venture by Dr S. Chelliah and Dr Bijender Singh. This paper is an attempt to trace the origin of the words 'dalit' and 'subaltern' and then moves on to explore Dalit and subaltern consciousness projected in the fictional world of the select Indian novelists. Beginning with the treatment of this age-old theme in Rohinton Mistry's *A Fine Balance*, this article moves on to explore the feelings of subaltern as female in Mahasweta Devi's *Mother of 1084* and this is sprinkled with quotations to substantiate and support his ideas. The highlights of the article include Amitav Ghosh's treatment of subalterns in his renowned work *The Hungry Tide a*nd the space for subalterns to voice their longing sentiments and feelings as captured by Aravind Adiga in *The White Tiger*.

The second paper entitled "The Doubly Oppressed: The Portrayal of Dalit Women in Bama's *Sangati*" is written by Dr Shalini Saxena. Her paper is an attempt to explore the trials and tribulations faced by Dalit women in Bama' *Sangati*. It tries to examine varied underlined and invisible ways of sufferings embedded in the lives of the Dalit community, particularly women as portrayed in Bama's *Sangati*.

The third paper of this anthology is written by a renowned Dalit personality, Harish Mangalam who is the founder member of Gujarati Dalit Sahitya Akademi. In his article entitled "Gujarati Dalit Poetry and Commitment," he has tried to illustrate and highlight the Gujarati Dalit Poetry which has been created with full commitment. The Dalit Literature cannot exist without commitment. He has originated novel rumination and divided such Dalit writers in three categories, i.e. (i) Committed Dalit Writers (ii) Wavering Dalit Writers and (iii) Fallen Dalit Writers. This classification will strengthen the Dalit literary movement. In a nutshell, he has given an outline on the complete Gujarati Dalit Literature in his paper.

The next paper entitled "Journey of Marginalisation towards Fruition in Urmila Pawar's *The Weave of My Life*" is a joint work by Dr M. Richard Enrico and Dr V. Nagarajan. This paper verifies the problems of Dalits and their journey towards supremacy from Urmila Pawar's autobiography *The Weave of My Life*. This paper is an eye opener for those who treat Dalit people without contemplating the part of society and they should be considered as a human being. The paper further explores the sufferings, pains and suppressions faced both in the inner and outer worlds faced by Dalit women with the point to show how they are always marginalised by the society in general and marginalised even more by the men of their own community.

Dr C. Ramya's research paper entitled "Orthodoxy – A Shameless Pursuit of Identity: Dr B.R. Ambedkar's Ultimatum Attack on Brahmanic Theories from *Who were the Shudras?*: A Historical Documentation" attempts to answer the question, "how the Shudras became the fourth varna," discussing Babasaheb Dr B.R. Ambedkar's views on the sacred books of Hindus in his book *Who Were the Shudras?* and the role of Brahmanical law-givers in assigning the degraded social status of the Shudras.

Dr Suruchi Sharma has explored the anguish of the chamar caste in her paper entitled "Tyranny of Caste Hierarchs: An Analysis of Rohinton Mistry's *A Fine Balance*" and it is a humble effort to criticise the arbitrariness of the upper caste people. Through this paper, she has tried to explore how the upper caste people remain the mute spectators and do not come to help the poor and low-caste people.

Dr V. Nagarajan and Dr F. Vincent Rajasekar's paper entitled "Portrayal of the Conditions of Dalits in Mulk Raj Anand's *Untouchable*" expresses the impact in the Indian Literature focused on liberty and equality of Dalits. Dalit Literature is about Dalits written by Dalit or non-Dalit in the cause of Dalit in human society. Some caste people have a suppressed mode in the society. They are dominated by the race of community and the high class people. It expresses the broken heart of the segregated class and their soul burning in the form of contradictory society. Today Dalit Literature is slowly elevating to the level of conventional literature like short-stories, plays, novels, dramas, poems and autobiographies.

Unlike mainstream literature, Dalit Literature is dedicated to developing a consciousness among the non-dominant caste-people and instilling in them a spirit to act against their oppressors. Neha Raina's paper entitled "Meena Kandasamy's *Touch*: Vocalisation of Dalit Ordeal" is a modest attempt to explore the thematic concerns of Dalit consciousness with special reference to the poems in her collection entitled *Touch*. The poems have been articulated well and they act as an embodiment of active resistance and revolution against the Hindu-Brahmanical section of society who acted as perpetrators of caste differences and suppression. A beacon call of upcoming revolt and revolution marks the undertone of almost every verse in *Touch*.

The ninth paper entitled "Silence of the Subaltern in Dalit Writings" written by Dr V. Nagarajan and Dr S. Pushpalatha" neatly explores how the society got fragmented by casteism and class discrimination considering Dalit autobiographies as something revolutionary making a clarion call for Dalits and the subaltern sector of society to move towards power centre.

Dr Ishrat Jahan's paper explores Dalit movements as a form of resistance against discrimination based on caste and religion. Her study shows how Dalit movements through various mediums such as rap music, contemporary trend of resistance of oppressed people, are creating awareness among them. The paper also analyses some of the famous rap songs of young social activists like Rup Lal Dhir's Dalit folk songs, Ginni's viral songs *Danger Chamar* and *Fan Baba Sahib Ki*, Dhamma Wings's Dalit Rap song *Jai Bheem-The Song of Pride* and Sumeet Samos's Dalit Rap Videos like *Let me Tell You What You Have Done*. The only intention of their songs is to protest and raise a voice against inequality without shedding a drop of blood and how these youth singers have used fusion-form of their mother-tongues with other languages such as Hindi and English etc as a medium of resistance.

K.M. Keerthika's paper "*A Weave of My Life: A Dalit Woman's Memoirs*: A Brief Analysis" explores the sufferings, pains and suppressions faced both in the inner and outer worlds faced by Dalit women with the point to show how they are always marginalised by the society in general and particularly by the men of their own community.

Sanjay Kumar's paper entitled "Journey from Marginalisation to Liberation: A Critical Appraisal of Omprakash Valmiki's *Joothan: A Dalit's Life*" showcases the saga of sorrow of Omprakash Valmiki and the other Dalits of his village. This paper is a critique on the caste discrimination and it delineates that how the Valmikis of his village were segregated from the upper caste people of their village. They had to live under inhuman conditions and they had to eat left-over or stale food like dogs or other stray animals.

S. Divya Bharathi's paper "Picture of Motherhood in *Mother of 1084* and *Bayen* by Mahasweta Devi: A Critical Analysis" attempts to show the Indian playwright Mahasweta Devi's Anglophone play *Mother of 1084* as the play which is known for its reference to feminist ideology and mother-son relationship. Through the characters of Sujata and Nandini, her powerful exploration of female characters is revealed and the play is picturised as a tragedy of a political mother.

Unsympathetic behaviour of the husband becomes the cause of troubles for children. It is double standard of morality and civil laws.

N. Kaushi Reddy's paper "Projection of Dalit Womanism in Gogu Shyamala's Selected Short-Story Collection *Father May Be an Elephant and Mother Only a Small Basket, But...*: An Analysis" is an attempt to project the Dalit writer Gogu Shyamala as one who has been acquired and created a space for herself in the literary world. Gogu Shyamala demonstrates differences rather than subsuming to the universalised mainstream practices of the so-called concept 'feminism.' The hardships of Dalit women are not simply due to their poverty, economical status, or lack of education, but also due to severe exploitation and suppression by the upper classes. Gogu Shyamala has depicted inhuman practices in her works such as brutal patriarchy, violence in their domestic life, and discrimination on the basis of gender and caste through her short-stories. The paper explores the harsh realities of the suppression, struggle and torture experienced by Dalit women who are forced to live miserably.

The fifteenth paper entitled "Malayalam Dalit Poetry: A Reflection of Cultural Marginality" written by Dr S. Chelliah and Dr Kishore Ram explores how existence itself is a trauma for the Dalits and how conversion, education and employment, the three options before the Dalits to improve their social status, have failed and this failure is a major theme in most of the poems written by Dalit writers.

Guni Vats' paper entitled "The Daughters That Weren't: The Saga of Dalit Feminism" is a voice for the suppressed Dalit women. The preamble to the Constitution of India promises security to all its citizens. But in the years of development, it has conveniently pushed Dalits to the margins denying them any voice in the society. Dalit women have suffered a worse fate. They are denied the right even to be recognised as humans. They are triple marginalised for their caste, class and gender. Her paper tries to bring out the politics that has silenced Dalit women not only outside their house but also inside their house.

Disha Sharma's paper entitled "A Threefold Oppression in Bama's *Karukku* and P. Sivakami's *The Taming of Women*" attempts to highlight this discrepancy prevailing in the modern time of the country through one autobiographical accounts of Dalit women writer Bama from *Karukku* and a fiction *The Taming of Women* by P. Sivakami. The idea is to draw a comparison between the crude reality as portrayed by Bama in *Karukku* and the sugar coated truth in P. Sivakami's novel. Both will gradually frame out the subjugation of not one class only but a gendered lens of the society that somewhere gets retaliation with awareness.

S.F. Filomine White Sheela's paper "Subaltern Voices and Dalit Issues in Bama's *Karukku*: A Critical Analysis" explores the plight of the socially underprivileged, which casts light on the most agonising and wretched lives of the Dalit women with the focus on Bama's voice for those who are silenced by caste oppression envisioning the empowerment of the Dalit people through education. This paper is an attempt to show how the voices of the Dalits are raised in *Karukku,* and how Bama has found the right way to explore the sufferings of Dalit women. The conditions of Dalits were very bad with the form of discrimination based on identity akin to racism. Her own life experiences urge her to actively engage in alleviating the sufferings of the oppressed. Thus, Dalit Literature may be substituted by subaltern studies.

The nineteenth paper of this anthology is written by Dr Kusum Kanger. Her paper entitled "Dalit Marginalisation and Caste Atrocities in Sheoraj Singh Bechain's *My Childhood on My Shoulders*" is an attempt to throw light at the pathetic conditions of Dalits and their involvement in the blind-belief, traditionalism and narrow-mindedness. The poverty and traditional notions of Sheoraj Singh's family members failed to save his father's life. Consequently, Sheoraj Singh's family members had to see very bad days in their life after this death.

Dr Prachi Priyanka's paper entitled "Looking at Caste, Gender and Dissent in Baburao Bagul's *Mother*" is about the marginalisation of Dalits and it depicts the struggle of a Dalit widow who is fighting a fierce battle to maintain a balance between her physical, emotional and economic needs. The paper examines how Pandu's mother carries the burden of being a Dalit woman all her life – as she is assaulted by her husband's hands, her son's suspicions and the overseer's desires. The paper aims to explore the various reasons that are detrimental to the loss of love and understanding between mother and child, and how caste and gender become the cause of the double oppression of a Dalit woman.

A.P. Pavithra Bhuvaneshwari's paper entitled "Juxtaposition of Dalit Narratives with Afro-American Slave Narratives in the Vicinity of Emancipation: A Brief Comparative Note" sheds light on the dexterous literatures brought forth by Dalits and African-Americans and explores adroitly the aspect of parallelism in both the literatures by articulating the vibrant 'Dalit consciousness' and 'slave consciousness' through their narratives, thereby negotiating the pains, agony, anguish, subjugations undergone by the Dalits and Afro-Americans in an identical way.

Dr Jayashree Hazarika's paper "Pariah or Harijan: The Struggle of a Lifetime" takes into consideration how despite so many years of independence, India has still a long way to go in the case of uplifting the life of the Dalits, especially their women. Comparison is also done on the two monumental works on the life of Dalits: Mulk Raj Anand's *Untouchable* and Viramma, Josiane Racine and Jean-Luc Racine's *Viramma: Life of an Untouchable*. The paper explores the writing trends on Dalit Literature and the feminists stand on it.

Dr Pallavi Saxena's paper entitled "Ventriloquising Dalit Repression in Aravind Adiga's *The White Tiger*" is an attempt to debunk the real face of Indian society. It tries to explore how the caste that one is born into affects not only the past and present but also the future of the subaltern class, especially the Dalits. It tries to delve deep into the consciousness of the underclass and delineates how, after leading a life of repression and subjugation for ages, in the democratic set up of today, the underclass has geared up to overcome the obstacles of caste system and ensure that nothing can stop them from achieving success in life.

Dr Sumitra Singh's paper entitled "Unheard Agonies: An Analysis of Caste in Balbir Madhopuri's *Changia Rukh: Against the Night*" is a modest effort to trace out the agonies of the Chamar caste. It depicts the pain of the exploited people and how the upper caste people turn deaf ears to the agonies of the marginalised sections of the society. Dr Kusum Kanger has focused how Dalit people are ostracised from the mainstream society and they are kept at the margins. She has analysed the pain of Balbir Madhopuri and the whole leather-workers in this paper.

Dr Sakunthala A.I.'s paper entitled "The Hunted Body and the Haunting Retaliation in Mahasweta Devi's *Draupadi*" tries to explore the trials and tribulations of a Dalit woman. It sheds lights how Dalit women are kept at the marginalised positions and they are considered just as a play tool for men.

The last paper of this anthology is written by Dr Sadhana Agrawal. Her paper entitled "Tribal Crime, Hunger and Pain of Caste: An Exploration of Laxman Gaikwad's *Uchalya: The Branded*" analyses the dehumanised status of the Uchalya community. It shed lights how Laxman Gaikwad had to see the utter poverty conditions in his community and even police also, instead of helping, exploit them. The tyranny of the upper caste and the police, depiction of starvation and tribal people's repression are the central concerns of her paper.

This book entitled *Dalit Literature: Journey from Repression to Resistance* came into existence only after the co-operation and suggestion of a good number of teachers / scholars who deserve our thanks and regards. For bringing out this book, the editors have been depended on the support of many people who have been immensely generous with their love and affection, time and knowledge, out of whom special mention has to be made of Dr V. Nagarajan, Associate Professor & Head, Department of English of Alagappa University College, Karaikudi (TN) for he has been a source of strength and inspiration to three of his PhD scholars who too joined hands with him for contributing research articles for inclusion in this anthology. Thanks are expressed in abundant measure to Filomine White Sheela, K.M. Keerthika, S. Divya Bharathi, Kaushi Reddy, A.P. Pavithra Bhuvaneswari for their keen interest and involvement in research pursuit and preparation of research articles and their concerns and warmth are, no doubt, beyond words. Dr C. Ramya's analytical study reveals a sensitive critical response and sociological insight into Dalit consciousness in literature with reference to Dr Ambedkar's social concern and insights, for which she richly deserves appreciation and heartfelt thanks from all and sundry. Sincere thanks are expressed, that too, in fullest measure to V. Kavithanjali, PhD scholar-cum-clerk of the Department of English & Comparative Literature of Madurai Kamaraj University, Madurai for helping the editors in every possible way with her valuable computerised work and assistance.

We are immensely thankful to Harish Mangalam for not only writing a scholarly paper on Gujarati Dalit Literature but also providing all support to the editors. We are highly thankful to Sanjay Kumar, Neha Raina, Disha Sharma and Dr Prachi Priyanka for their timely contribution, Dr Shalini Saxena, Dr Pallavi Saxena, Dr Ishrat Jahan for their generous cooperation, Dr Suruchi Sharma and Dr Kusum Kanger for every help and Dr Sakunthala A.I. and Dr Sadhana Agrawal also for their scholarly contribution.

We are immensely thankful to Mr Amit Garg, the Managing Director, Kalpaz Publications, New Delhi and his whole editorial and production team for bringing out this anthology so spectacularly and flawlessly. Our special thanks are due to Dr Sheoraj Singh Bechain, a highly acclaimed Dalit writer and Professor of Delhi University for keeping in constant touch with the editors and writing the foreword to this book. Above all, we sincerely acknowledge the power of almighty God with a complete submission to His will for steering us out of all the hurdles and difficulties encountered in the course of this endeavour.

Editors

Dr S. Chelliah and Dr Bijender Singh

Notes on the Contributors

1. Dr S. Chelliah is a Professor, Head and Chairperson of School of English and Foreign Languages, Madurai Kamaraj University, Madurai, Tamil Nadu, India. He has produced 17 PhD scholars, more than 176 MPhil scholars and 104 MA projects. He has published 6 books and 222 papers at various national and international journals. He has served as chief guest/guest speaker/special invitee at various national, international, UGC seminars and conferences and also served as an evaluator/adjudicator for more than 30 PhD dissertations at various universities. He has served as Dean for curriculum development of Madurai Kamaraj University, Director for Board of Studies Section, director for Spoken English Institute of Madurai Kamaraj University, Coordinator for CBCS Wing, liaison officer for SC/ST Cell of Madurai Kamaraj University and member of Board of Studies of both UG/PG of Pondicherry University, Manonmaniam Sundaranar University, Bharathidhasan University, Trichy, Bharathiar University, Coimbatore and Gandhigrahm University and an examiner of various colleges/universities both PG and MPhil levels and also coordinator for UGC Remedial Coaching Scheme for SC/ST/OBC and minority categories.

2. Dr Bijender Singh (MA, MPhil, PhD, UGC-NET, U-SET, M-SET, HP-SET, H-TET) earned his first PhD from USA for his voluminous doctoral dissertation entitled "Female Protagonists in Shashi Deshpande's Novels" and he wrote another voluminous PhD dissertation entitled "Notion of Nation and Yelp for Self: A Study of V.S. Naipaul's Selected Works" for his second PhD in English in 2018. He works as an English lecturer, editor and writer. He writes in English, Hindi and Haryanavi. He has done Sanskrit Honours (Shastri), Art &

Crafts Teacher Course and Multi-Purpose Health Worker (Male) Course. He has been the proud recipient of the Ambedkar Sahitya Ratna Award, Editorial Excellence Award and Dr B.R. Ambedkar National Award. He is the Editor-in-Chief of *The Expression: An International Multidisciplinary e-Journal*. He has written a few essays, some short-stories and many Hindi and English poems. He has published many articles in peer-reviewed national journals, international journals, seminar/conference proceedings and edited anthologies. Many research papers/articles have been written and published on his poetry books. He has published 18 books till date and his books are available at the libraries of international repute.

3. Dr Shalini Saxena currently works as an Associate Professor and Head in the Department of English in KR (PG) College, Mathura, Uttar Pradesh and she has nearly 30 years of teaching experience. She is a recognised PhD guide and has been a member of the 'Board of Studies' for many years in Dr B.R. Ambedkar University. She is also in the panel of examiners and paper setters of many universities. She has authored a book on the acclaimed Booker Prize winner novelist Kingsley Amis. She has presented around 20 research papers in many seminars and conferences of national and international repute. She also has 25 published research papers in various literary magazines and peer-reviewed journals. Her areas of interest include feminism, diasporic studies and Dalit Literature. She specialises in Postmodern Literature.

4. Harish Mangalam is the Founder Member and General Secretary of the Gujarati Dalit Sahitya Akademi, Ahmedabad. He was an Additional Collector in the Government of Gujarat. He has published 14 books in different genres and apart from these books; he has 30 edited anthologies to his credit. He has received 12 literary awards from various organisations including Gujarat Sahitya Akademi, Government of Gujarat, Gandhinagar and Gujarati Sahitya Parishad, Ahmedabad. He has successfully organised national and international seminars/conference under the banner of Gujarati Dalit Sahitya Akademi, Ahmedabad. Since 20 years, he is the editor of *Hayati* quarterly – a mouthorgan of the Gujarati Dalit Sahitya Akademi. As a general secretary of the Gujarati Dalit Sahitya Akademi, he has published 110 titles of Gujarati Dalit Literature in Gujarati, Hindi, English and Sanskrit etc. He has presented his scholarly papers and delivered speeches on Dalit Literature in different universities and organisations all over India, including at the prestigious Indian Institute of Advanced Studies, Shimla. He is a leading figure among all the Dalit authors because of his commitment to raise Dalits' issues through his Dalit literary creations and field work of 'Annadhamm Yojana'.

5. Dr V. Nagarajan currently works as an Associate Professor and Head of PG Department and Research Centre in English, Alagappa Govt. Arts College, Karaikudi, Tamil Nadu, India. He has put in 20 years of teaching experience at UG/PG level and he is a research supervisor of MPhil and PhD candidates. He has served as NSS Officer of Alagappa College for 3 years, NCC Officer from 25.09.2009 to till date, he has produced 40 MPhil scholars and produced 12 PhD candidates and published 10 articles in refereed national journals.

6. Dr M. Richard Enrico currently works as an Assistant Professor and Head of the Department of English, Ananda College, Devakottal, Tamil Nadu, India. He has put in some 10 years of experience and has published 4 papers in national/international journals and has worked as a research assistant in UGC major research project on "Enhancing Scholastic Achievement of Primary Children with Mild Mental Retardation through a Competency Updating Teacher Training Programme for Inclusive Education." His areas of interest are Green Literature, Black Literature, Ecocriticism and Canadian Literature.

7. Dr C. Ramya currently works as an Assistant Professor of English in E.M.G. Yadava Women's College, Madurai, Tamil Nadu, India. She has completed her master's degree in English, master's degree in Business Administration, master of philosophy in English and holds her doctorate degree in English. She has five years plus teaching experience and she has published more than 40 research papers in peer reviewed international journals. Her areas of interest are Psychoanalysis, Spiritual Studies and Literature.

8. Dr Suruchi Sharma (MA, PhD, UGC-NET) is an Assistant Professor in RKSD College, Kaithal, Haryana. She has done her PG from KMV College, Jalandhar, Punjab. She has been awarded PhD in English on Khalid Hosseini. She has presented her papers in many national and international seminars and conferences. Her papers have been published in many national and international journals and seminar/conference proceedings and several edited anthologies.

9. Dr F. Vincent Rajasekar currently works as an Assistant Professor of English at Lakshmi College of Education, Gandhigram, Tamil Nadu, India. He has published 2 papers in national journals and attended 4 conferences and 8 workshops related to literary subjects.

10. Neha Raina is an Assistant Professor of English in Govt. SPMR College of Commerce, Canal Road, affiliated to Cluster University of Jammu. She hails from the state of Jammu and Kashmir. She obtained her master's degree in English Literature from the University of Jammu and has qualified State Eligibility Test (SLET) also. She has actively participated and presented her research papers at various national and international seminars, symposiums, conferences of repute. Her areas of interest include Indian Writing in English, Literary Theory, Diasporic Studies and Subaltern Literature. Besides, she loves to compose poetries and write short-stories as activities in leisure time.

11. Dr S. Pushpalatha is as Assistant Professor of English in the PG Department and Research Centre in English at Alagappa Govt. Arts College, Karaikudi, Tamil Nadu, India. She has 20 years of teaching experience at UG /PG levels. She has published 10 papers in national journals and attended 10 seminars at national and international levels.

12. Dr Ishrat Jahan has done PhD from English Department of Maulana Azad National Urdu University, Hyderabad. Her PhD topic was "Dalit Images in Selected Urdu Short-stories." Her MPhil project was entitled "Orality and Performance: A Study of the Revival of Dastangoi." Her research interests include Dalit Literature, Oral History, Folk Literature, Subaltern Studies, Trauma Literature, Urdu Literature, Diaspora Studies, Comparative Literature, Human Literature, Marginal Studies, Gender Studies and Post-colonial

Studies. She has published one chapter entitled "Reflection of Social-Cultural Issues and History: A Post-Colonial Study of *Dastangoi*, An Urdu Storytelling Tradition" in *Reflections on Postmodern Literature*, edited by Vijay Choudhari. She has published several articles in UGC approved national and international journals and has presented papers at national and international conferences also.

13. K.M. Keerthika is a full-time PhD Scholar in the Department of English and Comparative Literature working on the topic entitled "Women's Stoicism and Self Identity in the Select Novels of Bharati Mukherjee, Chitra Banerjee and Jhumpa Lahiri: A Psychospiritual Approach" for her PhD thesis. She has been an outstanding student of MA English at Lady Doak College, MPhil English at S.F.R. College, Sivakasi. She has published 3 papers in international peer-reviewed UGC approved journals and attended one international conference on "Relocating Subalternity: Changing Configurations" organised by the Department of English of Thiruvalluvar University, Vellore.

14. Sanjay Kumar (MA, BEd, HTET, CTET, UGC-NET, HP-SET) is a PhD Research Scholar at Lovely Professional University, Phagwara, Punjab. He has done his MA in English from Kurukshetra University, Kurukshetra, Haryana. He presently works as a primary teacher in GPS Cooperative Farm, Pehowa, Kurukshetra. His areas of interest are Indian Writing in English, Gender Studies, Dalit Literature and Postcolonial Literature.

15. S. Divya Bharathi is a full-time PhD Scholar in the Department of English and Comparative Literature working on the topic entitled "Projection of Social Justice and Human Values in Select Novels of Mulk Raj Anand and Bhabani Bhattacharya: A Thematic Evaluation" for her PhD thesis. She has been an outstanding student of MA (English) at MKU College, Madurai, MPhil (English) at Madurai Kamaraj University, Madurai. She has published 3 papers in international peer reviewed UGC approved journals and attended one international conference at Thiruvalluvar University, Vellore.

16. N. Kaushi Reddy is a full-time PhD Scholar in the Department of English & Comparative Literature working on the topic entitled "Thematic Concerns and Stylistic Devices as Projected in the Fictional

World of Bharati Mukherjee: An Evaluation" for her PhD thesis. She has been an outstanding student of MA (English) at Cauvery College for Women, Trichy and MPhil (English) at Bharathidasan University, Trichy. She has published 2 papers in international peer reviewed UGC approved journals and attended one international conference at Thiruvalluvar University, Vellore.

17. Guni Vats is PhD Scholar at the University of Lucknow. She has completed her MA in English Literature from Central University of Rajasthan and she has earned her Honours in English Literature from the University of Delhi. She is a keen reader, budding researcher and an enthusiastic writer who takes immense pleasure in looking at diverse aspects of life from a psychoanalytical bent. She loves to experiment with themes, subject and writing styles. She is keen to research on the Indian women writers and carves a niche for them in the predominantly masculine world. Some of her works have been published in edited anthologies and journals.

18. A.P. Pavithra Bhuvaneshwari is a Guest Lecturer in the Department of English and Comparative Literature of Madurai Kamaraj University and a part-time PhD scholar of Madurai Kamaraj University working on the topic entitled "Juxtaposition of Dalit Narratives with Afro-American Slave Narratives in the Vicinity of Emancipation: A Brief Comparative Note" for her PhD thesis. She has been an outstanding student of MA (English) at DDE/MKU, Madurai and MPhil (English) at Madurai Kamaraj University, Madurai.

19. Disha Sharma is a PhD Research Scholar in the Department of English in the University of Jammu. She has done her master's degree also from the University of Jammu. She has published many research papers in different national and international journals. Her areas of interest are Dalit Literature and Gender Studies.

20. S.F. Filomine White Sheela is full-time PhD Scholar working on the Novels of Chitra Banerjee Divakaruni for her PhD thesis. She has been an outstanding student of MA (English) at SFR College, MPhil (English) in the Department of English and Comparative Literature, Madurai Kamaraj University, Madurai. She has published 4 papers in international peer reviewed UGC approved journals.

21. Dr Kusum Kanger (MA, PhD, UGC-NET) is an Assistant Professor in BAR Janta College Kaul, Kaithal, Haryana. She has been awarded her doctoral degree from NIMS University, Jaipur. She has earned her MPhil from Kurukshetra University, Kurukshetra. She has presented and published her papers in many national and international seminars and conferences. Her papers have been published in many national and international journals and edited anthologies.

22. Dr Kishore Ram is an Assistant Professor of English at NSS College, Kottiyam. He has put in some 14 years experience and has published 20 papers; at present guiding 6 PhD candidates and 3 candidates are awaiting PhD viva-voce examination and he has attended more than 20 conferences national/international levels.

23. Dr Prachi Priyanka is an Assistant Professor at School of Languages and Culture, Sharda University, Greater Noida, Uttar Pradesh. She has earned her doctorate in English literature – an inter-disciplinary study of the convergences between poetry and painting that aims to explore, analyse and understand how art, literature and society in different ages absorb and reflect commonalities in various aspects. She enjoys weaving articles on various topics that range from academic writings to art criticism and book reviews. She writes in both English and Hindi and her articles, stories and poems have been published in various online magazines, reputed journals and short-stories anthologies. Her research papers that specialise on South Asian Art, Partition Literature, Feminist Literature and Diaspora Writing have been published in various books and conference proceedings. Her book *Thistle and Weeds*, published in 2016, is a collection of eleven stories that dwell on the complexities of love, life and relationships.

24. Dr Jayashree Hazarika is an Assistant Professor at Manav Rachna International Institute of Research and Studies where she currently teaches Indian English Literature and Communication Skills. She is a traveller by heart. After completing her master's degree with first class from Guwahati University, she worked as a content writer in Delhi and also worked with publishing houses like Rupa Publications. Then she moved on to BITS Pilani to complete her PhD.

She has also worked as an assistant professor in Amity University. Despite settling in Delhi, she constantly indulges in her love for travelling and her works reflect that.

25. Dr Pallavi Saxena works as an Assistant Professor in the Department of English, Dronacharya Government College, Gurugram. She has more than twelve years of experience as an English teacher and has done her research work on the acclaimed Booker Prize winner novelist Kingsley Amis. She received her doctoral degree from Dr B.R. Ambedkar University in 2003. Her academic interests fall mostly into the areas of contemporary British fiction but her areas of specialisation remains Indian English Literature. She has ten published research papers to her credit and she has presented scholarly papers in many conferences and seminars of national and international repute.

26. Dr Sumitra Singh is an Assistant Professor at Amity University, Noida, India. She is the editor of *International Research Journal of Humanities, Engineering and Pharmaceutical Sciences.* She holds PhD in Afro-American Literature. She has presented her research papers/articles in around 70 national and international conferences/seminars and workshops. She has published many papers in various national and international journals of repute. She is also associated with various Community Outreach Activities.

27. Dr Sakunthala A.I. presently works as an Associate Professor of English at MPMMSN Trusts College, Shoranur, Palaghat, Kerala. She has been in the teaching profession since last 28 years. She has done her MA from University of Kerala, MPhil from Madurai Kamaraj University and PhD from CSJM University, Kanpur and pursuing DLitt on Dalit Studies at Bharatiyar University, Coimbatore. She has published two books *Image of New Woman in the Fiction of Anita Desai and Margaret Atwood* and *Dalit Voices in Indian Poetry: A Study of Malayalam and Marathi Poems*. She has presented papers in various national and international conferences and she has published 18 articles in various international journals with ISSN.

28. Dr Sadhana Agrawal (MA, PhD) is a Professor of English at Maharani Laxmibai Govt. College of Excellence, Gwalior (MP) which is one of the best known colleges of Gwalior – Chambal region affiliated to Jiwaji University, Gwalior. She has around thirty-three years of teaching experience of English Language and Literature. She has attended various national and international seminars/ conferences and presented her scholarly papers there. She has published 42 research papers in national/international reputed journals/books. She has completed two minor research projects in English sanctioned by UGC/CRO, Bhopal. Her areas of interest lie in Indian English Literature, American Literature, British Literature and English Language Teaching.

1

Dalit and Subaltern Consciousness as Projected by Select Indian Novelists in their Fictional World: A Critical Appraisal

— Dr S Chelliah and Dr Bijender Singh

'Dalit Literature' is uniquely Indian as it is a byproduct of an evil caste system that existed for many years in this country. Even though the Constitution of India has abolished the caste discrimination, it still lingers in many walks of life with its grasp as firm as ever on the minds of its people. It may be compared with the slavery in America and apartheid in Africa. The literature that arises as an outburst against casteism is Dalit Literature. The word 'Dalit' comes from the Sanskrit meaning 'ground,' 'suppressed,' 'crushed' or 'broken to pieces.' It was first used by Jyotirao Phule in the nineteenth century in the context of the oppression faced by the erstwhile 'untouchable' castes of the twice-born Hindus. The very primary motive of Dalit Literature is nothing but the liberation of Dalits. Dalit Literature got impetus in Maharashtra because of the legacy of Mahatma Phule and Babarao Ambedkar. Poems, short-stories, novels and autobiographies written by Dalit writers like Bandhu Madhav, Shankarao Kharat, Baburao Bagul etc did richly provide useful insights on the question of Dalit identity. Now the subaltern communities found a new name by coming together with the perspective 'Dalit is dignified,' thereby rejecting the subhuman status imposed on them by the Hindu social order.

The term 'subaltern' was first used by Antonio Gramsci, an Italian thinker, for the 'economically dispossessed' individual. In the Collins Cobuild English Language Dictionary, the 'subaltern' means any commissioned officer in the army below the rank of the Captain (1456). The denotative meaning hints at its connotative meaning 'subordinate position under compulsion.' The term 'subaltern' acquired popularity by the use of Gayatri Chakravorty Spivak in her article "Can the Subaltern Speak?" (1985). *Subaltern Studies* under the editorship of the Indian historian Ranjit Guha came into being in the early 1980's and it owes its theoretical inspiration to a creative and eclectic reading of Hegel, Marx, Mao, Levi-Strauss, Saussure, Barthes, Jakobson, Foucault and others. The associates in the first venture of Guha were Shahid Amin, David Arnold, Partha Chatterjee, David Hardimen and Gyan Pandey. Subaltern Studies began as an exploration of the politics of the subordinate classes in colonial India. The word 'subaltern' in *Subaltern Studies* represents:

> ...special nature of class relationships in India where the relationships at almost all levels, are subsumed in the relations of domination and subordination between members of the elite and subaltern classes – 'Subalternity' – the composite culture of resistance to the acceptance of domination and hierarchy – to characteristic of class relations in our society. (Chakravorty 376)

Partha Chatterjee quotes Gramsci to expand the theory of subaltern consciousness. Gramsci imparts a political criterion for a critique of subaltern consciousness. Gayatri Chakravorty Spivak defines subalternity different from Guha, Chakravorty and Chatterjee Spivak poses a rhetorical question "Can the Subaltern Speak?" She asked this question sometimes in the 1980's. Since then, it has become a watchword for the subdued and oppressed women in the postcolonial world. In a word, 'subaltern' is German word which means 'inferior rank' or 'secondary importance.; The concept of 'subaltern' is also defined by Julian Wolfreys, "It contains the groups that are marginalised, oppressed and exploited on the cultural, political, social and religious grounds" (Wolfreys 25). Thus, Subaltern

Literature reflects various themes such as oppression, marginalisation, gender discrimination, subjugation of lower and working classes, disregarded woman, neglected sections of society, deprived classes etc. Becoming "Dalit" is the process through which the caste subaltern enters into circuits of political commensuration and into the value regime of the "human" (Rao 264).

Subaltern Literature is one of the subdivisions of post-colonialism, primarily concerned with the themes such as those about the masses, Dalits, the deprived, oppressed, marginalised and neglected sections of society and such subaltern consciousness has got projected rather richly by a few novelists in Indian English fiction. One among the few is Rohinton Mistry, internationally acknowledged and one of the prominent writers of the post-colonial era who has the credit of being the author of three novels and a short-story collection set amidst the closely knit and isolated Parsi community in Bombay. His novels generally deal with the theme of exploitation basing on the political, economic and social aspects stressing the necessity of social purpose in fiction. Untouchability has been India's gravest social evil since time immemorial and it is still practiced in various parts of India especially in rural India and Rohinton Mistry's *A Fine Balance* is a novel in which he deals with plight of untouchables. The so-called, down-trodden or lower caste people are denied from educational opportunities because education may enlighten them to their rights as citizens. The caste discrimination and repression is found as a common practice among the Hindus in India. Rohinton Mistry tried his level best to voice the cruelty and oppression experienced by these muted untouchables in his novel *A Fine Balance* which clearly exposes class and caste disparities of Indian society.

Rohinton Mistry describes about 'Chamars' born into a leather-working and shoe-making family and provides a clear picture how the upper caste people treat them brutally in a distressing manner. The proof of the inhumanity of upper castes is shown in the lines that follow:

> For walking on the upper-caste side of the street, Site was stoned, though not to death-the stones had ceased at first blood. Gambhir was less fortunate; he had molten lead poured into his

> ears because he ventured within hearing range of the temple while prayers were in progress. Dayaram, reneging on an agreement to plough a landlord's field, had been forced to eat the landlord's excrement in the village square. Dhiraj tried to negotiate in advance with Pandit Ghanshyam, the wages for chopping wood, instead of settling for the few stick he could expect at the end of the day; the Pandit got upset, accused Dhiraj of poisoning his cows and had him hanged. (Mistry 222)

The downtrodden were cruelly treated by the upper caste people. It is clearly visible in their activities such as stoning Sita just for walking in the streets of the upper castes; pouring molten lead into the ears of Gambhir just for hearing the prayers of temple and compelling Dayaram to eat stool of the landlord just for asking wages and so on. Such inhuman actions by the upper castes have become routine affairs and phenomena. The untouchability is a kind of disease which denigrates not only Hindu culture but it is also a blot on Indian society. In the words of Rohinton Mistry:

> What is this disease? You may ask. This disease, brothers and sisters, is the notion of untouchability, ravaging us for centuries, denying dignity to an fellow human beings. This disease must be purged from our society, from our hearts, and from our minds no one is untouchable, for are all children of the same GOD. Remember what Gandhi says that untouchability poisons Hinduism as a drop of arsenic poison's milk. (Mistry 163)

In fact, Rohinton Mistry is in favour of untouchables and subalterns. There are four characters – Dina and Maneck who are Parsis and two tailors, Ishvar and his nephew, Omprakash. The lives of the tailors' forefathers, who were in fact 'Chamars' or 'Mochis,' mirror the ruthless cruelty of the caste-system in the rustic India where unbelievable oppression is carried out on the lower-caste people by the upper caste people such as Jamindars and Thakurs.

These subalterns are subjugated and they receive heartless treatment at the hands of the upper caste people. For example, Dukhi's wife, Rupa was victimised and raped by the Zamindar's gardener for stealing fruits and milk from upper caste houses in order to feed the children. Her disgraceful exploitation by the gardener is Mistry's ruthless observation on the dual standards existing in the contemporary Indian society in the form of untouchability. Even in the local elections, the blank ballets were filled in by the landlord's men. At every stage of their lives, the untouchables encounter oppression which is one of the themes of Subaltern Literature.

Mahasweta Devi's *Mother of 1084* is a self-conscious reconfiguration of the third world intellectual as a subaltern and a subaltern woman at that. It takes us here to take to heart Spivak's caution that the subaltern as female is even more deeply in shadow (*Post-Colonial Studies Reader* 28).

Next writer dealing with subaltern consciousness in Indian English fiction might be Amitav Ghosh, the most contemporary novelist whose novels deal with the most contemporary issues like modern man's perennial problems of existential crisis, problems of alienation, problems of restlessness, rootlessness and unsettled problems of marginalisation etc. In his novel *The Hungry Tide*, he has beautifully depicted the unfulfilled hopes and aspirations of the post-war and post-partition subaltern classes of the subcontinent. His echoes of identity crisis, sense of alienation and displacement of the migrants' rootlessness, homelessness, cultural and linguistic identity, all resonate through his novel. Amitav Ghosh in his novel defines the space of home in relation to nation and in relation to the global village. *The Hungry Tide* summarises the events at Morichjhapi in 1979 and subaltern consciousness that Nirmal finds in the novel. He not only emphasises with the world but also identifies with the refugees as he understands the universal yearning of the wretched of the earth, the millions without a home.

In the novel *The Hungry Tide*, Amitav Ghosh delineates the post partition influx of population from East Bengal to West Bengal. In this novel, Nirmal's diary entries narrating Morichjhapi and the plight of the Fokir's mother Kusum serve as a true reality of the subalterns. The refugees fought for survival, became the victims of Morichjhampi after the water and food supplies were cut off to the islands to coerce the refugees to flee. The deprived classes termed as the subaltern agents sit there rather helplessly and silently listening to the policemen making their announcements, hearing them say that their lives were just like dirt or dust. The refugees of the novel who are the victims of the constructed East Bengali Muslims as the ontological 'other' are everywhere depressed, oppressed and also marginalised. The eminent scholar-critic of subalterns is Gayatri Chakravorty Spivak whose epoch-making question, "Can the Subaltern Speak?" is fully apt, implying that silence is the critical component of subaltern identity. The massacre, the tiger killing, Kusum's father and Fokir's vulnerability to the state official are instances in *The Hungry Tide* that depict the marginalised people's predicament as well as the subaltern consciousness.

Mahasweta Devi's short-story *Breast-Giver* (*Stanadayini*) and Bama's *Sangati* project some sort of subaltern consciousness. Devi's *Breast-Giver* revolves round the life of Jashoda, a poor Brahmin woman. She acts as a wet nurse for the new-born children of the Halder family just to earn livelihood for her invalid husband who lost his leg at an accident, her own children and also for herself. Her breast, which is a gift of nature and a source of nourishment, thus becomes a commodity. Finally, Jashoda develops a lump on her breast which is diagnosed as breast-cancer and she dies a painful death, thrown of both by the Haldar family and her husband. The well-known Tamil writer Bama's *Sangati* (1994), which means in English 'events,' is a plethora of events. The narrator describes the events of which she has been an eye-witness or she had heard her. Lakshmi Holmstorm, the English translator of *Sangati* writes about it, "Sangati – moves from the story of individual struggle to the perception of a community of 'Paraiya' women." Thus, both Devi's *Breast-Giver* and Bama's *Sangati* attest to the fact that gender discrimination is something that worsens the state of the female subaltern in every society.

Aravind Adiga's *The White Tiger* which won the Man Booker Prize in 2008, has earned popularity among a large circle of readers because it reserves much space for the subalterns to voice their longings, sentiments and feelings. Marx brought a sea change in the thinking of the intellectuals by dividing the world into 'haves' and 'have-nots.' Here is a novel in which the hero, the son of a 'have not,' a rickshaw puller, achieves what he longs to achieve by fair or four means. For him, existence matters not the system that the society prescribes. Balram, the hero, is rightly named by the school inspector 'the white tiger' because he possesses the devilish energy with which he kills his boss in order to be the boss – the killer instinct gets portrayed by Adiga in appropriate language. The entire novel is designed on the designs of a subaltern Adiga aptly answers Spivak's question, "Can Subaltern Speak?" Here Balram champions the cause of the underdogs, downtrodden and the neglected. Born as Laxmangarh the neglected corner of India, Balram suffers, struggles, rises on the social ladder – the story of a have not to have something in life nourshing subaltern consciousness in his life.

Works Cited

Chakraborty, Dipesh "Invitation to a Dialogue" *Subaltern Studies Vol. IV*. Ed. Ranjit Guha. New Delhi: Oxford U P, 1995. Print.

Chaturvedi, Vinayak, Ed. "Introduction." *Mapping Subaltern Studies and the Postcolonial*. New York: Verso, 2000. Print.

Devi, Mahasweta. "Breast-Giver" *Breast Stories*. Trans. Gayatri Chakravorty Spivak. Kolkata: Seagull Books, 2010. Print.

Guha, Ranjit. "On some Aspects of the Historiography of Colonial India" *Subaltern Studies*. New Delhi: Oxford U P, 1984. Print.

Holmstrom, Lakshmi. "Introduction." *Sangati*. New Delhi: Oxford U P, 2010. Print.

Mistry, Rohinton. *A Fine Balance*. New York: Rosetta Books LLC, 2004. Print.

Prakash, Gyan. "Subaltern Studies as Postcolonial Criticism." *American Historical Review* 22 Dec 2010. Print.

Rao, A. "Who is the Dalit? The Emergence of a New Political Subject." *Claiming Power from below Dalits and the Subaltern Question in India*. Eds. M. Bhagavan and A. Feldhans. New Delhi: Oxford U P, 2009. Print.

Wolfreys, Julian; Ruth Robbins, and Kenneth Womack. *Key Concepts in Literary Theory*. Edinburgh: Edinburgh University Press, 2006. Print.

2

The Doubly Oppressed: The Portrayal of Dalit Women in Bama's *Sangati*

— Dr Shalini Saxena

Dalit Literature is no longer a monolithic concept. It is a literature of resistance which primarily focuses on the ostracisation and marginalisation of oppressed communities like scheduled castes, scheduled tribes and other backward castes. In the Indian social hierarchy, Dalits get the lowest status. In past, they were not allowed to enter into temples and had no access to education. Dalit Literature is a revolution against the age-old exploitation and humiliation of Dalits. Famous Dalit critic Neha Arora states that "It is enough to say that any piece of literature is Dalit Literature which concerns Dalits and which is inspired by the 'Dalit Movement" (Arora 161). It is a plea for equality, justice and freedom which have been denied to Dalits since time immemorial.

By reason of their caste, gender and low economic status, Dalit women remain in one of the most marginalised groups and are often misrepresented by writers. We can say that a Dalit woman is a Dalit among Dalits. She is doubly oppressed: first, being a woman; second, on account of belonging to the lowest community. Harish Mangalam believes that Ambedkar fought for women's rights and education, "While Manusmriti enslaved women, Ambedkar awakened their mind, ignited their heart, strengthened their energies and resurrected them as powerful human beings. He fought against the state and society to realise justice for women" (Mangalam 162).

Many Dalit writers like Bama, Pawar, Kamble, Bechain and Arjun Dangle came up with their shocking stories of subjugation, sorrows and sufferings. Dalit men writers started writing their stories in the beginning but later Dalit women also started writing their stories. Dalit women have sympathetic portrayal in Dalit works and they remain victim of domestic violence or rape. Dalit women writers delineate how they resist and fight back "[...] like any other victim of social oppression to guard their dignity" (Tomar 3).

South and West India abounds in a number of Dalit feminist writers. Among them Bama, Sivakami, Poomani have successfully explored subalternity and gender discrimination in their works. *Sangati* was originally written in Tamil in 1994. It was translated by Laxmi Halmstrom into English. The word 'Sangati' means events and the novel portrays the events that take place in the life of Dalit women through individual stories, anecdotes and memories. Observing the vulnerable condition of Dalit women, Bama expresses caste and gender problems both outside and inside the community. According to Bama:

> All women in the world are second class citizens. For Dalit women the problem is grave. Their Dalit identity has given them a different set of problems. They experience a total loss of social status. Even they are not considered dignified human beings. My stories are based on these aspects of Dalit culture. (Ranjana 2-3)

Sangati highlights gender discrimination faced by Dalit women since childhood. Girl babies are always considered inferior and taken less care of. Bama raises the issue of gender bias by saying, "If a boy baby cries, he is instantly picked up and given milk. It is not so with the girl. Even with breast-feeding, it is the same story; a boy is breast fed longer, with the girl, they bear them quietly, making them forget the breast" (Bama 7).

Dalit girls hardly enjoy their childhood. They have little time to play as they have to take care of their younger siblings, "Maikkanni is one such girl who has started to work from the day she learns to walk" (Bama 70). She has to go to work when her mother delivers a baby. When her mother becomes fit, Maikkani turns to take care of the new born baby. Bama shows gender discrimination meted out to Dalit women throughout their lives. The life of a Dalit girl is no doubt tormenting but the life of a grown up Dalit woman is even worse. Bama describes the life-style of Dalit girls as follows:

> Why can't we be the same as boys? We aren't allowed to talk loudly or laugh noisily; even when we sleep we can't stretch out on our backs or lie face down on our bellies. We always have to walk with our heads bow down, gazing at our toes even when our stomachs are screaming with hunger, we mustn't eat first. We are allowed to eat only after the men in the family have finished and gone. What Patti, aren't we also human beings? (Bama 29)

Bama feels disheartened to observe that in the patriarchal society, women are given second position these days and men a higher position everywhere. Bama shows gender discrimination meted out to Dalit women throughout their lives, "When we played 'buses' there were always boys at the start and finish of the rope as driver and conductor, who allowed the girls to enter in the middle, and shouted at them. And when we played husband and wife they were the ones in authority; they took the role of policeman and ship-owners" (Bama 31).

Bama realistically portrays the physical violence like lynching, whipping and canning that Dalit women suffer at the hands of their fathers, brothers and husbands. Bama cleverly ropes in the prevailing subordinate condition of women through the ages as a girl, woman, a bread winner for the family and her place in the church. Through the characters of Mariamma and Thaayi, she presents the theme of universal gender issues, unhappy married life, humiliation and oppression. Their husbands also humiliate them by beating them mercilessly and cutting their hair. But they never revolt against it. When the narrator asks about it to her mother, why she does not leave this fellow, her mother replies, "It's not so easy to get away, once you are married. Once you've put your head in the mortar, can you escape from the pestle? No, she must continue to suffer until her head rests on the earth at last" (Bama 44).

Women have to suffer both mentally and physically at home. And if they dare to revolt, it causes violent repercussions or their deaths. When Bama asks her Pattii about the violence, she asserts angrily, "You ask me why? Because the man was crazy with lust. Because he wanted her every single day. How could she agree to his frenzy after she worked all hours of the day and night, inside the house and out? He is an animal, that fellow. When she refused, he practically broke her in half" (Bama 10). Bama delineates another scene of women's pitiable condition:

> Suddenly a woman thudded past us, running as fast as she could. She was pregnant....her husband came chasing, a stick of firewood in his hand....he caught up with the women and dragged her along by the hair....how dare you to defy me!' Because she was heavily pregnant, her whole stomach dragged on the earth as he pulled her along. Shocked at the sight, people shouted at him, you brute, you animal, haven't you got even a drop of human feeling or compassion in you? How can you torture her like that, without even caring that she is pregnant? (Bama 62)

Inequality between men and women is one of the main concerns of Bama. Male domination is rampant in all arenas of Dalit women's life. Caste-courts and religious institutions are male dominated and rules of sexual conduct apply differently for men and women. The story of Mariamma who is falsely convicted by the caste court is a typical example of the use of double standards for men and women. Patti who witnessed her daughter being tortured to death by her drunken husband tells Bama, "I reared a parrot and then handed it over to be mauled by a cat. Your periappan actually beat her to death. My womb, which gave birth to her, is still on fire. He killed her so outrageously, the bastard" (Bama 10).

Bama states that Dalit women do not have much time for their rest for themselves. They have to live such circumstances in where they work round the clock. Bama writes about them, "When they come home in the evening, there is no time even to draw a breath"

(Bama 59). From morning till evening, they work hard in the fields or have to do domestic works like collecting water, cooking food and husband etc. Even after doing all this, these women have no time to sleep soundly as, at night, one more duty is left for them – to satisfy their husbands. As she writes, "night after night they must give in to their husbands' pleasure. Even if a women's body is wracked with pain, the husband is bothered only with his own satisfaction" (Bama 59).

Bama voices out the grievances of the Paraiyya women who face inequality at every step of life. Obviously, the code of conduct that is ingrained into young minds since infancy is that men are entitled to greater privileges and entitlements. There is no justice for women. They can't eat food before their husbands even if they are pregnant or hungry. A song sung by young children can be considered as one such instance:

> Crab, O crab, my pretty little crab, who wandered through all the fields I planted, I pulled off your claws and put you in the pot, I gave the pot a boil and set it down. I waited and waited for him to come home and began to eat as he came through the door. He came to hit me, the hungry brute. He pounced at me to kill me. He struck me, he struck my child. He almost crushed the baby in my womb. He beat me until my legs buckled. He thrashed me until my bangles smashed. (Bama 30)

This is clearly an example of an instruction as to when women are supposed to eat i.e. only after men. That the person in question is pregnant doesn't give any concession in eating earlier. Dalit women are subjected to economic inequality also. Women are also wage earners and work equally as men in agricultural fields and building-sites but still earn less than men do. What is more ironical is the fact that the money that men earn is their own to spend as they please, whereas women bear the financial burdens of running the whole family, often even singly. If man goes off money he has earned, drinks as much as he likes, and eats in coffee-stands and food-stalls, then "how can a woman go out to work and earn enough money to fill her children's bellies and do whatever else is necessary in the house? How can she manage everything with just her wages?" (Bama 63).

Poor Mikanni is beaten by her father because she spent one rupee on ice cream from her wages.

Bama realises that the Dalit women are constantly under the threat of sexual harassment and are not safe in their work place also. A Dalit woman activist recently confided that "There is no girl in our Cheri who has not been coerced or raped by the dominant caste men when they go to the fields to fetch water or for work" (Basu 124). The story of narrator's cousin, Mariamma tells a lot about the sexual assault, the abuse faced by Dalit women and their inability to stand up against it.

Here Bama give the example of Mariamma whom an upper caste fellow tries to molest. Anyhow, she manages to escape from his hand and tells everything to her friends but they advise her to keep mum, "It is best if you shut up about this. It is you who will get the blame; it is you who will be called a whore" (Bama 24). They dare not to complain. Later on, the man fabricates a story that he had witnessed Mariyamma having sex with a Dalit youth named Manikkan. When the matter comes before the village headmen, Mariyamma is beaten and is fined as per the decision of the council of elders. The council never tries to verify the truth about Ayya's statement. In an attempt to appease the landlord, they give the verdict against Mariyamma knowing fully well that Mariyamma is innocent. The Naattaamai ends the proceedings by saying, "It is you female chicks who ought to be humble and modest. A man may do a hundred things and still get away with it. You girls should consider what you are left with, in your bellies" (Bama 26).

Arokkyam narrates another shameful story of her granddaughter's physical harassment, "Even last week, when my granddaughter Paralokam went to pull up grass for the cow, the owner of the field said he would help her lift the bundle on to her head. That was his excuse for squeezing her breasts, the barbarian. He's supposed to be the Mudalaali's son. He is supposed to be an educated fellow. The poor child came and told me and wept. But say we dared to tell anyone else about it" (Bama 26).

The Dalit pople are sometimes unable protect their women against the upper-caste atrocities. It is because of the organisation of the social structure on caste lines which makes Dalit men voiceless. What prompts silence in such grave injustices is the fear that if they question the upper-castes, they would be beaten up, their houses burnt down and their women raped.

Bama boldly reveals the discrimination of Dalit women in the Church also. In the wake of Dr Ambedkar's call to shatter the shackles of casteism, most of the Dalit men and women got themselves converted to Buddhism or Christianity. But the religion they were converted into, was often indigenised. In *Sangati*, Bama engages herself in a blatant criticism of both Hindu casteism and the rifts in Christianity also. She states that Dalits, who go on empty stomachs and take pains to make offerings like paddy, maize, millet, pulses, sesame seeds, or beans, or whatever was growing in the fields are "treated discriminately in celebrations or in making offerings even in the Church" (Bama 34). The Dalit women who crave to play the roles of Virgin Mary or even dressing up baby girls as infant Jesus are never accepted by the menfolk. Even "a peep into the sacristy" remains a dream unfulfilled for girls (Bama 32). Moreover, the Catholic priests are also gender biased and treat the converted Dalit women as inferior. They are humiliated even at Church, "they must lick the priest's shoes and we his slave, while he threatens them with tales of God, Heaven, and Hell" (Bama 35).

Bama's another work *Sangati* draws a comparison between the oppressed Dalit women and upper caste women. According to Bama, the arrogant behaviour of the upper caste women irks the Dalit women who show no any feeling of pity or compassion towards Dalit women but treat them contemptuously as if they are creatures of a different species having no sense of honour or self-respect, "They themselves lead lives shut up inside their houses, eating, gossiping and doing their husbands' bidding, and then they treat us like this" (Bama 66).

Bama is of the view that upper class women lead a substandard life than Dalit women. They are confined within the fourwalls of their home and find no way to express their pent up emotions. Upper caste women are not allowed to see cinema, they cannot do inter-caste marriage even though they are literate, "a girl who has a little education and has progressed somewhat, is not allowed to seek a like-minded man, and certainly not marry anyone of her choice" (Bama 109).

Bama accentuates the denial of Dalit woman's voice in public spaces with aplomb in *Sangati*. She maintains that in the phallocentric society, public spaces like streets, cinemas, chavady etc are often under the sway of men. Chavady is seldom the meeting space for the upper castes. However, it is the most popular public sphere where discussions are held by the Dalit men. This is an area where the Dalit women do not have any access. When the local court for settling disputes is called, women are restricted from entering. They are the "she-donkeys" who have to be shooed and "stamp[ed]" upon" (Bama 23). Bama criticises patriarchal attitude of the society, the caste panchayats where women have no role and they aren't allowed to bear witness or speak in support of the accused. As V. Geetha notes "for women ... to be in the public eye means risking their honour, and public speech by women is almost always considered an upstart act" (Geetha 150).

The process of law making and its upholding has from time immemorial been associated with men. The accepted social norms for a man and a woman are different. Regarding justice Paatti says, "What do we know about justice? From your ancestor's times, it has been agreed that what men say is right" (Bama 28). However, the young narrator has the audacity to question the "just" nature of justice delivered to Mariamma, "If only they had allowed the other women-who had gone..., with her to speak at the assembly, all the lies and all the truth would have come out" (Bama 28).

In this novel through different narratives Bama draws a pathetic picture of Dalit women's lives. She says that the women do not know to whom should they vote for? They vote to the person who was suggested to them by their husband according to the verdict of the caste panchayat.

It is quiet ironical that in the caste panchayat, the women are not allowed to speak but the Dalit patriarchy meets the same treatment at the hands of upper caste people. In *The Grip of Change*, a young Dalit male Rasendran attempts to speak regarding a hike of one rupee in the caste panchayat but the furious Kathamuthu can't withstand this audacity and roars, "Because you have learned to read and write doesn't mean that you can speak up in this forum.... Shut your mouth. I'll knock your teeth, if you don't" (Bama 69-70).

Bama is all praise for the freedom and empowerment enjoyed by the Dalit woman even though it is within a restricted domain. She points out that Paraiyar woman is economically self-dependent because she earns her own money by doing work in the field. She does not have to address her husband in a way she would address a superior. In a situation of dispute, word in response to word, abuse for abuse is the socially visible norm. In his book *Why I am Not a Hindu* Ilaiah debunks the truth that "Patriarchy as a system does exist among Dalit Bahujans, yet in this sense it is considerably more democratic" (Bama 34).

Bama also lays emphasis on the fact that the women of Paraiyar community lead a happy life in time of trouble and depression. She mentions it with pride that sometimes in the Dalit community; women are free to select a life partner or to remarry also. Some women marry a second time after the death of a husband. That is quite normal for them. On the other hand, "among the other communities of our village, you can see straight away, the indignities suffered by widows. In our street though, everyone is held the same: widows are not treated differently" (Bama 90). Women in other communities have no choice to do love marriage and if someone tries to do so, it may have a terrible or inhuman consequence.

Dalit women take recourse to variegated tools for survival. While Mariamma accepts what comes to her, Pecchiamma protests by walking on without her husband. Language is one of the effective tools they deploy against their oppressors. Women give vent to their feelings by calling their neighbours abusive names or shouting the names of their body parts. This, for them, is an effective defence mechanism to maintain their psychological equilibrium. It becomes evident through the fierce squabble between Raakkamma and her husband. When her husband beats her badly in the public place, she doesn't bear it meekly rather replies in the same manner by using obscene language. She has the courage to reply him back. She cries with pain but strongly replies. Bama asserts:

> She shouted obscenities; she scooped out the earth and flung it about. How dare you kick me, you low life? Your hand will get leprosy! How dare you pull my hair? Disgusting man, only fit to drink a women's farts! Instead of drinking today every day, why don't you drink your son's urine? Why don't you drink my monthly blood? And she lifted up her sari in front of the entire crowd gathered there. (Bama 61)

Bama's *Sangati* is replete with instances of simultaneous empowerment and disempowerment of Dalit women. One hilarious incident is when she tries to explain the reason behind women's use of obscene language, full of sexual connotations as well as the fights that took place daily between husbands and wives in the open street. They were both loud and aggressive and rather than behaving meekly or submitting to the husband's beating, women fought back showing the same aggression and violence that men exercised against them. Though the behaviour of the Dalit women might seem uncouth to people from higher castes but it was a ploy to justify their discrimination against the Dalit patriarchy:

> At first, when I saw what Raakkamma [a woman neighbour] did, I too was disgusted, and thought to myself, 'Chi, how can she expose herself like that?' But later, I realised that it was only after she screamed and shouted and behaved like that that he let her go. I realised that she acted in that way because it was her only means of escape. (Bama 62)

The youngest generation portrayed in *Sangati* reveals a fierce struggle for equal recognition. When Maikkani and her friends are abused at the factory by the children belonging to other castes, with a single voice of defiance, they refuse to work. They go back to work only when pacified by the maistri.

Sangati holds a mirror to the state of repression as well as the vigour, courage and the resilience of Dalit women even in the midst of all misery. After describing all the troubles and tribulations, she suggests that girls and boys should be treated alike and should be given equal freedom. It will bring about parity between man and woman in the long run. Then injustice, violence, and inequalities will come to an end, and the saying will come true that 'women can make and women can break.' She concludes her novel with an optimistic point of view saying, "I am hopeful that such a time will come soon" (Bama 123). In the end of this novel, the Dalit women celebrate their newly found identity and inner strength.

Works Cited

Arora, Neha. "The 'Anubhava' (Experience) Takes Precedence Over 'Anumana' (Speculation)." *Dalit Literature: Content, Trends and Concerns*. Ed. Harbir Singh Randhawa. New Delhi: Sarup & Sons, 2010.

Bama. *Sangati*. Trans. Laxmi Holmstrom. New Delhi: Oxford U P, 2005. Print.

Basu, Tapan. *Translating Caste*. New Delhi: Delhi University, 2002. Print.

Geetha, V. *Patriarchy*. Kolkata: Stree, 2007. Print.

Ilaiah, Kancha. *Why I am Not a Hindu: A Sudra Critique of Hindutva Philosophy, Culture and Political Economy*. Kolkata: Samya, 1996. Print.

Mangalam, Harish. "Twice Cursed Lives: A Study of Representation of Dalit Women in Tamil Dalit Fiction." PhD Dissertation. New Delhi: Jawaharlal Nehru University, 2014. Print.

Singh, Ranjana. "Dalit Women Identity in Bama's *Sangati*." *The Criterion: An International Journal in English* 4.5 (Oct. 2013). Web.

Sivakami, P. *The Grip of Change and Author's Notes*. Chennai: Orient Longman, 2006. Print.

Tomar, Ruchi. "Dalit Feminism: A Transformation of Rejection into Resistance." *The Criterion: An International Journal in English*. 12 (Feb 2013). Web.

3

Gujarati Dalit Poetry and Commitment

— Harish Mangalam

By following the unjustifiable and irrational law of *Manusmriti,* Bharatiya *Varnashram* (Indian four-fold stratification of caste-system) has turned untouchables into animals. In Buddhist writings, first time the protest against the *varnavyavastha* is noticed. It means, it is assumed; Dalit Literature has come into existence from that era. Buddha's thoughts on protest against the varnavyavastha, we could track the footprints in Buddha's writings. In this connection, in *Tripitaka,* castes, class, thoughts on highbrow, lowbrow and purity of lineage is considered as unsociable. In *Therigatha*, the consequences of caste-system are presented as it is presented in modern media. As far as it concerns to the Dalit writings, Dr B.R. Ambedkar's social reform movement has remained as the core of the writings. So, largely he is accepted as the father of modern Dalit writings. In Gujarat, first Dalit poem was published in 1912 in the compilation of folksongs by Ranjeetram Vavabhai Mehta is as under:

In one hand there is a *Hukka*[1] and his silver anklet
Uncle *Chunilal Mojanivala*[2] thus has gone to Dalits ghettos
Dalits ask what we can do for you brother
Dalits reply what we can do for you brother
Our wages are not paid,
Our money he has taken

We do not have clothes to cover our bodies
And how he would give us clothes?
If he dies, ends our all misery
(1. *Hukka*: smoking the hookah 2. *Mojanivala*: surveyor)

The second Dalit poem published by Amrutlal Sundarji Padhiyar in 1918 was "Antyaj Stotra" (Hymn of Praise of Untouchable):

Oh miserable *Antyaj Stotra*[3]
You face poverty because of cruelty
In spite of that you follow our Hindu religion,
So we respect you...
(3. *Antyaj Stotra*: Untouchable Verse)

The elabourate preface of that booklet was written by M.K. Gandhi. Thereafter, "Antarvedana" (Inner Pain) poem by Manor Jivram Gangera is unique one and it was published in 1928.

Oh mother in your lap, I am unhappy now
I am pained as I am known as *Antyaja*, untouchable
I worship Ram and Krishna, perform rituals,
Recite the *slokas* of *Bhagwat Geeta,*
I take care of cows but still misery of mine does not end.
I become happy to be born as a human being
But felt pain as insulted and live life like an animal.

During the above period, the thoughts of M.K. Gandhi impressed and influenced the intellectuals in Gujarat and across the nation. But in Maharashtra State, the ideology of Mahatma Jyotiba Phule, Shahu Maharaj, E.V. Ramaswamy Periyar, Narayam Guru and Dr B.R. Ambedkar influenced the intellectuals and it was thought provoking too. In Gujarat, literature was depicted during that period by pro-downtrodden sympathisers, so we call it the literature for sympathy (and not of self-experience as is being written now a days). After that in Maharashtra, there was a movement of *'Dalit Panther'* and the educated young people who were already aware and awakened by the ideology of Dr B.R. Ambedkar, started to revolt against injustice caused since ages, resultant which forceful resistance came out and sprouted in their writings. They write their agonies, protest against untouchability, inhuman discrimination, insult, low and high, four-fold stratified social system and exploitation etc. Now it has spread across the globe and known as 'Dalit Literature'. It is needless to mention here that Dalit Literature is committed literature.

The meaning of 'commitment' is already implied consent in 'Dalit' term. So, Dalit Literature is dedicated and committed to the ideology of the first Mahatma of India Jyotiba Phule, E.V. Ramaswami Periyar and Dr B.R. Ambedkar etc. Dalit Literature is inclusive of progressive, feminism, Marxism, tribals, and LGBT, over and above the untouchables and the people who have been socially, economically, educationally, politically and culturally exploited. The definition of 'Dalit' term is a broader one and there is no any scope for a narrow vision. In Gujarat, we do not find any foresightedness to narrowing it. In the other regions of our country, we observe that the definition of Dalit Literature has been made narrow and the writers cling to it that a Dalit writer who writes for only untouchables' cause is called Dalit Literature. Where as in Gujarat, apart from any castes and creeds, one can write for the above mentioned marginalised sections is called Dalit Literature. Because the term 'Dalit' is an adjective originated from a Sanskrit word *'Dalan'* means 'downtrodden,' 'crushed' etc. Therefore, 'Dalit' means not only an untouchable but it is obviously inclusive term of all the above marginalised sections. Ultimately, the myopic definition of 'Dalit Literature' will cut off its wings and maim its soaring.

I would like to cite a little incident of Abraham Lincoln's life. He was a lawyer. Like other lawyers of his time, he was not after money. He was not taking his practice fee from poor and he pleaded in the court without taking any money. A widow of the freedom fighter had complained him that a pension agent Mr Right had gluttoned half of her husband's 400 dollars. Hearing this, Lincoln became angry. He told his friend to get this money back, "I'll split Right's skin." Lincoln won the case in the court and he did not take any penny from the widow as his fee, but in addition to that he paid the money for the railway ticket fare to the widow. Lincoln's commitment to be with the oppressed and oppose to the oppressor is indeed worthy to salute. Dr Jaydeep Sarangi, a celebrated critic writes:

> Working on Dalit Literature is always activism which involves a social commitment leading to social change. The Dalit body of writings portrays the under-dogs and through them the writers expose social hypocrisy and taboos, class exploitation and class struggle, social and economic injustice. Its implied value is human freedom and primary concern is the liberation of *Dalits*. (Dr Sarangi, Jaydeep IVth title of *'Hayati.'*)

Dr B.R. Ambedkar was a warrior and an emancipator of Dalits of India. His determination was very firm for the welfare of all the marginalised sections of India. In 1954, in a Nagpur literary meet, he addressed to the writers:

> Human and cultural values, recreate through own literary creations. Don't keep own aims limited or conventional. Keep them vast and let them expand. Don't restrict your pens up to only your issues. Use your pens in such a way so that it can bring light to darkness of rural India. There is the vast world of Dalits and marginalised in this nation, this fact should not be forgotten. The misery and pains must be properly felt and by your writing try to make their life excellent, this is the genuine service to humanism. (Maheriya 333)
>
> It is also stated further:
>
> For the Dalit's liberty, equality and brotherhood, he dedicated his lifelong hard struggle. He also roared: "The caste, in which I am born, that Dalit community faced inhumanity, injustice, hatred and injustice connected with slavery, I will end them all. If I fail to do so, I will end my life with bullet." (Jyotikar 5)

Kanshiram is also very well-known personality influenced by the ideology of Dr B.R. Ambedkar. He was serving in an explosive research and development laboratory in Khadki (Maharashtra State). He had a bitter experience of discrimination by Hindus. In his office, some communal-minded officers cancelled regular holidays of Ambedkar *Jayanti* and Buddha *Jayanti*, and they declared holidays on Tilak

Jayanti and one more holiday was added to Diwali Festival. Scheduled Caste employees opposed it. Kanshiram resigned from the service in 1964 against this injustice. He firmly determined that "those who have cancelled these holidays, I will make them to go on leave permanently!" Over and above, he declared very firm decisions are as below:

1. I will never be married.
2. I will never possess property
3. I will never remain present in any *Kriyakand*, (portion of the Veda relating to ritual) lest it may be marriage ceremony, death ceremony or a party celebration.
4. I will never visit my home.
5. I will dedicate my whole life for the cause of Phule – Ambedkary movement.

   And we observed that he clung to his commitment till his death. He struggled very hard for the *Bahujan Samaj Party* and shouldered the responsibilities as a founder father.

Considering this ideology, keeping human beings and humanity at the centre, literature writings are coming up, that becomes known as committed Dalit writings. It is also known as visionary and committed to thoughts. So, the literature doesn't exist without ideology. Author always remains present as a link between society and literature, s/he understands and interprets the complex relationship of society and literature, s/he represents that according to individual's ideology.

Dr B.R. Ambedkar's commitment to the Dalits is clearly our eye opener at the Poona Pact time. On the issue of separate electoral he had clearly mentioned, "I am ready to talk on any issue, any positive solution. But not ready to reduce any rights of my Dalit brothers" (Jyotikar 39). Some rumour against Dr B.R. Ambedkar was spread at that time he warned and said:

> When there was a struggle to select one, either an individual matter or the concern to nation, I gave always priority to nation. When there will be critical condition to select Dalit's welfare, I will give priority to the Dalit's concern. If there is a temptation

> to appoint me as High Court Judge of Mumbai, even the offer to become the Viceroy of Hind, but I would reject. Before my eyes, not my individual but the future of my Dalit Community is and will remain. (Jyotikar 79)

Because of the rejection of Hindu Code Bill, Dr B.R. Ambedkar was extremely disturbed and resigned as the minister from the ministry (27th Sept.1951). He also started the great and only the water *Satyagrah* in the world *Chavdar Lake* (20th March, 1927). During his life time, he did so many movements for upliftment of the marginalised people. Dr B.R. Ambedkar, after deep study had come to the conclusion that cruelty committed to Dalits, are they committed to them by their Hindu neighbours, why? So the Hindu scriptures allow them to commit cruelty on Dalits. The roots of cruelty were scriptures, so on December 25, 1927 he declared to set fire to *Manusmriti*. He had also declared to blow up the scriptures. Dalit Literature is that dynamite.

Thus, following the ideology of Dr B.R. Ambedkar, nearabout 100 to 150 poets/writers are engaged in creating Dalit Literature in Gujarat. Some of them are Dalit writers who cling to write only and only Dalit Literature. They are resolute and firmly follow the ideology of Dr B.R. Ambedkar. They are writers-cum-activists. They are well aware of the philosophy of Dr B.R. Ambedkar. Such writers are welcomed as "Committed Dalit Writers". Whereas some Dalit writers prefer to write in both the streams i.e. *Lalit* literature and Dalit Literature! *('Lalit'* literature means mainstream imaginary literature written for the sake of entertainment.) I think, they have not gone through the books of Dr B.R. Ambedkar. They are totally unaware of Dr B.R. Ambedkar's philosophy. Such Dalit writers do not follow aesthetics of Dalit Literature, so they create confusion and contradiction in their own creations in a wrong direction. Knowingly or unknowingly, they try to carry favour with both sides. They encash milk and curd smartly as per the prevalence of the circumstances in form of awards from the both areas of '*Lalit*' and '*Dalit*' literature! Instead of a great deal of commitment, their goal in their mind has always been to grab double benefit in the centre. In absence of knowledge of the clear ideology, they feel that there is no harm in having the best of both the worlds!! Such Dalit writers are very harmful to the Dalit literary movement. We recognise them as "Wavering Dalit Writers." Though, we hope, they must deeply study the books of Dr B.R. Ambedkar to understand his philosophy for the cause of the marginalised society. Some writers come from untouchables, tribals and downtrodden community, even though they engage themselves in writing only and only *'Lalit'* literature instead 'Dalit' literature for their own and social causes!! Obviously this is against Dalit literary movement. I think, such writers have less concerns about any kind of ideology. They believe in 'Literature' only. Do not believe in divisive nomenclature. We always find such writers boasting, 'literature is literature; there should not be any sort of divisions in literary world. No *'Lalit'* no 'Dalit.' But when atrocities, insults, injustice, collective massive attacks, untouchability and communal riots take place then their boasting disappears there and then. In such a critical situation, they expose their deceit on their own as well as on downtrodden society. Such writers have no ideology so they are unable to create protest literature. Their imaginary literature written for the sake of entertainment only is of no use so far Dalit literary movement is concerned. Such writers are more harmful than the 'Wavering Dalit Writers' we may give name to such writers as "Fallen Dalit Writers" because, though they belong to marginalised sections, they do not engage their selves in creating committed Dalit Literature based on the ideology of Dr B.R. Ambedkar. It is the literature of their real life. It is the literature of protest and resistance against inhumanity and in its centre is 'Man' instead of 'God'. It is needless to say that a real artist welcomes the Dalit Literature based on humanism.

After dividing the Dalit writers in three categories as above, now let us have a look on the glimpse of Gujarati Dalit poems written by Committed Dalit poets only. The Gujarati Dalit Literature was started with the emergence of poetry in 1912 with the publication of compilation of folklore by Ranjeetbhai Vavabhai Mehta and Antyaja Strotra by Sundarjee Padhiyar in 1918. The period from 1912 to 1975 is a "First Phase" of Gujarati Dalit Literature. The period from 1975 to 1997 (i.e. starting of Gujarati Dalit Sahitya Akademi, Ahmedabad, a very important era) is a "Second Phase" and onwards till today running is a "Third Phase" which is a very important phase, because cultivation of Gujarati Dalit Literature is in its full swing in all genres of the literature.

At present, there are nearabout 100 to 150 poets and writers in Gujarati Dalit Literature including non-Dalits who are very active in cultivating all the genres of literature. The important Dalit poets are, Dr Pathik Parmar, Harish Mangalam, Arvind Vegda, Kisan Sosa, Madhukant Kalpit, Chandraben Shrimali, Sarup Dhruv, Praveen Gadhvi, Sahil Parmar, Raju Solanki, Shanker Painter, Dalpat Chauhan, Maheshchandra Pandya, Purushottam Jadav, A.K. Dodiya, Neerav Patel, Bhikhu Vegda, Priyanka Kalpit, Chandu Maheriya, Yashvant Vaghela, Chandu Mahesanvi, Dr Ratilal Rohit, Dr Rajesh Makwana, B.N. Vankar, Diinu Bhadresariya, Dr Dhiraj Vankar, Hasyada Pandya, Kantilal Katil, Mukesh Boricha, Dr M.B. Gaijan, Manilal N. Patel, Dr Mohan Chavda, Naginchandra Dodiya, Nillesh Kathad, Prashant Kedar Jadav, Rajendra Rohit, Silas Pateliya, Raman Vaghela, Satyam Barot, Samant Solanki, Vitthalray Shrimali, Dr Vinod Gandhi, Vijay Majadari, Thobhan Parmar and Brahma Chamar etc.

Praveen Gadhvi is a renowned Dalit writer. Though he himself is non-Dalit yet the ideologically he follows is the ideology of Dr B.R. Ambedkar, Jyotiba Phule, E.V. Ramaswamy Periyar, Shahu Maharaj and Narayan Guru. In his poem titled "Brainwash," he expresses protest and anger against graded inequality. In Indian society, *Varnavyavstha* has divided the society as well as our whole nation. *Manusmriti* has given the laws according to one is the best being and another is the lowest among the low. The poet strongly condemned *Manusmriti*:

Please give me scanty water from the *Ganges,*
And add Waters of six sacred rivers.
I want to wash thoroughly the brain hanging from the
Broken skull of this *Chittapavan* Brahmin.
Please give me cake of detergent
I want to wash each cell of his brain.
I want to remove thoroughly the rust developed on his

Consciousness since centuries.
This is the *brahmin'*s centre of hearing
Along with the hymns of *Vedas,*
Meters of Valmiki
Verses of *Upanishads,*
The stanzas of *Manusmriti* also are taped here.
Dear Brahmin, you are allowed to chant *Upanishadas*
On the bank of the *Ganges* in the early morning
But,
There is no need of venomous curses of *Manusmriti,*
This is the centre of the vision which has given me black
Identity since centuries.
Dear Brahmin,
See the blue sky of the winter, see the green woods,
Also, see the seven colours of rainbow.
But, why do you see the black colour of my skin?
This is the *brahmin's* centre of smell.
It is aroused by the smell of my perspiration,
My breath, my karma, my existence.
Dear Brahmin, there are flowers of jasmine on earth to smell.
And if there is odour,
It comes from corruption, hoarding and lies.
Why do you smell only my dour?
This is the *brahmin's* centre of touch, *Mahasweta's*
The centre turns green at the slight touch of breath.
But it turns bright red if it touches even my shadow.
Dear Brahmin, if we would have fought together unitedly
Against intruders,
We would have not become slaves in history.
There is the wrath of Durvasa *Rishi,*
Against reservation in this cell.
Here is disgust against me,

Here is egoism.

(Translated by Dr Rupalee Burke)

Sahil Parmar is also a very well-known Dalit poet. In one of his very famous poem titled "In Search of Optional Images," he presents his love for his beloved wife but in a post-modern poetic style. The poet has created original, new and challenging images against traditional and monotonous images. The Dalit poet has woven harsh realities of the labourers and poor people who reside in dirty, over populated houses in narrow lanes of Chawls surrounding with full of smoke of fire-pans. We can see this stance as follows:

As to boil hotchpotch you clean *Dal* and *Chawal*

With that much hurry, I sit to write a poem about you...

About writing a poem on you, about your tooth I'll not use simile of

Pomegranate seed but I'll use seed of maize.

Irregularly arranged in small and big in size. About your eyes,

I'll not use eyes of *Mrignayani* or a cup full of intoxication,

But your eyes are like broken small marble's pieces...

(Translated by Dr M.B. Gaijan)

The poem is very long and the poet goes on to compare the use up traditional symbols with new one created likewise, her face is not like a full moon but like a 'pestle' or 'full of scars of smallpox', Eyes are not like '*Mrignayani*' but like two pieces of marbles, after giving five babies her body is completely withered away and the poet would not like to say her withered away body with monotonous image like 'an empty cloud after raining,' 'a withered away flower' or 'a sucked stone of mango' but the poet creates his own images completely based on reality of his own living society and says, 'your body is like a thrashed out jujube tree after picking up all its' fruits by the *savarnas*!' Further, the poet says that I cannot imagine your black colour like Krishna or like a blue sky, but I would like to compare your colour with the 'colour of ashes of fire-plan or otherwise like very cheap jiggery!' I cannot say that your nature is like rosy, or sweet of sweetmeat, but I would like to depict that 'your nature is like baked fresh dry meat or taste of cold porridge.' I cannot believe that your love is a flow of Gange's or Jamuna's water, but I can imagine that your love is like 'warm water forcefully come out with hot air from the water pipe of Municipality in an early winter morning is snug and fresh' or 'like enjoying sweet melodious midnight joining hands to hands!' etc.

Sahil Parmar, in his other poem titled "Shambhuda's Mother," rejects unscientific and irrational thoughts of Hindu social system. The poet writes if a cow gives birth to male buffalo calf then the calf would be starved without milk, because that male buffalo calf would not give milk, if a female calf is there, then that would give milk when she becomes mother of calf. Her urine and dung are used for medical purpose too. For the economic purpose cow is considered a holy mother. The poet has also used abuses in dialect. Hindus people relate cow with teir religion. They practise holy-un holy, pure and un-pure thoughts. But there is a vast difference like a sky and land between their speech and practice! They are elegant in speech only and very cruel in actions. In their elegant speech, all are equal but in reality there are many high and low discriminatory folds among us, stratification of castes and practice of inhuman untouchability etc. Against such social pollutions, the poet's revolt is flared up with abuses. About the use of such type of abusive language, in one programme, a fellow from audience complained to Ramanika Gupta, the editor of very famous Hindi magazine *'Yuddhrat Aam Aadami'* about the use of such language. Then she replied, "Since thousands years you have committed injustice to Dalits, now they are educated, awakened, at that time, instead of using of abuses what would else they do, do they play flute for you?" Here are some lines from "Shambhuda's Mother":

Plenty are they who drink plenty urine of cow
Plenty are they who eat cows dung...
This is the medium to cross the river *Vaitarani,*
You being fools don't think anything else, she is the cow,
Shambhuda's Mother
I say the fact, cent percent fact, listen it,

It is a frying pan to fry poor.

(Translated by Dr M.B. Gaijan)

Dr Pathik Parmar's poetry collection "Bahishkrut" (Ostracized) is a collection of Dalit *Gazal*s, all *Gazals* express his commitment. This is a unique collection. In one of his Gazals titled "Chapati is not Acquired", the poet suggests to come out from the decaying culture and dogmatic practices. He says; if you want to come up, do not depend upon irrational practices like *Mantras*, vows etc.

By following *Karmkands, Chapati* cannot be acquired,

Chapati cannot be acquired by mere chanting the Mantras

Good is truth or truth is God, only wise discussing thus,

Chapati cannot be acquired.

Hardly can I manage everything,

At that time mere worshipping the *Sadhus,*

Chapati cannot be acquired...

How can I explain myself when fire provoked in belly,

By following the discrimination *Chapati* cannot be acquired.

(Translated by Dr M. B. Gaijan)

In his another poem, the poet makes satires and exposes malice intention of so-called higher castes people towards untouchables of India. Dr Babasaheb Ambedkar had made provisions for the upliftment of the downtrodden communities in the constitution and availing these fundamental rights, the suppressed now have got education, awakened and started to plight in the field of literature. The Dalit litterateurs depict their age old miseries, atrocities, inhuman insults and exploitations made by so called *savarnas.* The Dalit writers highlight their injustice and wrong deeds so they do not like it and again show their hatred towards downtrodden people. Here is an illustration:

When I start to write, something happens to them,

I write on my misery and something happens to them.

How cruelty is done by dividing on the name of religion,

Now, I change the religion and soothing happens to them.

(Translated by Dr M.B. Gaijan)

Arvind Vegda, a committed Dalit poet, in his poem "Push Aside," raises his furious voice against God, temple, belief and dogmatic practices:

White heads mysterious mystery, fluttering the temple flags dead
The cries crushed under the romances, get up and awake the dead body of the God,
Begin the battle, the light of untouchability
Before defiling each village, hoping the white wolves to swallow up the
Huts of Dalit, blunt the sharp teeth with scythes...
They are human beings. We are not human beings because we have
Carried the corpuses of shadows on our shoulders and we have learnt
Push aside the air.
(Translated by Dr M.B. Gaijan)

Brahm Chamar, a riser Dalit poet, writes how he shoots an arrow in his poem titled "Postponed":

Yesterday
God pleased me
And asked my name-
I replied, *"Brahma"*
Thy looking at me
With a steady gaze.
And asked, "What is your caste?"
With intoxication, I answered, *"Chamar"*
And God disappeared!
From that moment
I postponed to visit the temple.

Harish Mangalam's poem "Muse" targets the *'Lalit'* poetry which is written for the sake of entertainment only with no goal. The poet pens perception how to write poem. This poem is instructive one for the 'Dalit' as well as *'Lalit'* poets too, completely based on reality:

> O Goddess of Verse!
> I wish you to make you dance
> On the screen of reality.
> We have never experienced the thrill
> Of sighting a colourful rainbow in the sky.
> Seeing one star after another falling
> From the very sky
> I wish to leave India's kingdom
> And go back home
> Look! Fingertips restless among
> The ripples on the dung floor
> Have removed the tiles from
> The dilapidated roof and are waiting eagerly.
> It is easy to fly in the land of fairies,
> You may sprout wings, it is natural,
> But try to walk barefooted on thorny land.
> Stop riding cloud – horses,
> Here are children without
> Slate, chalk and school-bag.
> Unblinkingly they stand and stare
> Will their speech emerge from
> Your verbose being or not?
> Your ears are accustomed to symphony
> have you ever heard a human cry?
> As you recall your beauteous form
> Words become crippled
> And we are betrayed.
> You puff up, you flit like a sparrow,
> You become delirious on seeing
> A colourful design

But I want to make you dance
On the screen of reality
And explain to you
The meaning of the creeper's willing.
(Translated by Dr Rupalee Burke)

Core of the poems is the important characteristic of Dalit writing. One can understand the commitment depicted in Gujarati Dalit poetry. The area of interest of all the above-mentioned Gujarati Dalit poets is exclusively for cultivating Dalit Literature only based on the ideology of Dr Babasaheb Ambedkar. They are rational. They never go astray to grab awards given by the mainstream literature. They are activists-cum-writers. The Gujarati Dalit Sahitya Akademi, Ahmedabad has started an 'Annadhamm Yojana' after Una village (Saurashtra-Gujarat) cruel atrocity, for those who relinquish their traditional and imposed unclean job, for their immediate livelihood, store up grain and edible oil so that the downtrodden people could not be depressed. These writers are representative of the Gujarati Dalit Sahitya Akademi, Ahmedabad. They used to pay their visit to the concerned villages for such social cause. Here is the resistance against unclean job imposed on the basis of '*Varnvyavastha*' which is totally unscientific, inhuman and discriminatory against the provisions of our holy constitution. With the full determination, the Dalit intellectuals, thinkers, scholars, activists and writers will have to usher the right direction to the 'Dalit Literary Movement.' To attain the emancipation, will have to take up the challenge of the world saint poet Kabir:

Kabir is standing in the bazar with a stick in his hand!
Those who are free from worries, they can accompany us!!

Works Cited

Gandhi, M.K., Ed. *Gandhijino Akshardeh, Vol. XIV*. Navjeevan Trust, Ahmedabad, 2015. Print.

Jyotikar, P.G. *Aarshdrashta: Dr Babasaheb Ambedkar*. Ed. Ahmedabad: University Granthnirman Board of Gujarat State, 1990. Print.

Maheriya, Chandu. *Samtanana Senani: Dr Ambedkar*. Ahmedabad: Gurjar Sahitya Bhavan, 2015. Print.

Mangalam, Harish. "A Special Issue of Gujarati Dalit Poetry." *Skylark India, Aligarh*. Kothi Zaamirabad, Raghubirpuri. 1996. Print.

Mehta, Makrand, Ed. *Hindu Varnavyavastha, Samaj Parivartan ane Gujaratna Dalito*. Ahmedabad: Amee Publication, 1995. Print.

Painter, Shanker. *Vyatha Pachisi (A Collection of Poems of Sahil Parmar)*. Ahmedabad: Dalit Sahitya Sangh, 1984. Print.

Parmar, Pathik. *Bahishkrut (A Collection of Poems)*. Ahmedabad: Gujarati Dalit Sahitya Akademi. 2003. Print.

Parmar, Sahil. *Mathaman (A Collection of Poems)*. Gandhinagar: Parmar, 2004. Print.

Prasad, Sanjay; Harish Mangalam, Arvind Vegda, Praveen Gadhvi. *Samyak*. Ahmedabad: Mahatma Gandhi Labour Institute, 2016. Print.

Sarangi, Jaydeep. *Hayati Quarterly*. Title-IV. Ahmedabad: Gujarati Dalit Sahitya Akademi, March 2014.

Sinh, Tej. "Ambedkarvadi Sahityani Avadharana" Editorial *Apeksha,*' July-Sept 2004. Print.

Tulsiram. "Dalit Sahitya ka Mool Swaroop Bauddh Sahityase Uttpan Hai". *Dalit Asmita Vol 1.* Delhi. Quarterly. (Oct.-Dec. 2010): 92-92.

Vegda, Arvind. *Pageru (A Collection of Poems).* Ahmedabad: Gujarati Dalit Sahitya Akademi, 2012. Print.

4

Journey of Marginalisation towards Fruition in Urmila Pawar's *The Weave of My Life*

— Dr M. Richard Enrico and Dr V. Nagarajan

Dalits are those people who have been put at the lowest stratum of the society. They have been oppressred and marginalised at every possible way by the upper caste people. They are discriminated at every stage and are not given rights to participate in the social activites.

Before the Independence of India, untouchables had been described as "The oppressed of the oppressed and lowest of the low" (http:// www.quora.com). They had been treated as lesser human beings by the society. The attention of Indian society was drawn towards the miseries of untouchables or Dalits during the second half of the nineteenth century with the introduction of modern education.

It paved the way for Dalit people to have a platform of equality and respect. It is only education which yielded them knowledge and made them realise the purpose of their life. It gave them a life of self-esteem and dignity. All this could happen only with the revolutionary notions by many social reformers such as Dr Ambedkar, Phule and many more.

Aloysius Irudayam S.J. Jayshree P. Mangubhai and Joel G. Lee write in their book *Dalit Women-Speak Out: Caste, Class and Gender Violence in India*, "Schedule caste or Dalit women in India today number 80.517 million or approximately 48 percent of total Dalit population, 16 percent of total female population and 8 percent of the total Indian population" (http://ashvamegh.net). Thus, Dalit people have a huge population but they have to beg for their rights.

Dalits have recently started to show resistance against oppression through their writings. During the Independence of India, many writers like R.K. Narayan, Mulk Raj Anand, Bama, Baby Kamble, Arjun Dangle and Ambedkar wrote in Dalit Literature and some have come up with their own stories of pain and suffering. They narrated the agony of Dalit life and problems like poverty, enslavement, and untouchability.

So Dalit Literature came into existence with the writings by the Dalits. It forms an important and distinct part of Indian literature. Dalit Literature is the stories or any literary material written in order to highlight the issues concerning Dalits. There are so many great people who were deeply concerned about the plight of the untouchables and fought against all unjust divisions of society. Dalit Literature is an important stream of Indian writing in English and other languages in India. A tradition of Dalit writing can be traced from *Periyapuranam* written by eleventh century writer Cekkilar. Modern Dalit writings are founded on the works and ideological insights of Ambedkar, the chief architect of the constitution of India. Dalit writing is tied with Dalit Liberation Movements in various parts of India. This category of Literature become a significant presents in the 1960's in Marathi Literature and later in Hindi, Tamil, Kannada, Telugu and Malayalam as well as English poems, short-stories, novels besides autobiographies from the major genres of Dalit expression. Eisenstein states:

> As Dalit women were marginalised in their pursuit of knowledge, they preferred their own regional languages to write about their

agony through their autobiographies. Women's self-image is projected by the very means used to distance or detach themselves. In their life stories, a variety of forms of understatement in place of growing narratives, women tend to write in a straight-forward and objective manner about both their girlhood and adult experiences (Eisenstein 97).

According to Bhiku Parekh:

> First as a story of unique self, Autobiography presupposes a culture in which individuality is valued and cultivated. Unless a culture encourages men and women to make their choices form their views, take risks, look upon life as journey and in general to fashion their lives as they please, one man's life is no different from other's... the autobiography is only possible in a society with well developed historical manner of thinking (Parekh 250).

The Weave of My life is the best autobiography by Urmila Pawar who is the author of two acclaimed short-story collections *Sahava Bot* and *Chahuthi Blint*. She co-authored a book with Meenakshi Moon on the role of women in the Dalit Movement. She is also a former actor of radical Marathi theatre and a playwright. Urmila Pawar is one of the foremost literary figures in Marathi. Urmila frankly writes of the private and public aspects of the life. She has focused on her love with Harichandra as a young teenager, and marrying him in family's opposition. She also writes about familial and marital conflicts in this memoir. Pawar won the Laxmibai Tilak Award for the best published autobiography given by the Maharashtra Sahitya Parishad for *Aaydan*.

The original title of *The Weave of My Life* is *Aaydan* and it is translated by Maya Pandit in English. *Aaydan* is the Marathi term which is referred to items made from bamboo, such as trays, baskets and hand fans. As Urmila writes in her prologue of *Aaydan*:

> Before plastic began to be utilized for making different objects of everyday use bamboo was the most common material used to make baskets containers and other things in general utility of the household. Aaydan is a generic term used for the things made from bamboo; awata is another word. Outside the Konkan, the job of bamboo basket was traditionally being assigned to nomadic

tribes, like Burud community. In the Konkan region, however it was the Mahar caste which took this task" (Pawar 116).

Pawar's mother used to weave Aaydans. Urmila discovers a similarity between the weaving of bamboo strips by her mother and the weaving of words by herself. Like Aaydan, Urmila weaves through her words the life charts of Dalit women including her life. Pawar articulates, "my mother used to weave Aaydan . . . I find that her act of weaving and my act of writing are organically linked. The weave is similar. It is the weave of pain, suffering and agony that links us . . . when I asked my mother about 'motherhood', she replied in one word 'sacrifice' with pain on her fact" (Pawar ix).

This memoir traces the journey of Urmila Pawar from the Konkan region where men and women lived a life of hard work and drudgery to Mumbai where she fought for Dalit rights – as a Mahar, as a Dalit and as a woman who challenged the conventions of both caste and gender as a strong literary voice. In this memoir, Pawar charts the day-to-day life experience in the time of her grandmother, mother and in her childhood. These three generations of Dalit women struggled to overcome the burden of their caste as Dalits or Untouchables make up India's poorest class. She also talks about how things have changed for the Dalits during her lifetime.

The Weave of My life begins with the detailed description of the harsh landscape of the Konkan region in Maharashtra. She also portrays Dalit women of her village who used to walk in the barren landscape to sell their products or buy anything. She states:

> women from our village travelled to the market at Ratnagiri... with huge, heavy bundles on their heads, filled with firewood... Their loads would be heavy enough to break their necks...quite an exhausting trip...narrow winding paths full of jutting sharp stones and pebbles...two big rivers to cross...After crossing hills and rivers, the women had to walk on a long, dusty and dirty path till they reached the city (Pawar 1).

Dalit peole were generally not allowed to let their shadow fell upon upper caste people. They were not allowed to worship in upper caste Hindu temples or draw water from the same wells that those

Hindus used. They had their separate places to live in. In most of the villages in India, today also Dalits remain either at a corner or much segregated from the upper caste people. These thoughts can be read in Urmila Pawar's memoir *The Weave of My Life*.

Dalits were believed to be racially inferior for years and were therefore forced to live in isolated communities. Pawar grew up on the rugged Konkan Coast where the Mahar Dalits were housed in the centre of the village so that the upper castes could call them at any time. As Pawar writes, "the community grew up with a sense of perpetual insecurity, fearing that they could be attacked from all four sides in times of conflict. That is why there has always been a tendency in our people to shrink within ourselves like a tortoise and proceed at a snail's pace" (Pawar 1). This memoir *The Weave of My Life* reveals her experiences with caste discrimination.

Gyanendra Pandey writes in his book *A History of Prejudice*, "Dalit autobiography ... foregrounded the vicious history of cast prejudice. The very titles of numerous Dalit life writings indicate the history of stigmatisation, oppression and poverty" (http://www.livemint.com). But Pawar's family was somewhat unique from others. Her father performed duties of priest for their caste which were typically performed by Brahmins. She refers in *Aaydan* about her father as a teacher and a reformist for the community but inside her house, he was a typical patriarchal person. Both of her parents were also strong believers in the importance of education to propel their children into a better life. She has also narrated the submissive and oppressive character of her sister-in-law Parvati. She has no power in their house to eat or sleep on her own wish. Pawar's resilience and strong belief in herself and her abilities shines through in this candid memoir.

She has deep observation about her family members and acute cultural changes in her sister's language. Similarly, the language is tinged by caste discrimination. Brahminical language can create a barrier among Dalits instead of facilitates. Generally the use the more formal 'plural' form of 'you' of Marathi is to address their husbands. As Pawar writes:

> I used to feel so angry about Tai's imitating the Brahmin God bole family using and in-laws, indeed. Our uneducated illiterate

> village women were much better. I think Tai's use of honorific created distance between herself and her husband, which was never there in husband-wife relationship in our community (Pawar 61).

She has also given references of her school life and particularly the items of the lunch boxes which show the demarcation of upper middle class and Dalit community. She writes, "She couldn't think to talk to her family. Economic conditions were not permitting" (Pawar 121). Few incidents such as the teacher's asking Urmila to collect cow-droppings and her refusal, Urmila's consequent beating at teacher's hands underline societal attitudes. There are several other factors also which make her feel to be inferior to her classmates. She clearly reveals her bitter experience with the Muslim family who condemns her as 'Mahar'. Prandya Daya Pawar delineates in *The Discarded Share*, "The Dalit autobiographies or memoir served two purposes: It brought to life a Dalit hero and bestowed upon him validity. At the same time, it established Dalit history and Dalits as dignified...No one was such a fool as to believe that the writing would liberate the Dalits..." (http://www.livemint.com).

Throughout this memoir, Urmila Pawar explores double discrimination. At one point, she reminisces that her mother had banished her to a corner when she started menstruating with instruction not to touch anything as it becomes 'impure'. She wondered at this concept of purity and rules. She feels, "As if I was not discriminated enough by others outside, now family too, has set rules for me" (http://indianexpress.com).

The Weave of My life draws out the contradiction between caste and gender as Pawar goes against her family's wishes and marries a man whose family is somewhat below her in social status and who is less educated than her. After her family moves to Mumbai, Pawar becomes involved in the Dalit right movements and is recognised as a leading figure in the Dalit Literary Movement. She writes frankly about her husband's constant criticism and emotional abuse as she continued to do her social work. Her writing became famous and gained awards. She gives some information about Hinduism, Buddhism and the political movements that helped for the changes in the life of Dalits. But it directly impacted her life. She accepts the influence of Dalit Literature as well as the impact of Dr Baba Saheb's Movement of conversion from Dalit to Navbuddha. Urmila explained in her memoir:

> The pace of conversion picked up radically after the conversion to Buddhism. To begin with, there was tremendous interest in the new religion and in the images of Buddha and Dr Ambedkar. Initially, it was difficult to replace the images of Gods. To replace it with Buddha and Ambedkar's, the age old habits of praying to the gods for praying for difficult times, were to strong be given up (Pawar 119).

Eventually, Pawar was introduced to a women's organisation 'Maitrini' through her friend Hira Bansode. She has narrated various experiences while working with the Dalit Women Movement wherein she interacted with many Dalit families who were hiding their identities to obtain social approval. Though she had been awarded for her writings, and led an achievable life in her society of Dalit Women's Movement yet she could not lead a happy life personally. When she writes *The Weave of My Life*, she explores:

> I was a rebellious child and had numerous fights with my mother while growing up. But by the time, I wrote this book, I felt I had taken her place. Like her, I was attempting to make the most of my life in a patriarchal society; I had lost my husband and my son and my two girls misunderstood me because they could not understand my need to have a life beyond home. It's as if our lives had been juxtaposed (http://indianexpress.com).

At the end of the memoir, Pawar has experienced much loss and tragedy. She loses her son, her mother and finally, her husband taken to drinking and has died in a short period of time. She finds herself being blamed by the common people in her community for these misfortunes because she was not a traditional wife and mother. She emotionally identifies:

> Life has taught me many things . . . I don't know how much longer I am going to libe, nor do I know in what form life is going to confront me. Let it come in any form; I am ready to face it stoically.

This is what my life has taught me. This is my life and that is me! (http://www.goodreads.com).

There are so many socio-political changes during the life of Urmila in Mumbai. In *The Weave of My life*, Pawar not only shares her tireless effort to surmount personal tragedy but also conveys the excitement of an awakening consciousness during the time of profound political and social change. Her further act of conversation to Buddhism changes her life in the caste-based Hindu religion. Like for many Dalits of her period, this act led to personal growth in Urmila's case. The next step was her discovery of feminism, adding to her growth.

Urmila Pawar, an acclaimed writer for the betterment of the society, wants to transmit the ill-practice of discriminating people according to their caste. She fights for the rights for women, especially Dalits because they are not considered even as a human being. In the hands of God, all are equal and there is no supremacy has to be followed in the society. This memoir is a powerful portrayal of Dalit suppression.

The first half of the book is full of general stories about her relatives, her childhood, injustice done to Dalits, patriarchal domination, and the daily compulsion of poverty, problem faced in society, all gives us a look into their culture. The second half focuses on her life in city and changing times for the untouchable castes. Pawar is now a well-known writer in Marathi language. But this memoir, in the hands of Pawar, went beyond self-expression and historical record. *The Weave of My Life* was a vehicle for Dalits to assert their identity, challenge the social order and protest against the oppression of centuries.

Works Cited

Eisenstein. *Feminist Criticisms and Social Change: Class and Race in Literature and Culture*. London: Cambridge U P, 1963. Print.

https://indianexpress.com/article/india/we-dig-well-denied-water-we-make-idol-cant-touch-social-justice-minister-thawar-chand-gehlot-casteism-4606884/

https://indianexpress.com/article/lifestyle/notes-from-the-margins-Dalit-writer-urmila-pawars-autobiography-inspires-a-marathi-play/

https://www.goodreads.com/book/show/6727719-the-weave-of-my-life

https://www.livemint.com/Leisure/PyoN5tzeJFZireKtqQwEqM/A-brief-history-of-the-Dalit-memoir.html

https://www.mumbaitheatreguide.com/dramas/reviews/11-aaydaan-marathi-play-review.asp#

https://www.quora.com/Did-Brahmins-oppress-the-lower-caste-by-introducing-the-concept-of-untouchability-and-discrimination-What-do-they-gain-from-that

Pandey, Gyanendra. *A History of Prejudice: Race, Caste and Difference in India and the United States*. England: Cambridge U P, 2013. Print.

Parekh, Bhiku. *Colonialism, Tradition and Reform: An Analysis of Gandhi's Political Discourse*. New Delhi: Sage, 1989. Print.

Pawar, Daya. *Pradnya: Baluta*. New Delhi: Speaking Tigers, 2015. Print.

Pawar, Urmila. *The Weave of My Life*. Trans. Maya Pandit. New York: Columbia U P, 2009. Print.

Rege, Sharmila. *Writing Caste, Writing Gender: Narrating Dalit Women's Testimonios*. New Delhi: Zubaan, 2013. Print.

S.J., Aloysius Irudayam, Jayshree P. Mangubhai, and Joel G. Lee. *Dalit Women – Speak Out: Caste, Class and Gender Violence in India*. New Delhi: Zubaan, 2011. Print.

5

Orthodoxy – A Shameless Pursuit of Identity: Dr B.R. Ambedkar's Ultimatum Attack on Brahmanic Theories from *Who were the Shudras?*: A Historical Documentation

— Dr C. Ramya

> ...What goes by the name of sacred Books contains fabrications which are political in their motive, partisan in their composition and fraudulent in their purpose. (Ambedkar: *WWTS* 13)

Dr B.R. Ambedkar, lavishingly, stacks up his aggravated form of repeated offence on Sacred Literature, the so-called sacred books of his the Hindus in his "Who were the *Shudras*?" as they contain the doctrines responsible for the decline and fall of our country and our society. Bhimrao Ramji Ambedkar, Independent India's first Law Minister and the principal architect of the constitution of India, radically, re-interpreted *Buddhism* and formed a new school of *Buddhism* called *Navayana* that rejected *Hinduism*, challenged caste system and promoted the rights of *Dalit* Community. As a social reformer, B.R. Ambedkar, popularly known as Babasaheb, claims the Orthodox Hindus as a set of Selfish beings in the world who are prostituting their intelligence in order to reinforce the bestowed interests of their class.

Precisely comprehending about the *Shudras* or the magnitude of the trivial problems of the *Shudras* is impossible without understanding the Indo-Aryan's theory of *Chaturvarnya*. *Chaturvarnya* is the vicious system of dividing the society into four classes: *Brahmins*, *Kshatriyas*, *Vaishyas* and the *Shudras*. This graded inequality of classes in the name of *varnas* where the priests are categorised into the *Brahminsvarna*, the soldiers are grouped into *Kshatriyavarna*, the traders belong to *Vaishyavarna* and the menials are not the *Dalits* and *Scheduled Tribes* who do not belong to any *varna* are called a *Dalits*. Historically this classified inequality is not just notional but legal and penal. The *Shudra*, under the system of *Chaturvarnya*, in addition of being placed at the bottom of the gradation, he is subjected to the multifarious mortification and indignity and the triviality of this problem can be understood from its traces by studying the roots of the origin of this fourth *varna*, the *Shudras*.

The present day *Shudras* are a collection of racially different heterogeneous stocks of castes, who are aboriginal inhabitants of India just like the way how the Celtics tribes of England have become absorbed in the Anglo-Saxon race. The *Shudras* of Indo-Aryan Society is no more a distinct identifiable community and in course of time, there arise a change in the connotation of the word *Shudras* itself as the word become a general name for a low class people without civilization, culture, respect and position, rather than being a name of particular community. To answer the unanswered question, "Who were the *Shudras*, Babasaheb summarises the facts after his thorough investigations as, the *Shudras'* origin arises from the Solar race of the Aryan community who recognised only there *varnas* normally, *Brahmins*, *Kshatriyas* and from a separate *varna* because they ranked as part of the *Kshatriyavarna* in the Indo-Aryan Society. The reason why the *Shudras* were drifted down as a fourth *varna*, the lowest of all is that there was a ceaseless feud between the *Shudra* kings and the *Brahmins* in which the *Brahmins* were put through various ruthlessness and indignities. Babasaheb puts it as:

> Owing to the denial of Upanayana, the Shudras who were Kshatriyas, became socially degraded, fell below the rank of the Vaishyas and thus came to form the fourth varna. (Ambedkar 9)

The tyrannies and oppressions of Brahmins on the *Shudra* created in them an aversion and hence the *Brahmins* refused to perform *Upanayana*, one of the traditional rites marking the acceptance of an individual's entrance to a school in Hinduism, for the *Shudras*, as the *Brahmin*, the noblest of all the four classes is given the noblest function of being the custodian of knowledge and learning.

While Babasaheb, with historical references, answers the origin of *Shudras*, one becomes doubtful about how they came to be the fourth *varna* of the Indo-Aryan Society. The riposte for the riddle could be attained only by questioning the Sacred Literature, the literature which is the main stream of the material for the study of the problems of the social history of the Hindus and Babasaheb, undeniably, is uncritical and fact-based who answers with his authentic historical research with the attitude of unsparing condemnation.

The origin of *Charurvarnya* in the Indo-Aryan society is the factual venture of discovering the identity of *Shudras* and how they became the fourth *varna*. To start with, Dr B.R. Ambedkar proposes to notice keenly and research on *Purusha Sukta*, the ninetieth Hymn of Tenth Mandala of the Rig Veda. *The Purusha Sukta* is the theory of origin of the Universe, to put it in simple words, it is a cosmogony. *Purusha* is the cosmic being from whose body the four *varnas* were born. The Veda reads, "The Brahmin was his mouth, the Kshatriya formed his arms, the Vaishya his thighs; the Shudra was born from his feet" (Ambedkar 25).

The constitution of Indo-Aryan society has been prescribed by *Purusha Sukta* and named as *Chaturvarnya*. A Brahmin scholar would treat this Sacred Literature with uncritical respect and reverence as the whole objective of the Sacred Books is to sustain the superiority and privileges of the Brahmins, as the plan of equating different classes to different parts of the body of the creator, the *Purusha*, is not a matter of accident but deliberate. The gradation of the class, in turn, fixes the function of the class. Mouth of the creator is equated to the birth of *Brahmin* class as the mouth is considered the noblest part of the anatomy and he is given the noblest function of being curator of knowledge and learning. The arms of the creator give birth to *Kshatriyas* who were given the function of fighting, the art that precedes knowledge. Since the arms are below the mouth, the *Kshatriyas* are given an order of precedence next below the Brahmin and the *Vaishya*, accordingly are given the order of the precedence next below the *Kshatriya* and they are given the function of industry and trade. The *Shudra* is the lowest and most ignoble part of the human frame who is placed last in the social order and given a filthiest function, say to serve as a menial. Now, the judgmental question of Babasaheb is that why *Purusha Sukta* did choose to equate *Shudras* to the feet? If the Vedic Literature concerned with the wellness of the society, it would have maintained the dignified origin of birth of all the four classes with equality. He sarcastically criticises that the author should have been aware of one thousand heads of *Purusha*, that is enough to assign one species to be born from one of his heads and it wouldn't have been this complicated if *Purusha Sukta* said that the different classes were born form different mouths of the *Purusha*. The primary concern of the *Purusha Sukta* is to explain the four classes of the society and Babasaheb satirically questions the need for creating a literature which preaches the class composition is not just ideal and natural but exceptionally sacred and divine.

Sequentially, the later development of *Chaturvarnya* witnesses the creation of fifth class next below the *Shudras* and separation of *Shudras* from the first three *varnas*. Peculiar terms namely, *Savarnas, Avarnas, Dvijas, non-Dvijas* and *Traivarnikas* were given rise whose names themselves disclose the relative positions of these classes and their definitive rights and privileges they connote.

The connotations of these terms are *Savarna* is contrasted with *Avarna, Varna* refers to the social classes in Brahminical Books and *Savarna* is to one of the four *varnas*. A *varna* is a term denoting to the one who does not belong to any one of the four *varnas*. The *Brahmins, Kshatriyas, Vaishyas* and *Shudras* are included within *Chaturvarnya* and *Ati-Shudras* and *Untouchables* fall outside the *Chaturvarnya*. *Dvija* and *non-Dvijas* are contrasted with each other. *Dvijas* are twice born, the first-birth from the mother and the second from the investiture with the sacred girdle. In that second birth, the

Guru (the teacher) is the father and Goddess *Savithri* is the mother and they are the twice born people belonging to one particular class, the *Dvijas*. They have the right to wear the sacred thread. Since, the *Brahmins, Kshatriyas* and *Vaishyas* have the right to wear the sacred thread, they logically, are the *Dvijas*. The *Shudras* and the *Anti-Shudras* have no rights to wear the sacred-threads and hence they both fall into the category *non-Dvijas*. *Trivarnikas* are the three *varnas* who were the *Dvijas*. It conveys the same distinction that is between *Dvijas* and *non-Dvijas*. The only difference is that it is limited with the categorisation till *Shudras* and does not extend till *Ati-Shudras*. Babasaheb perplexes and scornfully condemns quoting, "Can there be a greater riddle than the riddle of the Shudras." Surely, it calls for investigation and explanation as to who they were and how they came to be the fourth *varna* in the Aryan Society" (Ambedkar 40)

The primary objective of Dr B.R. Ambedkar in his historical book, "Who were the Shudras?" is to discover the origin of *Shudras*. And he hypothetically finds a remedy by researching each piece of *Brahminis* Literature separately and study whether it paves way for the people to be socially and emotionally intelligent, thereby, building a strong nation or just evidently be conscious of the origin of four classes and of *Shudras*. On the thorough study of the *Shudras*, what explodes is the extensive list of torments and sufferings to which the *Shudras* as subjected to caused by the Brahmanical law-givers through the dire system. Here are the various *Brahmanic Theories* depicting the status of the *Shudras Kathaka Samhita* is also called as *Black Yajur Veda* which says that a *Shudra* should not be allowed to milk the cow whose milk is used for *Agnihotra* is usually performed by orthodox Hindu Communities. *Maitrayani Samhita*, the oldest *Yajurveda Samhita* that has survived and it says that the Shudra must not be spoken to when performing a sacrifice and a *Shudra* must not be present when a sacrifice is being performed. The *Aitareya Brahmana* is the Brahmana of the *Shakala Shakha* of the Rig Veda, an ancient Indian collection of sacred hymn which was attributed entirely to a single man, *Mahidasa Aitareya*. It says that a *Shudra* is a servant of another and cannot be anything else. In the later period of Manu and other *Smritis*, the growth of disabilities of *Shudras* faced an insanely frenzied speed which grew to an unthinkable extent.

Dharmasatra is a genre of Sanskrit texts referring to the treatises of *Hinduism*, *Manusmriti* is the first Sanskrit text to be translated during the British rule of India by Sir William Jones to formulate the Hindu Law by the colonial government. It is the ancient legal text among the many *Dharmasastras* of Hindusim. It presents that the *Brahmins*, *Kshatriya* and *Vaishya* constitute the twice-born castes, but the fourth, the *Shudra* has only one birth. The dead Shudras should be carried through southern town-gate but the dead twice-born by the western, northern and eastern gates.

One earns respect through his wealth, kindred, age, sects (and) knowledge and among the four *varnas*, the three higher castes are worthy of respect who possess the best of these five factors but a *Shudra*, in spite of possessing all these factors, is not worthy of respect except he has attained tenth decade of his life. But the one who knows the Veda completely is great among the other four *varnas*, irrespective of his age, wealth or kindred.

If a *Brahmin*, involuntarily, slays a *Kshatriya*, in order to cleanse himself, should give thousand cows and a bull and live in the foot of a tree with his locks braided and with subdued senses, for three years. If a *Brahmin* has slain a virtuous *Vaishya*, should give one hundred and one heads of cattle and practice the same expiation for a year. But the slayer of a *Shudra* should practice all the expiations and he may give to a priest ten white cows and a bull.

A *Shudra* might not have been taught law or enjoin him in any religious observances. The person who, indeed, does it would sink into the darkness, the hell, called *Asamvita*. Accumulation of wealth is legally not granted for the *Shudras* and if possessed it can be taken by a Brahmin with undisturbed peace of mind as the very sight of possession of wealth by a *Shudra* injures the Brahmin.

Duties for all the castes are ordinary by *Manusmriti* as, teaching, study, sacrifices, giving and receiving gifts are for Brahmins: defence of people, sacrifice, study are for *Kshatriya*; tending of castle, giving alms, sacrifice, study, trade and usury, and also agriculture are for *Vaishyas*; the only one duty assigned for the *Shudras* is serving all the other three twice-born castes.

Any individual reading the content of these Sacred Books would be stemmed and struck by the fact that the *Shudras* alone has been targeted and victimised by the Brahminic law-givers. It is quite critical and the readers of history would be wonderstruck as the ancient Brahminic literature oppressed a particular caste of Indo-Aryan Society i.e., the *Vaishyas* and not the *Shudras*. Now, the question is that why the *Vaishyas* were let off and the fury was directed entirely towards the Shudras?

Apastamba Dharmasutra is the oldest Sanskrit text that has survived into the modern age from the first Millennium BCE. It says that a *Traivarnika* shall never study *The Veda* in a burial ground nor anywhere near it. A *Shudra* and an *outcaste* are included by the term burial ground are included by the term burial ground and that one should avoid studying in the same house where the *Shudras* and *outcastes* dwell. Even if a student looks merely at a *Shudra* woman, the recitation of the Veda must be interrupted; the food touched by a Brahmin or other high-caste person becomes impure but does not become unfit to eat but if the food is brought by a *Shudra*, irrespective of it being touched by him or not, it becomes impure and unfit to eat.

The *Vishnu-Smriti* or *Vaishnava Dahrmasastra* or *Vishnu Sutra* is in the main collection of ancient aphorisms on the sacred laws of India which propounds that the members of the twice-born castes should never let a *Shudra* to be a part of their family even though he/she is their father/mother. If the parents are of inter-caste, say one from the *Dvijas* the other from the *non-Dvijas*, the son can take care of the parents of the high class. The *Vasishtha Dharma Sutra* is one more famous Dharma Sutra written by Rishi Vasistha to teach the Hindu society, the social laws and the duty of man. It posits that the food given by a physician, a hunter, a woman of bad character, a race-bearer, a thief, an Abhisasta, and eunuch or an outcaste must not be eaten. And if a Brahmin dies with the food of a *Shudra* in his stomach, the possible birth of himself in his next life would be a village pig or a member of that *Shudra* family. Even though the Brahmin recites the Veda, offers agnihotra, mutter prayers, nevertheless finds a path that leads upwards if his body is nourished with the essence of a Shudra's food. The abomination of the social laws reaches at its peak when it loathes even the food prepared by the *Shudra*. If a high-caste person has conjugal intercourse, even his sons begotten on a wife of his own caste would belong to the giver of the food i.e. to the *Shudra* and he would never be able to transcend to heaven. When there is tug-of-war between the communities of a single society, emotional turmoil and imbalances would be the chief characteristic of the individual in the society and thereby, civilization becomes meaningless in the absence of harmony and peace among the people. Daniel Goleman rightly puts the interlink between the social and emotional intelligence as, "All emotions are social... You can't separate the cause of an emotion from the world of relationships-our social interactions are what drive our emotions" (Goleman 83).

Any society would, undeniably, not be guaranteed with harmony and peace just by individuals' social awareness but by the actions associated with such awareness determines social faculty that includes concern, the care that we shoe towards others' needs and how we act accordingly. *Synchrony*, the smooth interaction between the persons at the nonverbal level, *Influence*, the involvement in shaping the outcomes of social interactions, all together paves the magnificent way towards social facility. In psychotherapy, the feeling of hurt is diagnosed with neural basis. Our brain activates stimuli causing distressing sensations of bodily pain when we are physically hurt. That exact stimulation is induced during social rejection too. Daniel Goleman stresses, "...We have a hardwired system that is alert to the threat of abandonment, separation, or rejection these were once actual threats to life itself, though they are only symbolically so today" (Goleman 114)

In a nutshell, Dr B.R. Ambedkar claims that his accusation on sacred literature as that contains abominable social philosophy responsible and urgency of social reform as it deals with life itself as Goleman says. Prof. Thorndyke rightly puts it as, "...that a man thinks is a biological fact, what he thinks is a sociological fact" (Ambedkar 15).

What Babasaheb opposes would be offensive only to a class of Hindus who are known as orthdox and they would not admit that there is any need for reformation at all a nothing is wrong with the Hindu social system as they believe. It is quite obviously natural for an orthodox Brahmin scholar to respect and revere the sacred literature of the Hindus as it is a literature which is almost entirely the creation of the *Brahmins*. The entire book *Who were the Shudras?* gives facts and figures on Brahminical Laws on the *Shudras* showcasing the unimaginable pains and penalties imposed upon the so-called low-caste people, "Had the Brahmin any cause to regard the Shudra as his special enemy" (Ambedkar 66).

About an average Brahmin's attitude towards these disabilities of the Shudras, Babasaheb states that his moral sense has become so dulled that he has ceased to bother about the 'why' and 'how' of these disabilities of the *Shudras*. It is, unconditionally essential to manifest to the world that these disabilities have no parallel anywhere in the world. The ultimate atrocity of the *Dharma Sutras* is that it says, "...it will be a crime for a Shudra to study the Vedas or hear it being pronounced and if he does commit such a crime his tongue should be cut or molten lead should be poured into his ear" (Ambedkar 75).

It is, concretely, evident that the orthodoxy by curbing one's right to education and freedom is no sanctity, but mere shamelessness clothed by civilization.

Works Cited

Ambedkar, Bhimrao Ramji. *Who Were the Shudras?* New Delhi: Samyak Prakashan, 2011. Print.

Goleman, Daniel. *Social Intelligence*. London: Arrow Books, 2007. Print.

6

Tyranny by the Caste Hierarchs: An Analysis of Rohinton Mistry's *A Fine Balance*

— *Dr Suruchi Sharma*

Caste and class have been a determining factor of a person's status, place and position in the social hierarchy from the ancient Vedic times to the modern era. Indian caste system is among the world's oldest forms of surviving social stratification. The caste system which was said to be introduced in ancient period to regulate and discipline the society and its smooth functioning has paved way to discrimination and degradation. It was the system that divided the society into four *varnas*: Brahmin, Kshatriya, Vaishya and Shudra providing social stratification in a hierarchical manner assigning people an identity by their work and limitising their social mobility. Dr B.R. Ambedkar said, "Caste system is not merely division of labourers – rather quite different from division of labour – it is a hierarchy in which the division of labourers' are graded one above the other." There are many castes in India which are considered backward and these castes are being exploited and suppressed by the upper caste people. By the efforts of Dr B.R. Ambedkar, the Indian Constitution has given a special privilege to these people and now the social status of these people has improved a lot.

Rohinton Mistry, a South-Asian Parsi writer, a social humanist, attempted his best to voice the cruelty and oppression experienced by Dalits in his second novel *A Fine Balance.* The novel exposes class and caste disparities of Indian society which also mirrors a visual rendering of those who endure its inequities. Dr Reman Kumari writes about this novel "*A Fine Balance* is a fictional presentation with three major strands in it – the stories of Dina Dalal, a Parsi widow who bravely strives for a free and independent existence; young Maneck Kohlah who grapples with problems of existence and the Chamar-turned-tailors Ishvar and Omprakash both of whom struggle for survival in a world that is hostile but occasionally allows them to find refuge in feelings of kinship and togetherness" (Kumari 87).

The novel *A Fine Balance* is set in Mumbai. Its theme is Dalit oppression and it has the Indian Emergency in its setting. The novel portrays the predicaments of Chamars (leather-workers) or untouchables very tactfully. It is a tale of four innocent persons snared in the grinding gears of history. The story revolves around four characters – Dina and Maneck who are Parsis and two tailors Ishvar and his nephew Omprakash. The novel begins with Dina's story as an unmarried girl:

> Dina Dalal seldom indulged in looking back at her life with regret or bitterness, or questioning why things had turned out the way they had, cheating her of the bright future everyone had predicted for her when she was in school, when her name was still Dina Shroff. And if she did sink into one of these rare moods, she quickly swam out of it. (Mistry 14)

Dina Shroff becomes Dina Dalal after her marriage with Rustom Dalal. She was from an aristocratic family. Her father was a physician. She was merely twelve years old at the time of death of her father. She remains under the care of her brother Nussawan. He was not a good boy and he treated her badly. He abuses her and compels her to do all the household chores. She remains under pressure. Though he helps her in some matters yet he keeps her under his full control. He stops her from going to school and hits her when she misbehaves. When Dina gets her hair trimmed without his permission, he says, "Fourteen is too young for fancy hairstyles, plaits are good for you. Besides, I cannot afford to pay for the hairdresser" (Mistry 23). Thus, Nussawan becomes very angry with her at times. His wife Ruby also dislikes Dina and they want to get rid of her. Dina finds her would be husband, Rustom Dalal at a theatre and marries him against the wishes of her brother and his wife Ruby. In fact, they become happy that this marriage has helped them get rid of their tension of Dina's marriage. But she remains unfortunate because their happy life comes to an end at the day of her third wedding anniversary, when Rustom dies after being hit by a car while on his bicycle. Dina does not want to return to her brother's house and under the guidance of her husband's surrogate parents, she becomes a tailor. After twenty years, her eyes gave out due to complicated embroidery work and she became jobless. She eventually met a lady, Mrs Gupta and on her advice of a woman, she started working for a company named Au Revoir Exports. She started taking contracts to make readymade dresses for this company. Having poor eyesight, she had to hire some tailors for her work and she hires Om and Ishvar for her piecework.

Maneck Kohlah was born in a mountain town to loving parents. His father owned a grocery store that had been in family for generations. He was sent to boarding school when he was in fourth standard. He was separated from his parents much against his wishes and his relationship with his parents deteriorated further, when he was sent to college. After a humiliating ragging session by fellow hostel students, Maneck's mother arranged a different living situation for him and he moved in with Dina Dalal.

Ishvar Darji and his nephew Omprakash Darji belong to chamar caste and they have to face many problems in their life. These people hail from different social stratum but destiny makes them together. Though there are many themes in this novel yet Dalit theme is one of the dominant themes. The novel describes the terrible story of the Dalit community. Om and Ishvar Darji come in the city to make their career as tailors but there was much tumultuous environment in their village. The novel tells the anguish of Dukhi Mochi who was a man of revolutionary thoughts. When he was eighteen years old, his marriage is fixed with Roopa who was now only fourteen years old. She gives birth to three daughters in the six years but unfortunately, none of the girls survives after few months of their birth.

Though he was a cobbler by profession and knew that his position is not much better in the village because he had to become a servant of the upper caste people. He somehow thought that his sons may get rid of this humiliating life and they may adopt some new profession. His wife, Roopa also favoured his decision and he sends his sons Narayan and Ishvar to the city so that they might become tailors.

There wasn't any good source of income in the family so the children were 'undernourished and ill-fed'. When Ishvar was a baby and Roopa's milk dried, she had to steal the milk of the landowners' cows. She took only little milk from the cows so that the landowners may not have doubt that the milk of their cows has been stolen by someone. It was a very risky work for a woman. She went to the orchards also to bring the ripe fruit at the dead of nights. One night, as she was filling her sack with oranges, a lantern suddenly raised and she saw a man sitting on a bamboo-and-string cot. After she had filled her sack, she thought of running but the man warned her not to run and also allowed her to pick more oranges. This man was hired by the landowner to protect the orchard. After picking few more oranges, she was expresses her gratitude to him.

But there was something else in the man's mind. He warns her that he would shout and call the landowner and his sons. On seeing her with sack of oranges, they would strip and whip her for stealing their oranges. The conversation between the two lays bares the plight of Dalits:

> "Don't go yet, take as many as you want," he said.
>
> "Thank you, I have enough."
>
> "You are sure? I can easily give you more if you like." He put down his stick and got up from his cot.
>
> "Thank you, this is enough."
>
> "Is it? But wait, you cannot go just like that," he said with a laugh. "You haven't given me anything in return." He walked towards her.
>
> Stepping back, she forced a laugh too. "I don't have anything. That's why I came here in the night, for the sake of my child."

> "You have got something." He put out his hand and squeezed her left breast. She struck his hand away. "I only have to shout once," he warned, and slipped his hand inside her blouse. She shuddered at the touch, doing nothing this time.

He led her cringing to the cot and ripped open her top three buttons. She crossed her arms in front. He pulled them down and buried his mouth in her breasts, laughing softly as she tried to squirm away.

> "I gave you so many oranges. You won't even let me taste your sweet mangoes?"
>
> "Please let me go."
>
> "Soon as I have fed you my Bhojpuri brinjal. Take off your clothes."
>
> "I beg you, let me go."
>
> "I only have to shout once." (Mistry 110-11)

The man molested her and she was helpless because the other step taken by her might have been worse than that. She would have lost her honour and she might have been whipped for her act of stealing. She took the sack and went home crying. Dukhi was not sleeping but he pretended to sleep. He heard her muffled sobs several times during the night and he had thought what might have happened with her. He wanted to go to her but he stopped himself because he didn't have suitable words to comfort her. He was very disheartened. He wept silently and his eyes were filled with the shame, humiliation and anger. He even thought to annihilate himself. By morning everything had become normal. Roopa behaved as if nothing had happened. Dukhi also said nothing to her and they ate the oranges in the morning.

Roopa gave birth to her second child who was named Narayan. When Ishvar and Narayan were ten or twelve years old respectively at that time, they were sent to learn tailoring work under the guidance of Ashraf. All the village people raised their voice against this step taken by Dukhi Mochi but he did not care for anybody's words. His step was really very bold, "Besides tanning and leather-working,

Dukhi learned what it was to be a Chamar, an untouchable in village society. No special instruction was necessary for this part of his education. Like the filth of dead animals which covered him and his father as they worked, the ethos of the caste system was smeared everywhere" (Mistry 106). This news made many people his enemy. They discussed, "Dukhi Mochi has gone mad. With wide-open eyes he is bringing destruction upon his household" (Mistry 105). They could not do anything but they were simmering from inside. Dr Dodhiya writes in this context, "They say that Dukhi dares to break the timeless chain of caste, which high caste people would not like at all" (Dodhiya 15).

These two brothers get full attention and care from Ashraf Chacha and his wife, Mumtaj. After some time they become expert tailors. Ishvar starts working and living with Ashraf Chacha while Narayan decides to return his village. His family has already earned the animosity of the higher caste people. After becoming a tailor, he does not work only for the upper caste people. He starts sewing the clothes of the lower caste people. He gets a good earning from his business and he makes a new house in place of his hut. He marries Radha after earning ample money. He has a son and a daughter. He is filled with self respect and refuses to sew the clothes of the upper caste people. The upper caste people of the whole village develop natural animosity and remorse towards him.

Narayan learns a lot from his experience and by the time he becomes aware of his fundamental rights provided by the constitution. When there were the Parliamentary Elections in his village, he refuses to cast his votes for the upper caste people. He shows his desire to cast his vote to the candidate of his choice. When he objects to cast his vote in favour of the landlord, the fumed landlord sends his goons. Narayan and his two fellows are forcibly captured by them. They bring them to the landlord's flat. The goons behave with utmost cruelty. They tie Narayan and his two fellows upside down from the twigs of the banyan tree. Their clothes are put off and they are beaten black and blue. They wanted to see them whimper in pain. At the evening when election is over and the landlord wins the election by his forgery, his henchmen thrust burning coals in their gentiles and mouths. They had to tolerate the unbearable pain and they cry loudly but nobody shows any sign of sympathy for them. They cry like the wounded or the slaughtering animals. Soon their tongues and lips melt away due to the burning coal. It was due to the fear of the Thakur Dharamdasi. Their screams are heard in the village but nobody comes for their help from the village. When they become silent, their bodies are taken down from the banyan tree, but still there is some movement in their bodies but they are killed by wrapping and pressing the ropes around their necks so that they may die of suffocation. In this way, Narayan and his two people die for their right of suffrage. But Thakur Dharamdasi is not satisfied with the death of these three people. He wanted to give the punishment of his disobedience to the whole family. He ordered his goons to bring and burn alive all the members of Narayan's family. He wanted to create terror in the village so that the villagers may not dare to raise their voice against him. That's why all the dead bodies are displayed at the village square. In order to save their lives, Omprakash and his uncle Ishvar somehow run away to a nearby village.

With the arrival of readymade garments business, the tailoring business of his uncle Asharaf has to suffer a setback. They are forced to live in the city for their survival but life in city is really tough. They had to face difficulties in the city until they get help from Dina Dalal who was also looking for some tailors. They manage to get a shack in the nearby slum.

Rohinton Mistry depicts caste discrimination as a stigma for the society. It is the caste and community differentiation that makes these people miserable. Rich people like Thakur Dharamdasi have all the power in their hands and they run the government. The people like Narayan become their prey and even police do not arrest them. In fact, it is the police that provide protection to such criminals. Here no FIR is lodged against Thakur Dharamdasi because he is the all-in-all of that area and even the police are under his control.

Thus, Mistry portrays the representations of Dalits in *A Fine Balance*. It brings a sensible and sensitive understanding of social exploitation inherent in the class structure of India and points out how a marginalised person loses his individual identity. I can be stated that "the search for the individual and social identities is palpable in Mistry's works" (Deivasigamani and Lakshmi 270). Jaydipsinh Dodhiya also writes about Mistry's novels, "One of the most remarkable features of Rohinton Mistry's fiction is that it brilliantly captures the crowded, throbbing life of India" (Dodhiya 02).

Conclusively, caste discrimination is a kind of disease that denigrates not only Hindu culture, but it is also a blot on Indian society and it is reflected in the words of Rohinton Mistry, "What is this disease? You may ask. This disease, brothers and sisters, is the notion of untouchability ravaging us for centuries, denying dignity to our fellow human beings. This disease must be purged from our society, from our hearts and our minds. No one is untouchable, for all are children of the same God. Remember what Gandhiji says, that untouchability poisons Hinduism as a drop of arsenic poisons milk." (Mistry 359) Bijender Singh also shares the same undercurrent that "The unity and awareness of Dalits can bring revolution in their lives and change their situation to the core" (Singh 47). Therefore, atrocities to the Dalit and Parsi community are the central concerns of this novel as Shabistan Zafar and Ajoy Batta opine, "*A Fine Balance* explores the injustices of caste and probes the implications of defying it" (Jafar and Batta 23706).

Works Cited

Deivasigamani, T., and G. Thibiga Lakshmi. "The Concept of Untouchability in Rohinton Mistry's *A Fine Balance*." *Language in India*, 18:3 (March 2018): 268-272.

Dodhiya, Jaydipsinh. *Novels of Rohinton Mistry: Critical Study.* New Delhi: Sarup & Sons, 2004. Print.

Gaikwad, Kamalakar B., and Vijay D. Songire. "The Subaltern Voice and Visibility in Rohinton Mistry's *A Fine Balance*." *Pune Research Journal: An International Multidisciplinary Journal*. 2.1 (2016): 1-6.

Kumari, Reman. "Untouchability and Rohinton Mistry's *A Fine Balance*." *A Publication of Trans Asian Research Journals AJMR*, 1.7 (2012): 87-91.

Mistry, Rohinton. *A Fine Balance* (1995). New York: Rosetta Books, 2004. Print.

Singh, Bijender. "Revisiting Dalitism in Rohinton Mistry's *A Fine Balance*". *Daltri Journal*. 2.10 (2013): 37-47.

Singh, Sumitra. "Exploring Dalit Aesthetics in Rohinton Mistry's *A Fine Balance*." *Indian Dalit Literature: Critical Ruminations*. Ed. Bijender Singh. New Delhi: Authorspress, 2015. 70-76. Print.

Zafar, Shabistan and Ajoy Batta. "Struggle for Identity and the Cultural/Social Difference in *A Fine Balance* by Rohinton Mistry" *International Journal of Recent Scientific Research*. 9.1 (Jan. 2018): 23703-06.

7

Portrayal of the Conditions of Dalits in Mulk Raj Anand's *Untouchable*

— *Dr V. Nagarajan and Dr F. Vincent Rajasekar*

Dalit Literature is the genre which plays a vital role in Indian literature. It had emerged in the 1960s and started with Marathi language and also followed in Hindi, Kannada, Telugu and Tamil languages in the aspects of literary phenomenon. The term 'Dalit Literature' was first used in the conference of 'Maharashtra Dalit Sahitya Sangha' in Mumbai in 1958. The word Dalit literally means 'oppressed.' Dalit is also called 'outcast'. It is a self designation for a group of people traditionally regarded as untouchables. Dalits are mixed population of various caste groups living not only in India but all over the world.

The word 'Dalit' comes from the Sanskrit word 'dal' which means downtrodden, suppressed, and crushed. It was first used by Jyothi Rao Phule, the champion of backward classes and other oppressed classes of Maharashtra in 19th century.

So many Dalit leaders carried out the Dalits' equality such as Martin Luther King in America, Nelson Mandela in South Africa and Dr B.R. Ambedkar in India. They sacrificed their life and helped the people get rid of their pain. Some of the most important writers are Mahasweta Devi, Daya Pawar, Arjun Dangle, Poomani, Bama,

Abhimani, Annabhababu Sathe, Arun Kamble, Urmila Pawar and Mulk Raj Anand etc who focused on the socio-equality of Dalits.

Maharashtra started an organisation in the name of Block Panthers. It was inspired by the 'The America Panthers' in America. It makes for the social and political rights of Negroes and some organisations are republication party of India such as Indian Panthers Party, All India Scheduled Caste Federation, Mala Mahanadu, Madiga Reservation Porata Samithi. All these organisations are built for the enrichment of the Dalit's equalities. The works and speeches of great social reformers, Martin Luther King, Nelson Mandela, B.R. Ambedkar and Jyotiba Phule continued to inspire the Dalits in modern world.

Dalit Literature got own literary place among in the mainstream literary genres. It is to develop the basic human values like liberty, fraternity, equality among the Dalit and non-Dalit people. They need identity with self enrichment and also develop the society. The writers of Dalit Literature have started tormenting experiences of Dalits exposed to the contemporary social, political, economic, educational and mental conditions of Dalits. Dalit people had affected by the necessary needs of food, clothes and self protest. They are suppressed by the higher caste brutal mankind.

Dr B.R. Ambedkar is one of the greatest leaders who struggled for the freedom and equality of Dalits. His famous books are *The Buddha and His Dhamma, Annihilation of Caste,* and *The Problem of Rupee in British India.* His book *Thoughts on Pakistan* makes him as a Dalit crusader. He started many periodicals like *Mook Nayak, Bahishkrut Bharat, Janata, Prabuddha Bharat* etc for the Dalit's rights. When he was practicing law in the Bombay High Court, he tried to promote education to untouchables and to uplift them. His first organised attempt was his establishment of the central institution Bahishkrit Hitakarini Sabha which was intended to promote education and socio-economic improvement as well as the welfare of outcasts, at the time referred to as depressed classes.

Arjun Dangle has defined Dalit Literature as "Dalit Literature is one which acquaints people with the caste system and untouchability in India. It matters with a sociological point of view and is related to the principles of negativity, rebellion, and loyalty to science, thus finally ending as revolutionary" (Dangle lii).) His work *Poisoned Bread* is the first ever attempt to anthologise Dalit Writings in English. Sharankumar Limbale has stated, "Dalit Literature is precisely that literature which artistically portrays the sorrows, tribulations, slavery, degradation, ridicule and poverty endured by Dalits. This literature is but a lofty image of grief" (Limbale 30).

Dalit writers also write short-stories and novels to express Dalit sensibility suitably. The short-stories like Anna Bahu Sathi's "Fakira" and Sankar Rao Kharat's "Davindi" are important in this context. Mulk Raj Anand is the insisting writer to touch upon the genre of Dalit Literature in his novels *Coolie* and *Untouchable*. It mainly aims at creating awareness of Dalits about their social conditions in the society.

Mulk Raj Anand is one of the first and foremost writers to focus on the theme of 'untouchablilty'. His literary career was launched by his personal experience about the caste system. The novel *Untouchable* was written by caste Hindu Mulk Raj Anand. Many publishers had rejected it. His first major novel *Untouchable* was published in 1935. It exposed the day-to-day life of a latrine cleaner Bakha. The novel portrays the social evils of high caste community and the innocent behaviour of the untouchables. It focuses on many social evils prevalent in the society and the cruel caste system prevalent in India. Mulk Raj Anand has thrown light on the tyranny of the upper caste Hindus and the physical and psychological tortures of Dalits. Most of the events of the novel describe the poor and dehumanised status of Dalits. The protagonist, Bache's sufferings are instinctively the study of hard realities of out caste society. E.M. Forster observers that:

> The sweeper is worse off than a slave, for the slave may change his master and his duties and may even become free, but the sweeper is bound for ever born into a state, from which he cannot escape and where he is excluded from social inter course and the consolations of his religion. Unclean himself, he pollutes others when he touches them. (Forster iv)

The novel *Untouchable* delineates the issue of the caste discriminations through the main protagonist, Bakha. He is eighteen-year-old Dalit boy exploited and suppressed by the society. He works labouriously to clean the public latrines of the town. As he was a Dalit boy and his work was of an inferior quality, the Hindus render him an untouchable. Such illustrations from the novel expose the author's empathy with the Dalits of India and the novel further tells about the mentality of upper class Hindus.

M.R. Anand delivers the novel's major ideas and concerns through his character Bakha. They have to work continuously and the pain, sorrow, slavery and humiliation are a part of their life. The outcast people struggle to live in the world of financial instability and they have to face the ill-treatment and humiliation by the upper caste people. The major characters of the novel are Bakha and Sohini. Both of them are the victim of caste discrimination and they have to suffer the tyranny, exploitation and subjugation of the caste system. The novel portrays that the Dalit people's life style remains much degraded. The protagonist, Bakha has to face many major and minor sufferings of his own experience.

The novel opens with Bakha's father yelling at him. The cleaning of public latrines is the routine work of Bakha. Bhakha's father is Lakha in the novel who is a domineering person. The morning conversation between Bakha and Lakha about the toilet cleaning is indicative of their real status in the society. Bakha is ignoring his job. Singh, a famous hockey player, yells at Bakha just because he has to done the petty work of toilet cleaning and he is a poor low-caste boy. Afterwards, Singh encourages him and says that he will give him hockey stick later. This was the happiest moment for him. After meeting Singh, Bakha finishes toilet cleaning and returns his home much tired and hungry.

Sohini is Bakha's sister. She also has to work as a sweeper. When she was going to well to draw water, some people remained in the lookout to molest her. Gulabo had a superiority complex and she was the mother of Bakha's friend. She hates Sohini and also gets angry about her son's friendship with Bakha. She belongs to upper caste than Bakha. Bakha gets again cleaning work at town square and the temple instead of his father, Lakha. He feels fake illness. It is a miserable moment for Bakha because Bakha knows everything that the father's activities also suppress him. But he cannot raise any question against him and he gets ready for going to the job.

Bakha eats the candies and unfortunately, touches a high-caste man. The man feels angry with him and scolds him. A large crowd gathers there to see this scene. At this moment, the Muslim crosses the way and disperses the crowd. Before leaving the crowd, the man slaps Bakha's face. Bakha feels ashamed at that time, but he can't show any action of gallantry against him. He cries, collects his things and moves aside of the temple.

At the moment, Bakha hears the fearful sound from aside of the temple. Later, he finds that it was his sister, Sohini's voice. Behind her fearful sound, Pundit Kali Nath, priest of the temple, was giving sexual torture to her. Bakha saves his sister and fights against him but Sohini yanks his brother and protects him.

Bakha's family has to beg food for their daily needs. Bakha makes a friendship with Ram Charan and Chota. Ram Charan and Chota belong to higher caste than Bakha. Bakha goes in the marriage of Ram Charan's sister with melancholy mode. His friends find him and asking about his disturbance. Bakha tells about the slap and also Sohini's sexual assaults. Bakha's friends become indignant. But they do nothing.

Bhaka goes to Charat Singh's house to receive the hockey stick and he goes to play with his friends. While playing, a dispute arises among the two groups and a boy gets injured. When Bhaka takes the injured boy to his home, his mother accuses Bakha for her son's injuries. He returns his home, his father also banish him away from their house. He feels alone under a tree. The chief of the local Salvation Army, a British man named Colonel Hutchinson convinces him to reach to the church. The colonel's wife becomes furious and she shouts at the act of her husband. Bakha leaves the place suddenly.

Bakha has no idea about the way he was going. Finally, he reaches at a train station. When he hears the Gandhi's speech about untouchables, he feels a bit relaxed and cool. After he analyses their ideas and words, he feels that he has a widely power of his life. At the end of the novel, Bakha returns his home.

The novel is a mixture of self supporting ideas from the awareness speech about the issue of society. Bakha raises his power of thought after attracting the speech programme about the untouchables. It is used to follow the thought of Gandhi and some organising workers. It is such great development of the Dalit or outcaste people's mental stability and also the identity in the society. It is used for making better society. In the words of Marlene Fisher, "...Anand's first novel, then, is at one and the same time a fine piece of creative work in terms of its own artistic integrity and an indication of it author's humanistic commitments and future novelistic directions" (Fisher 15). Asserting the importance of Dalit Literature, Arundhati Roy has observed:

> I do believe that in India we practice a form of apartheid that goes unnoticed by the rest of the world. And it is as important for Dalits to tell their stories as it has been for colonised peoples to write their own histories. When Dalit Literature has blossomed and is in full stride, then contemporary Indian literature's amazing ability to ignore the true brutality and ugliness of the society in which we live, will be seen for what it is: bad literature. Jaydeep Sarangi considers Dalit Literature as a culture specific upheaval in India giving importance to Dalit realisation, aesthetics and resistance. (Introduction to "Dalit Voice" 2018)

Dalit Literature emerged from the suppressed society to develop equality in the society. So, the people mentioned the oppressed character as protagonist in their novel like Bakha in Mulk Raj Anand's *Untouchable*, Coolie's *Munoo* and Thangam of P. Sivakami's *The Grip of Change*. These novels portray the sorrows, tribulations, slavery, and poverty of Dalits. The society shows a clear depiction of a casteist mindset of people. People can unite without thinking about the caste system and the lands also should be divided equally without thinking about any caste or community.

As a conclusion, Dalit Literature emerged as a revolutionary power to save the life of Dalits. In this way, education and the idea of democracy awaken the suppressed society. Many minor things also create confidence, pride and self-esteem. The ultimate aim of Dalit Literature is, to bring the equality, liberty and freedom for everyone irrespective of caste, class, gender, race or ethnicity. It automatically provides the fraternity among the people.

Works Cited

Bagul, Baburao. "Dalit Literature is but Human Literature." *Poisoned Bread: Translations from Modern Marathi Dalit Literature*. Ed. Arjun Dangle. Bombay: Orient Longman, 1992. Print.

Dangle, Arjun. "Introduction: Dalit Literature Past, Present and Future." *Poisoned Bread: Translations from Modern Marathi Dalit Literature*. Ed. Arjun Dangle. Hyderabad: Orient Blackswan, 2009. ixx-liv. Print.

Forster, E.M. "Preface". *Untouchable*. Mulk Raj Anand. London: Penguin, 1985. Print.

http://en.m.wikipedia.org, Dalit Literature

http://www.gradesaver.com, study-guide

Limbale, Sharan Kumar. *Towards an Aesthetic of Dalit Literature*. Trans. Alok Mukherjee. New Delhi: Orient Longman, 2004. Print.

Marlene Fisher. *The Wisdom of the Heart*. New Delhi: Arnold Publishers, 1985. Print.

8

Meena Kandasamy's *Touch*: Vocalisation of Dalit Ordeal

— ***Neha Raina***

Dalit Literature forms an important and distinguished part of Indian English Literature. It emerged in the decade of 1960, starting with the Marathi vernacular; it soon appeared in various other languages viz; Hindi, Kannada, Telugu, Bangla and Tamil etc, employing narratives of poems, short-stories, and mostly autobiographies, which stood out due to their stark portrayal of reality and the Dalit political scene.

On reading Kandasamy's collection of poems *Touch*, it is seen that the anger and frustrations of this neglected marginalised community is vividly used as motifs of suppression, subjugation, hegemonical structural framework of society, with rebellion and revolution as means to achieve elevation and upliftment. Each poem in *Touch* is a telling-tale of woe and worry of Dalits in general and Dalit women in particular. This paper is a modest attempt to bring to fore the sufferings and dilemmas of Dalits which Meena Kandasamy has used as weapons of change and reform; yearning for a holistic and humanistic betterment of this subaltern class. *Touch* contains a Foreword by Kamala Das where the renowned poetess writes, "Older by nearly half a century, I acknowledge the superiority of her portico mission" (Touch 7). Meena follows the psychological tradition of Sylvia

Plath and Langston Hughes, a fabric rare and strange. Meena herself regards her poetic corpus as a process of coming to terms with her identity and consciousness. She knew, she says that "my gender, language and castelessness were not anything that I had to be ashamed of....I wrote poetry very well aware of who I was" (Source: Poetry International Web). A Dalit women writer is herself Dalit among Dalits. Her active engagement as editor of a Dalit magazine "The Dalit" and association with the Dalit Panthers of India (A Militant Activist Dalit Organisation) has further honed her awareness of what it means to be a woman in a caste-ridden nation; the outcome of which is glowing volume of poetry that arises "not out of mere reading but out of active engagement." (Source: Meenupress.com)

As a writer Meena Kandasamy mainly focuses on caste-discrimination, feminism and linguistic identity. As a fierce critique of academic language; in an interview which appeared in Sampsonia Way Magazine, she says, "Poetry is not caught up within larger structure that pressure you to adopt a certain set of practices while you present your ideas in the way that academic language is." (Kandasamy: "Angry Young Women are Labelled Hysterics" 39)

Dalit Literature is an emerging genre in Indian Writing. The writers including the Dalit writers have faced a lot of criticism and hardships. Dalits (Dal-broken), underestimated and neglected since ages, got a new current of ideas to vent their dilemma and disillusionment with the upper caste discrimination against them. A new team of Dalit and non-Dalit writers writing for Dalits make an important sub-genre in Indian English Literature. Fearless and far-visioned; this literature voiced against the perpetuation of Dalits in general and the Dalit women in particular; their pathos and pain flowed in glowing letters penning down their struggle against all odds of social stratum.

The early Dalit fiction got sharp momentous through the writings of P. Sivakami, Bama, Abimaani, Poomani, Sukirtharani, Prathibha, Jayachandran, Chanakya, Dharman, Yahan, Adhi etc and it is expressing the tale of gloom, apathy and resentment among Dalits. *Touch* (2006) is a collection of eighty-four poems mainly centred on the issues of marginalisation of Dalits especially women to their social superior counterpart.

In an interview once Meena said, "My poetry is naked, my poetry is in tears, my poetry screams in anger, my poetry writhes in pain. My poetry smells of blood, my poetry salutes sacrifice. My poetry speakers like my people." (Kandasamy: "Let-there be light". www.jpcs.in)

In one of her poem, "Touch" the sensations of touch is discriminated on the basis of normal touch and the touch given by an outcast or low-caste. She laments:

You will have known almost
every knowledgeable thing about
the charms and the temptations
that touch could hold.

But, you will never have known
that Touch-the Taboo
to your Transcendence
when crystallized in caste
hear a Paraphernalia of
undeserving hate. (36-41)

She equates this sense of aloofness among the humans as a failure, a failure of one human to identify with others; the only reason springing from caste difference.

And the only failure, that ever came:
the only gross betrayal
was from your own skin. (7-9)

In another poem "Advaita: The Ultimate Question" from her book *Touch*, Meena raises fundamental question of ultimate oneness with the supreme God.

Non Dualism
Atman self
Brahman God
Are equal

Are same
So I. (1-6)

Curiosity and thirst to find equanimity with other class finds vent in the lines:

One More
Final Question
Can My
Untouchable Atman
And Your
Brahmin Atman
Ever Be
One? (16-23)

Her poem "Prayer", questions the ultimate fate of Dalits:

An irked Rajput surged forth
And smote the untouchable with an iron rod.
He, warrior caste lion couldn't tolerate encroachment.
At the temple. By a Dalit. Deathly howls of a feeble – voiced
Rent the air, fervently seeking holy intervention.
....
Caste crueller than disease, emotionless, dry, took its toll
Confirming traditional truths: Dalits die, due to devotion.
Where did this poor man's sixty five-year old soul go?
To Heaven – to join noble martyrs who died for a cause?
Or to Hell – Where the God reside, making caste laws? (27-29)

The question Meena raises here is of worth consideration. Her inner self witnesses a whirlpool of emotional upheavals. She voices her concern whether this man-made law of caste discrimination also exists where the almighty lives. Her question whether the poor man who died gets 'Heaven' or 'hell' is deep and perturbing one.

"Becoming A Brahmin," a poem which talks about a 'Shudra' or 'Outcaste' to convert into a Brahmin by following an algorithm records the sad plight of the outcaste at the hands of their social superior.

Begin:
Step 1: Take a beautiful Shudra girl.
Step 2: Make her marry a Brahmin
Step 3: Let her give birth to his female child.
Step 4: Let this child marry a Brahmin.
Step 5: Repeat steps 3-4 six times
Step 6: Display the end product. It is a Brahmin.
End. (1-6)

This poem is actually based on a documentation prepared by Preiyer, a Dalit intellectual on the speech of Gandhiji at Tirupur on 20th September, 1947. The poem is a mockery of this weird notion of marrying a Shudra girl to a Brahmin boy and many of her coming generations to follow the same footsteps in order to get final product a Brahmin and further Meena continues to say that "We await another father of the Nation to produce this algorithm." ("On Becoming a Brahmin" 13)

Her poem "Another Paradise Lost: The Hindu" presents story of a serpent and her conversation with it. The serpent narrates self story that once it was a Monarch named Nahusa, the Great; who was held with high honour on the Earth and in the heaven too.

Long long ago, I was a mighty monarch on earth,
Feared and respected. I was Nahusa the Great.
My subjects were happy, the kingdom prosperous.
And I ruled for twelve thousand years. (55)

He raised questions before Gods in heaven about the caste system and propounded the notion of equality, freedom and fraternity. He was labelled a rebel and was then awarded a punishment to return back to earth in the form of serpent. The serpent discloses:

I wanted to know why caste was there,
Why people suffered because of their karma,
I questioned the gods and the learned sages there.

I asked them what would happen if a high-born did manual work
Just like the low born. (59-63)

The serpent says the gods up above in heaven plotted against him owing to his curious questions of lack of equality even in the abode of God's kingdom and his concern for the Dalits.

The Gods plotted against me,
The deciding that I was trouble. I was cursed to turn into a vile snake.
I was banished from paradise. For sixty million years, I shall roam the
Earth, and then I return. This was a different case of the paradise lost. (67-71)

Few poems like "Liquid Tragedy: Karamchedu 1985," underline the ill-fate meted out to low-caste women and men folk on account of their appeal for common questions of equality and freedom to live. Meena here brings the tragic massacre of Karamchedu which took place on July 17 in 1985 in state of Andhra Pradesh where six Madiga (low-caste) men were killed and three Madiga women were raped by the upper caste men. This massacre turned ugly side when a low-caste women protested against the washing and cleaning of cattle in the pond where these Dalits; Madigas drank water.

Buffalo baths, Urine, Bullshit
Drinking water for the Dalits
The very same Pond
Practice for eons.
A bold Dalit lady
dares to question injustice.
Hits forth with her plot.
Her indignation is avenged.
Fury let loose.
Violence, Rapes, Killings. (1-9)

These lines "Buffalo baths, Urine, Bullshit, drinking water for the Dalits" speak in volume the inhumanitarian mental attitude. These upper class people assumed and so perpetrated atrocities towards the neglected and marginalised sections of society. Dalits were even denied the basic human rights to clean drinking water and they were forced to drink from the same water body where their cattle drank, bathed and urinated. The woman folk who rebelled against such malpractices were not only molested, harassed but also raped to appease their raging voices. Meena explores the heart-wrenching voices of weakened souls:

> Dalits exist – weary of the persecution
> And wander all over the Nation
> Again, a Dalit exodus.
> Total surrender. (16-19)

Her poem "Narration" narrates the voiceless voicing of the Dalit women who were exploited, molested and physically abused by rich upper-class landlords.

> I'll weep to you about
> My landlord, and with
> My mature gestures-
> You will understand. (1-4)

The questions of discriminations on the grounds of low caste in our society and no apathy in molesting a 'Dalit' woman find expression in these lines:

> The torn sari, dishevelled hair
> Stifled cries and meek submission
> I was not an Untouchable then. (5-7)

The predicament of Dalit women at the hands of their own husbands who inflicted domestic violence and hushed their voices can well be understood in these lines:

> How can I say
> Anything, anything
> Against my own man? (56)

The inability to quench their thirst for gaining freedom to live with equality and recluse in seclusion and silence is well poeticised here:

So I take shelter in silence
Wear it like a mask.
When alone, I stumble
Into a flood of incoherencies... (19-22)

Poems like "Aggression," exemplifies Dalits struggle for existence and longing for some favourable time to come where they can live with equality, fraternity and freedom as their right as equivalent to 'upper class.'

Ours is a silence
That waits. Endlessly waits.
And then, unable to bear it
Any further, it breaks into wails. (1-4)

The line "Ours is a silence that waits. Endlessly waits" gives a deep peep into the psyche of outcastes whose voices were muted and there struggle to find expression of self in long years. The silent voice uproars a coming revolutionary change to come soon:

Sometimes,
The outward signals
of the inward struggles takes colossal forms
And the revolution happens because one dreams explode. (7-10)

These ending lines have wider implications:

Most of the time:
Aggression is the best kind of trouble-shooting. (Line No?)

This fire in their eyes for a better futuristic life is self-evident in yet another powerfully scripted poetic work titled "Fire" which echoes the soul-voices of Dalits experiencing indifferent and inhumanistic behaviour from the 'other class' people:

Black satanic fumes

Shroud the blank blue skies
in puffing jet black soot;
few flashy cameras record
glimpses of destruction
(for tomorrow's papers).... (1-6)

The gloom of negligence and compulsive suffering is penned in the below lines:

Up there
Reverberate and sound as loud
as snail shells crackling under nailed boots
and perhaps as distinct and defenseless
This double catastrophe projected in sights
and shrieks evokes ...
No response. (20-26)

The agony of enraged mind is given vent when the poetess says, "Those above are (mostly): indifferent bastards." "Shame" poeticises how this society of indifference treats the Dalit women who negate the crimes like rape, molestation and physical abuses by upper caste men due to their social affiliations, ultimately forcing the girls to find recluse in committing suicide:

"Gang Rape"
Two severe syllables
Implied in her presence
Perpetuate the assault
...
Public's prying eyes
Segregate her-the victim
But the criminals have
Already mainstreamed
Their caste is classic shield. (1-9)

The heinous crimes of rapes and molestations of a Dalit girl are thought to be a commonplace thing which aggravates the pains of the suffered soul:

> "Dalit Girl Raped"
> Is much too commonplace.
> Humiliation gnaws
> The sixteen years old.
> Gory scars on a wrecked body,
> Serve as a constant reminders
> of disgrace, helplessness. (10-16)

Left with gloom and despair; to end life means – life to them:

> Bravely, in search of
> a definite solution,
> and elusive purification,
> She takes the test of the fire-
> the ancient medicine for Shame. (22-26)

Radical in thoughts and carrying a streak of sharp critical views; her poetry poeticises the grim and grieved mental agonises. This marginalised minority section was tormented with since antiquity. As a Dalit woman writer, her medium of writing is English language for she finds it apt to bring her issues to the global platform. It was also that she selectively chose the genre of poetry herself because to her, poetry is the best medium to articulate the upsurge of violent emotions, brewing inside her when females and Dalit issues in society are concerned. Kandasamy said in an interview that language is the site of subjugation and oppression and it is poetry to challenge the oppression of language and its inequalities. By choosing to write in English language she assumes to bring the anti-caste strain in Indian English Writing.

Protest against age-old systems work in society for the supremacy of upper section of society. Upper caste people vouch for their 'divine origins.' Instead of bearing the trauma in "endless silence," she chooses to speak out vehemently and more forcefully. Revolutionary in its verbosity and revolutionary in actions; this saga of struggle and resistance for caste-annihilation makes it ample clear what needs to be corrected and reformed without any further delay.

In "Hymns of a Hag" Meena devises a methodology to take revenge on the upper caste. She fancies herself as a 'witch' who wants to fly to the 'temple street' hunting oppressors (non-Dalits) to shave their heads and cut their holy threads.

> I fancy myself being a witch.
> Broomstick born and black as pitch. (2)
>
> Thin, stark-naked and with fire for eyes.
> Killing men whom I despise. (4)
>
> Haunting oppressors to shave their heads
> Cutting all their holy threads. (12)

The long-long history of relentless urge to gain freedom of expression and equality among Dalits is expressed when they take revenge:

> Experiencing joy as they bleed.
> Dance, rejoice my black black deed.
>
> Leave one farewell note, an obscene cue:
> 'Judgement day is long since due.' (24)

The numerous incidents of witch-hunts in India can be seen. Most of the Dalit and Adivasis women are accused of practicing sorcery and they are brutally murdered, such themes are addressed in her poetry. When woman folk find an urge to take a stand for themselves against the patriarchal domination in the society and demand their fair share of property or demand the respect they rightfully deserve, they are branded as 'witches'. In an essay *Dangerous Dalit Woman and Witch-Hunters*, published in *Ultra-Violet*, Kandasamy gives a detailed view on the alleged 'Witches' and the reason for terming them so:

> The helpless 'Witches' are hounded and punished by being stripped naked, paraded around the villages, their hair is burnt off or their head tonsured' their faces blackened, their noses cut

> off, their teeth pulled out (they are supposedly defanged) so that they can no longer curse, they are whipped, they are branded, sometimes, they are forced to eat human faces and finally, they are put to death (here again the Indian imagination takes over: the victim is hanged, impaled, hacked, lynched or buried alive). And you have got it all wrong if you assumed that such stomach-churning, toe-curling torture is done in dingy, shadowy places: vast, open village lands come in particularly handy as favoured locations, and the cheering crowd can fill a modest stadium. (Kandasami)

The poems "Eklaivan" exemplifies the differences meted out to low-castes since time immemorial.

You don't need your right thumb,
to pull a trigger or hurl a bomb. (6-7)

This note comes as a consolation. Here are few more lines by the same poet:

You can do a lot of things
With your left hand.
Besides, fascist Dronacharya warrant
Left-handed treatment. (1-4)

It underscores the false notions based on inequalities of caste and creed in the gurukul of Guru Dronacharaya since mythological times. Eklaivya was a talented disciple who devotedly obeyed what his master ordered to him in gurukul; but owing to his low –birth he was not given the equal treatment as his fellows of upper caste enjoyed. Rather, he had to cut his right hand Thumb in order to prove his dedication and entrust towards his master which was not in justification to any grounds. In poems like "Fleeting" a graphic heart-rending painful picture of Dalit experiences is explored.

One history is lost,
Perhaps destroyed
And efforts at recollection
Entail in melancholy. (1-4)

She continues to lament:

Caste perennially remain
a scheming bulldozer
Crushing only the Dalits-
And renewing, revoking the bitter past. (7-10)

Meena Kandasamy not only fights the questions of Dalit struggle for existence but challenges the age-old caste system and rigidity of society. The lines 'Crushing only the Dalits - And renewing, revoking the bitter past" is an ample proof of the struggle and desire to break away the shackles of caste stamped on them since long times. The sorrow of grief-stricken lot is embedded in the lines:

We move about, measuring our ages in sorrows.
But when can we get to live our lives in retrospect?

Her stand in all 'grey and white' sparkles in these lines from poem, "Dignity":

You stick to your faith,
The incurable sickness
of your minds,
we don't stop you
from continuing
to tend centuries
of cultivated superegos. (7-13)

But, don't suppress
One rightful share of dignity
It might even prove helpful
If you ever learnt
That virtue
Though inherited
Was nothing beyond
The appearance
Of the footprint

Of a bird
On water... (17-27)

In the poem titled "Immanuel," the mythical character of Immanuel is chosen which carries deep-rooted meaning and provides insightful message to the people.

God he was, in those short living years,
When he lifted the lowly and put down
The mighty from their thrones. (Immanuel 1-4)

Like Immanuel the Messiah of the Jesus, there will be Dalit heroes who will uplift the lowly and put down 'the mighty' from their thrones. Irony and dark humour in her pieces of poetries make her verses of repression and resistance more appealing and worth reading.

And he became a greater God,
With his brutal death, that incited
Many deaths and a significant liberation.

It was a warriors passing,
....
The Jewish carpenter's son. (10)
Now, if there be any mourning
Let it be for our heroes
Yet to die, fighting.... (13)

Here is an excerpt from interview:

Q/N: How do you see the situation of Dalits today and in the future? How do you think that your writings will initiate changes in the sociological paradigms as envisaged by the Dalits?

Meena: The struggle to annihilate caste will be victorious, and it will owe a great deal to the Dalit people and their relentless struggle. It is not an overnight change, but the change has to come about. I don't think I'm an author of history, or an agent of change to comment upon your second question.

All that I can safely say is that if people are made to rethink about caste, and if they can be convinced that it is self-defeating in the long run, they will not have trouble letting it go. Caste protects a lot of selfish interests and that is why it seems as if it were to stay. Next, there is a great deal of animosity against the Dalits because caste-Hindus think that they are beneficiaries of the reservation policy. I think such a manner of harbouring grudges is not going to serve any purpose. If the reservation policy wasn't there, India would have witnessed its first and real revolution. What we also need right now is sanity: realising that caste is one of the most insane instruments of discrimination and that casteism is actually a real psychological condition. "If people understand that caste exists in the mind and nowhere else, all its cruel physical manifestations like segregation and untouchability, can be erased. And I think it is in the hands of writers to make people think about it. Writers have the power of the written word, all done they can plead with people to unite for change." (Ujjwal Jana). "Last Love Letter," another piece of poetry in *Touch*, creates a paradoxical statement which negates the effects of the discrimination based on caste and colour perpetuates on lovers who belong to two different classes of society:

....Our passionate love,
Once transcended caste.
Let it now
Transcend mortality...
Fear not beloved,
In love
Love is not compulsory. (1-7)

The dehumanised behaviour with the socially uprooted, marginalised lower section of society and the gender differences meted out within their own community etc views are well written in poem "We Will Rebuild Worlds":

We will rebuild / world's from shattered glass/
and remnants of holocausts. (1-2)

The brutalities and suffering imposed by the upper caste on Dalits have been beautifully penned down in these lines:

Once impaled for our faith/and trained to speak in
voiceless whispers/we'll implore/you to produce the list/
/from hallowed memories/of our people disgraced /as
outcastes/degraded/as untouchable at /sixty-four feet/
denied a life/and livelihood and done to death/

in so many ways it would take/an encyclopaedia to
describe and steven-spielberg/or some-such guy to
produce the special effects for a blockbuster version/
not just the stories of how/you charred to death forty-four
of our men and women and children/because they asked
for handfuls of rice/ (11-13)

Even the young boys and girls who dared to love beyond caste differences were made to face deadly punishments publicly:

Poured poison and pesticide through the ears-nose-mouth/
Or hanged them in public/because a man and a woman
dared to love
And you wanted/to teach/other boys and girls/the
Lessons of/how to/whom to/when to/where to/continue
their caste lines. (23)

The final beacon call is given loud and more fiercely:

We will learn/how to fight/with the substantial
spontaneity/with which we first learnt/how to love.
So/now/upon a future time/
there will be a revolution. (43-46)

The powerful surging voices of marginalised lot find expression when they declare a coming revolution for their rights and a better future life:

It will begin when never/resting we will scream/until
....
India, what is the caste of sperm?/India, what is the cost of life?
and the rest of our world's will rush/

In this silenced earth/
Like the rage of a river in first flood. (70-76)

Works Cited

Abrams, M.H., and Geoffrey Galt Harpham. *A Handbook of Literary Terms*. Stamford: Cengage Learning, 2015. Print.

Anand, Mulk Raj, and Eleanor Zelliot. *An Anthology of Dalit Literature*. New Delhi: Gyan Publishing House, 1992. Print.

http://meenakandasamy.wordpress.com

Jana, Ujjwal. "The Struggle to Annihilate Caste will be Victorious". Meena Kandasamy in Conversation with Ujjwal Jana. *Postcolonial Text*. 4.4 (2008): 1-7. Print.

Kandasamy, Meena. http//:www.meenu.wordpress.com

—. *Touch*. Mumbai: Peacock Books, 2006. Print.

Sarangi, Jaydeep. "Rev. of *Touch* by Meena Kandasamy." *Mascara Literary Review*. n.d. Web. 24 July 2015.

9

Silence of the Subaltern in Dalit Writings

— *Dr V. Nagarajan and Dr S. Pushpalatha*

"Every day millions are crushed and killed in spirit; ever so often some of them are killed physically as well" (Anand Teltumbe). The terms like 'race' and 'caste' came into existence as a result of the oppression and despair of the lives of the marginalised class of nations were observed. Arjun Dangle defines Dalit Literature in the following words:

> Dalit Literature is one which acquaints people with the caste system and untouchability in India...It matures with the sociological point of view and and is related to the principles of negativity, rebellion and loyalty to science, thus finally ending as revolutionary. (Dangle 54)

The marginalised groups or the subaltern as they called all over the world have a similar system of subjugation but the titles differ as per the class. In the western world, it was under the pretext of race whereas in India, it was under the name of caste. The silenced subaltern sections were distanced from the power centre and they were always on the periphery.

Whether it is race or caste, inequality and exploitation form the core of marginalisation. Insecurity and injustice have resulted from marginalisation. Based upon race and caste marginalised literature came into being. The term 'race' gives rise to literature of the slaves and 'caste' gives rise to literature of the untouchables. Dalit communities and Black American communities underwent similar kind of experiences which give rise to cumulative shame as well as anger.

Dalits were always on the marginalised 'other' side of Indian society. After many centuries of silence about themselves, the subjugated Dalits started voicing their personal and collective suffering which paid way to Dalit Literature depicting the assertion of human rights, self-pride, revolt against social injustice and hopes and aspirations for a new society which would be devoid of discrimination. According to Shrankumar Limbale, Dalit Literature artistically portrays the sorrows, tribulations, slavery, degradation, ridicule and poverty endured by Dalits. Limbale asserts that Dalit Literature is a lofty image of grief.

'Dalit' is a Hindi word which bears the meaning 'oppressed' or 'broken'. The term was used in the 1930s as a Hindi or Marathi translation of 'depressed classes'. So 'Dalit' is not a caste. It can be called a symbol of change and revolution. In the year 1992, Arjun Dangle published his work entitled *Poisoned Bread* in which he attempted to anthologise Dalit writings. He anthologised all the genres available in Marathi literature: poetry, short-stories, public speeches and autobiographical excerpts. The primary aim of Dalit writings is to effectively threaten the Brahmanic hegemony from literature. It also focuses on stirring up thinking in Dalit intellectuals and catalysing creation of organic intellectuals of Dalits.

Jyotirao Phule, a Marathi Dalit writer dedicated his book *Gulamgiri* to the then Negroes in America for their sublime disinterestedness and self-sacrificing devotion in the cause of Negro slavery. Mahasweta Devi, Namdeo Dhasal, Daya Pawar, Arjun Dangle, Sachi Rautray, Poomani, Imayam, Basudev Susani and Abhimani are some of the writers who contributed to Dalit Literature immensely. There are also writers who are not Dalits by birth but write Dalit Literature. Mulk Raj Anand, Kumaran Asan, Sarah Joseph and Premchand are some of the well-known writers who have contributed to Dalit Literature.

In India the caste system as an exploiting system adheres to a set of values always favouring it. It is said that, to keep the torch of power unextinguished, social inequality and untouchability were retained by the early rulers. It is very pathetic that exploitation affects Dalits doubly for being Dalit and being poor. Immersed by the socio-cultural predicaments the Dalits of India lived a life of poverty, ignorance, injustice and humiliation. Caste system and the hierarchy structured through caste continues to exist in every part of the life. Social position of the Dalits does affect their everyday life. Hegemonic upper class cultural values exclude Dalits as inferior in the mainstream society. B.R. Ambedkar opined that a slave is free from the slave owner but an untouchable is not. Slavery is conscious and physical whereas untouchability is both conscious and it involves unconscious belief that enslaves an untouchable both in mind and body and pervades the whole of social life.

The cultural norms that are set for the upper castes differ from those of the Dalit caste. Upper caste cultural norms would confine Dalits to be inferior on the one hand stigmatise them as inferior on the other hand. In Indian society, the caste-based divisions of labour makes Dalits do the most menial jobs in the society. They are denied education, self-respect, religion and human dignity. Upper caste norms are considered to be superior and worthy of imitating.

Dalitism does not mean being silent about caste. Upper castes might think that not mentioning caste would be a civilized act and a well-mannered position. Being silent about caste would not eradiate caste discrimination. Education and caste awareness only could make Dalits reject the humiliating ways in which they are treated. Ambedkar's philosophy brought such awareness on caste. Ambedkar suggests that the subversion of visible symbols of untouchability and slavery and rejection of Hinduism is a must to bring about revolution. Though Dalits are not slaves in the strict sense, untouchability and caste system enslaves them.

Dr Ambedkar who made an uncompromising struggle and E.V. Ramasamy who took relentless reformative measures are the two important figures in making an anti-dote to counter the widespread virus 'Dalitism'. Dalit Literature is "basically in the affirmation of Dalit identity by discarding the Brahmanic language and symbolism. It is in their use of their own language, idiom, metaphor and imagery" (Wankhede 31).

Many Indian women writers like Bama and Baby Kamble, through their autobiographies, depict the injustice and humiliations forced on Dalits by the upper castes. Though many writers have focused on the horrendous experiences of Dalits in Indian society, Bama's novels have a new perspective. With a moral and social purpose, Bama has penned down the real conditions of Dalit community in the form of fiction. She strongly believes that if the inherent spirit of her people is properly kindled by the right type of education and employment, they will come out in flying colours. In her novel *Karukku* Bama presents the development of the protagonist's mind through varied experiences and her search for identity in the world. *Karukku* has a two-dimensional spiritual development – nurturing of her belief as a Catholic and her realisation of herself as a Dalit. She finds similarities between the saw-edged palmyra tree and her own life. She says, "Events that occurred during many stages of my life cut me like Karukku and made me bleed...Later they also become the embryo (Karu) and symbol that grew into this book" (13).

The dangerous effect of casteism on the voiceless subaltern is painfully depicted in *Karukku.* As a little girl Bama, once happened to see a man from Dalit community who was working in the fields of Naicker and he "brought something like vadai or green banana bhajji in the packet, because the wrapping paper was stained with blood. He came along holding out the packet by its string, without touching it" (13).The man was not allowed to touch the parcel because he was a Dalit. The protagonist was shocked to see the deep rooted untouchability prevailing in Indian society.

Bama watched that the households of upper castes survive on the labour of Dalits. The village is rich in resources but Dalits do not have share in it. She angrily watches Dalits cleaning the filth every day. Both Bama's maternal grandmother and paternal grandmother worked in Naicker's house. The way they were dominated and addressed even by small children in Naicker's house made Bama understand how powerful the hierarchies of upper castes could be.

The grandmothers were given only the left-overs in Naicker's house. Bama observes:

> The Naicker women would pour out from a height of four feet, while Paatti and the others received and drank it with cupped hands held to their mouths. I always felt terrible when I watched this. My other Paatti was the same. As soon as dawn broke, she would go to the Naicker houses, sweep out the cowshed, collect up the dung and dirt, and then bring home the left over rice and curry from the previous evening. And for some reason she would behave as if she had been handed the nectar of the gods. (14)

Brushing aside the mental trauma and psychic tension, Bama could become the topper in her S.S.L.C. examination among the Dalit students. She decides that she should be more rigid and try to overcome the worst effects of casteism. She was agonised when she saw the upper caste women feeling reluctant to share the seat with her. Bama painfully records, "Wherever we go we suffer blows and pains" (24).

Arundhati Roy's debut novel *The God of Small Things* is one of the most celebrated novels in the field of Indian writing in English and the novel forcefully discusses the issue of casteism, male patriarchy and class exploitation. The story weaves around the tragic episodes of Ammu and Velutha in whose life subalternity or untouchability or marginalisation becomes the death knell. Velutha, in the novel represents the whole Dalit community. His relationship with Ammu, a Syrian Christian woman was considered as a sacrilege by Ayemenon, because Velutha was an untouchable who should not try to come to the power centre. Velutha had to pay a high price for being an untouchable.

Velutha's father is terror-stricken to see "what his Untouchable son had touched. More than touched" (78). The past of the marginalised people is very well reflected in the novel. Veutha's grandfather had embraced Christianity along with a number of Pullayas and Pellayas in order to escape from the scourge of untouchability. It is a disgusting fact that even after their conversion to Chriatianity, they have been treated as untouchables or Dalits.

R.G. Jadhav writes, "Dalit is a Sanskrit word and means downtrodden or oppressed or exploited or condemned to peripheral leavings" (39). The cry of the subaltern diminishes in the eternal silence of the infinite crowds of upper castes.

When Mammachi comes to know about the relationship between Ammu and Velutha, she spits and wonders how her daughter could stand the particular smell of a Paravan. The relationship between a high caste woman and an untouchable can never be digested by a Syrian Christian and it is a disgrace for her. The love affair between Ammu and Velutha is being crushed by the orthodox forces on account of the power politics of caste. K.N.M. Pillai, a communist party leader is essentially a political man and a professional omeletteer. He does not come to stand by Velutha at the time of crisis. He represents those who merely make a show of being reformers. In the police station, he pretends as if he does not know Velutha when he is brutally beaten to death.

Velutha is portrayed as a victim of casteism. In Mammachi's time, the untouchables were experiencing the highest level of humiliation in the society where the so-called upper castes dominated. The untouchables were not allowed to walk in the public roads, to cover their upper bodies and carry umbrellas. The untouchables were treated as if they were cursed beings. The parameters for the untouchables were set by the upper castes. Mammachi tells the twins, "Paravans were expected to crawl backwards with a broom, sweeping away their footprints so that Brahmins or Syrian Christians would not defile themselves by accidently stepping into a Paravan's footprint" (73-74).

Velutha is a man imbibed with the excellent skill of carpentry. Mammachi often says that if Velutha had not been a Paravan, he would have become an engineer. She thinks that skills and potentials are the sole property of the men belonging to the high castes. She extracts the maximum amount of work from Velutha but she pays him less. He is not entertained like other touchable workers in the factory. Roy succinctly exposes the vulnerable conditions of Dalits through Vellaya Pappan and Velutha.

Women writers like Bama and Urmila Pawar focus on women Dalits who experience double marginalisation. All men and women are created by the same God, but man makes the society fragmented by casteism and class discrimination. Subalternity or marginality is a wide spreading virus that could be demolished by means of education. By the emergence of Dalit Literature, a profound change is taking place in the Indian society.

Space for Dalits in the police department and other departments of bureaucracy has recently been provided through reservation which is a good sign. The pro-Dalit laws should be implemented by the people who are not caste-free. Dalit autobiographies are revolutionary and they make a clarion call for Dalits, the subaltern sector of society, to move towards the centre of power. Urbanisation and upward mobility will put an end to the atrocities forced on Dalits. Following the theory of Derrida on deconstruction the Dalits can be brought to the centre.

Works Cited

Bama. *Karukku*. Trans. Lakshmi Holmstrom. Chennai: Macmillan, 2000. Print.

Dangle, Arjun. *Poisoned Bread*. Trans. Mumbai: Orient Longman, 1992. Print.

https://bahu-virupaksha.sulekha.com

https://www.hindustantimes.com/Dalit-killed-for-digging-own-well/

Roy, Arundhati. *The God of Small Things*. New Delhi: Atlantic, 1999. Print.

Surendran, K.V. *The God of Small Things:* A Saga of Lost dreams. New Delhi: Atlantic, 2000. Print.

Wankhede, M.S. "Dalit Voice in India: The Protest Literature." *Cyber Literature* XXI.1 (2008): 25-40. Print.

10

Performing Resistance or Caste-Pride Celebration: A Study of Selected Indian Dalits Folk-Rap Music

— *Dr Ishrat Jahan*

> Caste is not a physical object like a wall of bricks or a line of barbed wire which prevents the Hindus from co-mingling and which has, therefore, to be pulled down. Caste is a notion; it is a state of the mind.
>
> (Ambedkar, *Annihilation of Caste* 46)

Dalit Literature needs no introduction in present time. Almost, all scholars as well as non-scholars are now more aware about what is Dalit Literature and what are its objectives. More reputed universities have included Dalit Literature as a core subject for their students. Dalit Literature is a kind of experience writing about subjugations and oppressions of Dalits that has a very long history itself. Dr Bhim Rao Ramji Ambedkar is worshipped as the *Messiah* among Dalits and other oppressed communities who penetrated the thoughts of self-identity and the rays of caste-free society. Consequently, Dalit movements have come out as the result of human discrimination and humiliation of untouchable people that they were forced to experience. It has been undoubtedly observed that Dalits are the victims of violence and brutally crushed whenever they raised their voices against injustice. For an instance, Radhika Vemula demanded justice of her son, Rohit Vemula's institutional murder in January, 2016 but her efforts remained fruitless. A number of media persons have witnessed the physical violence and her dragging on the road.

In nineteenth century, Dalit movements, for the empowerment and self-recognition of low-caste people were initiated by non-Brahmins of South India. Subsequently, it developed into different regional literatures. Dalit movements are associated with marginalised people and those who are laggard behind socially and economically. The only objective of Dalit movement is to bring social, economic and cultural changes in their lives. (Limbale, *Towards an Aesthetic* 10-12). From past few years, we have been observed that TV news channels and other social media portals are organising many debates over this matter and unjust forms of the protest. Generally, the meaning of 'resistance' is an act of resisting and opposing against discrimination on the basis of gender, caste and religion. The act of resistance demands for courage and a vigorous heart to confront the hegemonic oppression and systematic violence as it happens in Dalit Literature which encourages people against the religious injustice and requires a command on power holders as well. The literary meaning of 'resistance' is 'to stand against' in critical political-cultural sense. Some critics considered Dalit Literature as the 'literature of resistance.' It is defined as a struggle for survivor and pain, fear, repression, violence, discrimination based on caste and religion. Power and courage are key words of it. As per definition of Oxford Advanced Learner's Dictionary, resistance means dislike of or opposition to a plan, an idea etc., refusal to obey or the act of using force to oppose somebody or something.' From last few decades, there is a growth in different types of resistances against on-going caste discrimination and dehumanisation led by Dalits and non-Dalits for Dalits' rights. In present time, Dalits assertion is quite visible across the country. In April 2018 all Dalits came together and angered over the decision of the Supreme Court on the dilution of SC/ST. Now, there is a heightened sense of casteism and discrimination based on that among educated youth. They have more consciousness to understand those political theories what led protest movements. The resistance of an oppressed community as in case of Dalit Literature has an aim of the progress of humanity and establish equality among people (Deka, "The Dalit Awakening" *India Today*). Undoubtedly, resistance is a social dynamite which can be revealed by physical expressions but keeping silence, or through using other weapons; written-literary works or oral such as protest speech, of other art performances. Dalit Rap music performance is also a kind of resistance which doesn't harm the oppressor. This is a peaceful way of opposing of someone. Therefore, music is a non-violent way of protesting against injustice and discrimination with Dalits.

Earlier, literary works were limited with the educated people only. So as a result of that, that printed writing emerged as a revolution among people especially Dalits who got to know about their self-esteem and basic rights in the society. Among those movements, Dalit music has flourished as a trend-cum-movement. Rap music is basically a western propounded cultural practice. For an instance, during 1990s, for the popularity of Basketball and Football in the slums of Brazil, and to spread African hip-hop, their dialectic raps were used to make awareness among youth. And youth had seen more consuming social mobility. Thus, youth consumption became an index to reach it global level. In the context of Rap in India, it was popularised in south India as a form of Hip Hop. In nineties, it has been more practised in Northern parts of India. Indian Diasporic artists such as Baba Sehgal introduced Hindi raps like *Thanda Thanda Pani*, *Dilruba*, *Main Bhi Madonna*, *Manjula* and *Dil Dhadke* in Bollywood. His album *Thanda Thanda Pani* sold more than 100,000 copies in just three and half months. (Phillip, "Meet the Brazilian Singer..." *TIME*)

However, it is obvious that rapping is another form of entertainment and famously used to elate, to educate, to instruct and to create an inner awakening among people towards socialism. Dalit music in India has undoubtedly seen as a best instrument to resist caste based discrimination and inequality as well as to mobilise youth. The resistant tradition of highlighting the social issues through verses or other performative art forms has a long history itself. In 13th century, the most famous Bhakti Movement was flourished from south region to north region of India. A saint of that era translated

Bhagwadgita into *Bhavarthadipika*, popularly known as the *Dnyaneshwari* which stressed on singing those verses rather than lecturing. After it, many saints Visoba Khechar, Janabai, Savanta, Goroba, Kahnopatra, and Chokhamela sang many devotional songs of God. During 19th century, there were two art forms: *Tamasha* and *Shahiri* in which Dalits used to perform their bitter realities and sometimes to entertain Brahmin courtiers as well. *Shahiri,* a performative art form recently depicted in award winning film *Court* (Vaz, "From Dnyaneshwari to Dalit rock." *Scroll.in*).

In my PhD thesis, I have examined that the prominent writers initiated different creative expressions like singing and performance of their folk songs, to spread Dalit awakening towards Dalit movements. Thus, I write:

> Some creative works took place in it such as *Jalsa* (to give a message through singing and performance). Around 1950s, few young educated men started to write serious writings. This coincided by a number of Dalit conversion into Buddhism. For instance, Anna Bhau Sathe, a prominent Dalit writer wrote about volatile surroundings not only in his literary works but also in other art forms like Lavni and Tamasha to make an awareness among Dalit masses. Anna Bhau Sathe named tamasha as Loknatya. He transformed this art form to suit the audience, time and content. (*Dalit Images* 38)

More than one decade ago, Gurkanwal Bharti gotimmense popularity as a Dalit pop singer for her songs *Fan Babasaheb Ki* and *The Danger Chamar.* Both of her songs went viral on YouTube. Here is the translation of *Fan Baba Sahib Ki* into English from Punjabi. It says:

> I am the daughter of Baba Sahib who wrote the constitution.
>
> We are earning our bread by what he wrote.
>
> I am such a fan of such thinking,
>
> I am a fan of such thinking who gave sacrifice for us.
>
> He was a lion who made his pen an arrow.
>
> He fought for rights and truth and changed our destiny.

He became an angel for the community.
The whole world knows this."
(Elephant, "The Danger Chamar" *The Red Elephant*)

Here, she narrates that she is a whole-hearted devotee of Baba Sahib and also reminds the people how Dr B.R. Ambedkar fought for social justice, rights of marginalised and the underprivileged groups of India. He gave the equal opportunity for all citizens by writing Indian Constitution. This was his victory over feudalism and slavery. Therefore, he proved that proverb, "the pen is mightier than the sword." Her song is like a devotional song for her as Dr B.R. Ambedkar sacrificed his life only for the betterment of downtrodden people. In her track "Haq" (Rights), she sings about fighting for rights and how Babaseheb has taught Dalits to speak up.

Ginni is the daughter of Rakesh Chandra Mahi and Paramjeet Kaur who belong to Chamar community. They are true devotees of Saint Ravidas and Dr Bhimrao Ambedkar who strongly supported to equality among the people of all religions. For his daughter's singing, he resigned his job and started to record Ginni's songs and videos. He firmly supported for her education. She is popularly known as Ginni Mahi who protested through her songs. And, her performative protest in the form of songs proved as mass appeal among people to change such social conflicts. Influenced by Ginni's popularity in youth, Amar Audio, a recording company signed her for her 'Dalit Folk' and produced her two more devotional albums *Guran Di Diwani* (2015) and *Gurupurab Hai Kanshiwale Da* (2016). In her interview with Malu, a journalist, Ginni says:

> I had sung for multi-singer albums before but didn't have a solo album. I began singing professionally when I turned 12. We began with devotional albums because any work should begin with the name of God. I have been inspired by Dr B.R. Ambedkar and try to bring his views about equality and justice through my music. (Molu, 17 Years-old Ginni, *Homegrown*)

In same interview, Ginni explained the intention behind her singing as well as reason. She accounts:

"Everybody is right in what they are doing. I would only do songs

> that an entire family can listen to together. I want to sing about unity, equality and end discrimination among castes because it is man-made. I believe that a singer doesn't have a caste and I myself don't associate with any caste. I believe I am an Indian and human first. Every singer is doing great things, I am still a child, I am nowhere near them. Everybody gets the result of the efforts they put in," she said. A panel of 5-6 family members choose the songs lyricists send them. "We see what suits her image the most and is not bearing any ill-will towards anybody. We don't want to put anybody down through our songs. We just want to uplift. What matters most is the audience reaction. We always try to give the audience what they need and what are their wishes." (Molu, *Homegrown)*

Ginni's native place is Doaba region of Jalandhar city in Punjab state. A study says that this is the place which is dominated by SC caste. In 2001, the census recorded it was 40.46% out of total population. A large number of people are true followers of Ravidas (79, Jodhka, *The Ravi Dasis of Punjab)*.There are many more singers from same region who expressed anguish and plight of these poor Dalit people through their Dalit folks. Roop Lal Dhir, another Chamar caste Dalit sang about 'Dalits' rights and their bitter realities.' He confessed that now whenever he sings these Rabidasian devotional songs, getting low fare but now he intentionally has joined "Jai Bheem Mission" and "Caste-Pride Celebration." Now, more other Dalit singers have joined this mission.

According of an article "Calling People 'Harijan' or 'Dhobi' is Offensive: Supreme Court" published in *The Wire* (Indian Web Publishing), using of the word 'Chamar' is banned by the Supreme Court as it is the sign of human slurs. It follows:

> The Supreme Court enumerated under Section 3 of the SC/ST Act are offences which, to say the least, denigrate members of Scheduled Castes and Scheduled Tribes in the eyes of society and prevent them from leading a life of dignity and self-respect, the bench explained. "Such offences are committed to humiliate and subjugate members of the Scheduled Castes and Scheduled

Tribes with a view to keeping them in a state of servitude" (The Wire Staff).

But here, Ginni and her team has made in that manner that everyone feels proud on own caste and celebrates in Dalit-folk songs in Punjabi.

In her songs so called 'Caste-Pride Celebration,' Gurkanwal Bharti alias Ginni has defended Ambedkarite philosophy and hope for a peaceful humanity among people. This unique technique of resistance has emerged not only in Punjab, north region of India but existed in the other performative forms such as 'Dalit Youth Music Band' in other parts also, a long time ago. For instance, *Dhamma Wings* is the first 'Dalit Buddhist Rock Band' that's motto is to address not only caste based stratifications in the society and injustice associated with them but to replace those social evils with the teachings and the principles of Dr B.R. Ambedkar and Buddha. In 2011, this rock band was officially founded as *Dhamma Wings* by Kabeer Shakya, an engineering student with his friends. In initial years, his band didn't get much response from public but soon, got academic audience support when they started to perform in distinguished institutions like TISS (Tata Institute of Social Sciences, Mumbai). Even their videos on Facebook and YouTube went viral and got popularity. The most popular song of the *Dhamma Wings* is *Jai Bheem-The Song of Pride.* The words of the lyrics are given below:

RAPP BOI:

How would you feel? Waking up to a morning,

Knowing that you won't be witnessing the sun of another morning

Oppressed for caste oppressed for colour religion and personal opinions

It's democracy jai hind

Hai ladayi yeh zaat ki zaat-o-jamaat ki

Din-o-raat ki firqo mein bate aap ki

Par aaj bhi yeh duniya nahi tere baap ki

Aur aakhri khat mera hai azaad bhi

Shaheed hu main shaheed ek sipahi
Du gawahi har ek zulm ki aleef se elaahi
Dar wallahi ab main wo nahi jo tujhse dargaya
Ghut-ghut ke jeeraha tha ya ghut-ghut ke margaya
Good morning I won't be around when you read this
I ain't blaming no one but you know about my hit-list
I love science I love stars, I love nature more than cars
But you talk about caste? You don't deserve some water
Dalit lives matter human lives matter.
I always wanna be a writer writer like Carl Sagan
10 milligrams of sodium a good rope with some reason
got much stress on my mind so I became a monster.

(Album: Death Rap Hyderabad)
(Source: SoundCloud.com)

This famous rap-song is multilingual which has a hope of peaceful world where unequal, discrimination based on caste, gender and religion wouldn't have place. The rappers, Kabeer and his team stress that we all either divided by caste and religion are the children of one God. Untouchability based on caste is man-made concept and the miserable condition due to that. Like others, Dalit also are human beings and should be treated as same. Like upper caste people, they (Dalits) too have dreams. Due to their humiliation and caste based victimisation, from long centuries ago, they have become more conscious about their identities and equal rights especially Ambedkarite movements.

Among these youth icons, Sumeet Samos is another rapper who has just completed his Masters in Latin American Literature (Spanish) from Jawaharlal Nehru University (JNU). He belongs from Tentulipadar, a village in Koraput district of Odisha. Dalit movement in India has perhaps seen the use of music to mobilise youth, but now post-graduate student in Jawaharlal Nehru University (JNU) Sumeet Samos is rapping to spread awareness about the atrocities faced by Dalits. In the rap video put out by 'The Print on Twitter,' Samos is seen rapping about how Dalits are not treated as human beings. While Samos is able to question caste discrimination with these powerful lyrics, he tells *The Print* in an interview that there was a time he did feel inferior because caste was so internalised.

In an interview "Watch: JNU Student's Dalit Rap Takes on Casteism" with Rohini Chatterjee, Sumeet Samos who belongs to Koraput in Odissa, talks about the atrocities he faced as a child, "The print speeches (on caste) can be long and dry...Sometimes people don't even listen. With rap, I can sum up our message crisply and powerfully." (Chatterjee, Huffpost) He raps:

> Let me tell you what you have done,
> The pain is still not gone,
> You made me question my parents, my birth, my human existence,
> My appearance, my food, my clothes, my smell, etiquette, mannerism.
> I could never find the logic, no human reason.
> Season after season in all of life's motion,
> You did constant vilification.
> I saw my parents' tears, with caste humiliation.
> (Chatterjee, HUFFPOST)

Here, Samos raises the questions on caste discrimination and considers the root cause of his and the identity of his family, citizenship, sorrow, humiliation and their segregation from society. He also asserts that there is no valid reason of their abasements. Thus, he concludes caste based discrimination is man-made and not made by God.

Language plays an important role to establish individual's identity and recognition. In his book entitled *The Post-Colonial Studies Reader,* Bill Ashcroft defined language as a technique which provides us the power of knowing about the colonised people, place and culture as well. Then he says, "Language provides the terms by which the world may be known. Its system of values – its suppositions, its geography, its concept of history, of difference, its myriad gradation of distinction – becomes the system upon which social, economic and political discourses are grounded" (283). Language has become more powerful to express and to target on hierarchal power structure of the society. Language reveals user's social engagement in the society. The way in which language is used by a person, may be helpful to discover the identity of individual as well as his cultural richness. In present time, Indian youth has adopted various ways of resistance. The only intention of these above pop-cum-folk singers is to spread an awareness among people about the atrocities faced by Dalits for centuries ago by using different art forms such as rap songs, live stage performances and technologies like Facebook and YouTube, to engage audience, to get emotional support and to mobilise them into mass. Using these fusion performative art forms, Dalits now assertively establish and redefine their traditional identities. Hence, language works as a tool of resistance against injustice.

The young generation is using mother tongue as a tool with pride and has added more flavours of local folks and cultures in their performance to protest aggressively. Now their protests are more instructive for the people of all classes. For instance, Ginni sings in her own mother tongue, Punjabi folk to reach maximum people and to have emotional connectivity. *Dhamma Wings Band* and Sumeet Samos's Rap video *Let Me Tell You What You Have Done* are targeting students' groups and other elite groups to have an understanding for more debates and discussions, to take further step for Dalits' rights. The later groups are using more English words in their songs. It is generally known that English is a global language. Therefore, they are making it to reach these Dalits' issues and concerns on global standard.

Works Cited

Abedi, Zakir. *Contemporary Dalit Literature: Quest for Dalit Liberation.* New Delhi: Arise Publishers. 2010. Print.

Ambedkar, Baba Saheb. *Annihilation of Caste: With a Reply to M. K. Gandhi.* New Delhi: Samyak Prakashan. 2003. Print.

Ashcroft, Bill, et al. *The Post-Colonial Studies Reader*. Routledge, Taylor & Francis Group, 2006. Print.

Chaterjee, Rohini. "Watch: JNU Student's Dalit Rap Takes on Casteism." *HUFFPOST,* April 30, 2017. A5. Print. https://www.huffingtonpost.in/2017/04/30/watch-jnu-students-Dalit-rap-takes-on casteism_a_22062014/

Chandrasekaran, Lalita. "Social Mobility Among the Madiga of Karnataka." *Sociological Bulletin*. 41.1/2 (1992):119-144. *JSTOR*, www.jstor.org/stable/ 23620176.

Dangle, Arjun, (Ed). *Poisoned Bread: Translations from Modern Marathi Dalit Literature*. New Delhi: Orient BlackSwan, 2009. Print.

Deka, Koushik. "The Dalit Awakening." *India Today.* April 5, 2018. A5. Print.

https://www.indiatoday.in/magazine/cover-story/story/20180416-Dalit-protest-bharatbandh sc-st-act-supreme-court-judgement-1206277-2018-04-05

Elephant, Red. "The Danger Chamar." *The Red Elephant Foundation.* March, 2017. A5. Print. http://www.redelephantfoundation.org/2017/03/the-danger-chamar.html

Gaikwad, Rahi. "An Equal Music." *The Hindu Newspaper.* 20 August, 2016. A4. Print.

https://www.thehindu.com/features/magazine/An-equal-music/article14580390.ece

Jaffrelot, Christophe. "Caste and Politics." *India International Centre Quarterly*. 37.2 (2010): 94-116. *JSTOR.* www.jstor.org/stable/23006438.

Jahan, Ishrat. *Dalit Images Selected Urdu Short-stories.* Hyderabad: MANUU, 2018. Print.

Jodhka, Surinder S. "The Ravi Dasis of Punjab: Global Contours of Caste and Religious Strife." *Economic and Political Weekly*. 44.24 (2009): 79-85. *JSTOR.* www.jstor.org/stable/40279109.

Krishnaiah, B. *Dalit Movements and Literature: Emerging Issues and Challenges.* New Delhi: Prestige Books International, 2011. Print.

Limbale, Sharankumar. *Towards an Aesthetic of Dalit Literature: History, Controversies and Considerations.* Trans. Alok Mukherjee. New Delhi: Orient Blackswan, 2010. Print.

Lukose, Ritty. "Consuming Globalization: Youth and Gender in Kerala, India." *Journal of Social History*. 38.4 (2005): 915-935. *JSTOR*, www.jstor.org/ stable/3790482.

Muktibodh, Sharatchandra. "What is Dalit Literature?" Trans. Anil Ragunath Kulkarni. *Poisoned Bread*. Ed. Arjun Dangle. New Delhi: Orient Blackswan, 2009. Print.

Phillips, Dom. "Meet the Brazilian Singer Drawing Crowds with his Stinging Social Critique." *TIME,* Dec. 8, 2014. A5. Print.

http://time.com/3624155/brazilian-rapper-criolo-and-his-socialmessage/

Panther, Red. "Dalit Resistance and Violence." *Counter Courrents. Org,* Jan, 2018. A4. Print.

https://countercurrents.org/2018/01/06/Dalit-resistance-violence/

Sherinian, Zoe C. "Musical Style and the Changing Social Identity of Tamil Christians." *Ethnomusicology* 51.2, 2007238-280. *JSTOR*.www.jstor.org/ stable/20174525.

Vaz, Urami Chanda. "From Dnyaneshwari to Dalit Rock: The Evolution of Maharashtra's Revolutionary Music." *Scroll.in*, 2017. A5. Print. https://scroll.in/magazine/844792/from-dnyaneshwari-to-Dalit-rock-the-evolution-of-maharashtras-revolutionary-music

11

Urmila Pawar's *The Weave of My Life: A Dalit Woman's Memoir* – A Brief Analysis

— *K.M. Keerthika*

Literature critically views reality. Over the past many decades, Dalit Literature has emerged as a separate and important category of literature in India. Dalit Literature came out with a new emergence giving voice and identity to the people who are discriminated, exploited and marginalised because of their caste and culture. Dalit Literature came into existence only through the political movement spearheaded by Ambedkar.

The literal meaning of the word 'Dalit' is 'cut off,' 'oppressed,' 'downtrodden,' 'broken' or 'reduced to pieces.' It comes from the Sanskrit root 'dal.' Thus, the word 'Dalit' represents "those separated or distanced from the rest of humanity" (Kanipayyur 540 qtd. in https://docplayer.net). A person who faces discrimination and suppression in her life finds a voice through Dalit Literature. The ultimate goal of Dalit Literature is liberation of Dalits. According to Limbale, "Dalit Literature is the writing about Dalits with a Dalit consciousness and its primary motive is the liberation of Dalits" (*Towards an Aesthetic of Dalit Literature* 19). Dalit people are often called as 'Shudra' and 'outcaste Hindu'. During 19th century, a social reformer named Jyotiba Phule in Maharashtra first used the term 'Dalit' to get rid of the words 'Shudra' and 'outcaste Hindu'. Later, the word Dalit was also used in Hindu and Marathi as a substitute word to the term 'depressed classes that the British government used to describe what is now called the Scheduled Castes. Dr Ambedkar used the term to give a new scope and respect to the people who are called as 'untouchable' castes and he gave the term as 'Harijan' (which means 'Children of God').

The main focus of Dalit Literature is to represent the typical social, historical and cultural aspects of the Dalit community. Through Dalit Literature, writers struggle for their identity, social equality, justice and they want to get rid of all the sufferings, discrimination and economic exploitation. Dalit Literature forms an important and distinct part of Indian Literature. In 1960's, it emerged in Marathi language and later it was translated to Hindi, Kannada, Telugu and Tamil Language. Dalit Literature used all literary forms – poetry, short-stories, novels, plays and autobiographies in various languages. Poems, stories, novels, biographies, autobiographies produced by Dalits established a new body of literature in which for the first time the downtrodden took the centre stage. Before 1960's, there were writers like Baburao Bagul, Bandhu Madhav, Shankaro Kharat, Narayan Surve who expressed about Dalit people and the conflicts in their life.

Baburao Bagul wrote in Marathi, a collection of short-stories titled *Jevha Mi Jat Chorali* (*When I Had Concealed My Caste*) published in 1963. It brought a new momentum to Dalit Literature in Marathi because it brings out about the cruel society and social exploitation. Later, it is seen by many critics as epic portraying lives of the Dalits. Namdeo Dhasal founded an organisation called Dalit Panther; in order to expand Dalit Literature movement to India. Other prominent voices of Dalit writing in Marathi are Arun Kamble, Laxman Gaikwad, Laxman Pawar, Daya Pawar, Waman Nimbalkar, Tryambak Sapkale, Arun Dangle, J.V. Pawar, Kishore Shantabai Kale, Narendra Jadhav and Urmila Pawar. All these writers believed that through Dalit Literature and through their writing, they can question about society and culture. This may give them equality, human dignity. Most Dalit writers believe that the primary purpose of writing literature is to bring about social change rather than recreation. Baburoa Bagul rightly observes:

> Dalit Sahitya is not a literature of Vengeance. Dalit Sahitya is not a literature which spreads hatred. Dalit Sahitya first promotes man's greatness and man's freedom and for that reason it is an historic necessity...Anguish, waiting, pronouncements of sorrow alone do not define Dalit Sahitya. We need literature heroically full of life to create a new society.

As years pass on, Dalit Literature has also begun to give space for separate category as women writers from Dalit communities. Dalit feminism comes a long way with many milestones, to achieve this process. They took it as an opportunity to define their identities.

The first generation of Dalit women writers are Baby Kamble, Shantabai Dani and Shantabai Kamble. They are the direct followers of Dr Ambedkar. According to Baby Kamble, she took Dalit movement as 'struggle for truth.' These women writers explored their community culture in a more sensitive manner than the male writers. During 18th century, the society had got its change significantly and there it gave raise to second generation women writers. Writers like Kumud Pawde, Jyoti Lanjewar, and Urmila Pawar belong to second generation women writers. These women project their autobiographies in their works, through their regional languages like Marathi and Tamil.

Women in general are always marginalised by patriarchy, so Dalit women are more marginalised than Dalit men. They face a lot of struggle and many obstacles because of their own men. The plight of Dalit women is more depressing than Dalit men. Women's life is more pitiful and humiliating in the hands of men. Dr Ambedkar in his speech to the Dalit Mahila Federation in 1942 stated that "the progress of Dalit community should be measured in terms of the progress made by its women folk. Every woman should stand by her husband, not as his slave but as his contemporary, as his friend" (qtd. in Saran 84).

There were so many Dalit women writers who were considered as famous writers. They are Bama, Shantabai Kamble, Baby Kamble and Urmila Pawar who wrote about their plights and their works have been translated into English from various regional languages. Through their writings they try to bring out patriarchal reorganisation in the contemporary society and the life of women at both private and public places. Urmila Pawar, a creative writer whose autobiography *Aaydan* won accolades represented the strong sense of political and cultural identity as educated middle class Dalit women. Her work *Aaydan* projects how new modernity had transformed and intensified their gender and caste oppression "Caste is hidden like a prowling beast in the forest."

Urmila Pawar is an Indian writer of Marathi language. She is best known for her writing. She was awarded Maharashtra Sahitya Parishad for her literary work. According to Dharmarajan, her works reflect her experience of the difficulties of being a woman and a Dalit. Pawar was born and brought up in Konkan region of Maharashtra state. She was born in May 1945 at Adgoan village of Ratnagiri District. Even as a child, she was aware of her caste identity, she even faced discrimination in her school and other places. She received her MA from the University of Bombay and for many years she worked in the department of labour welfare for the government of Maharashtra.

In the present scenario, she is known as a feminist writer and leader of women's liberation movement. As a Dalit writer, she has established herself as a prominent voice of Dalit Literature after Daya Pawar, Baby Kamble and Shantabai Gokhale. Pawar was much sensitive about her caste, and she was aware of the limitation of person of lower caste and meaning of poverty. When Pawar was doing her schooling, she won't share her lunch with others, as the upper caste students bring variety of attractive items because of her economic condition at home. She never talks about it at home. Urmila Pawar was not good in English and she often felt small in her English classes when his English teacher used to call her names for having poor command over the language. Urmila Pawar writes about the caste discrimination:

> The upper caste girls always used words like 'Ladu', 'Modak', 'Karanjya', 'Puranpolya'. They brought such novel items in their tiffin boxes as well as at times we went on excursions. However, I never asked myself the stupid question, why we do not prepare such dishes at home? We were aware, without anybody telling

us, that we were born in a particular caste and in poverty, and that we had to live accordingly. (Pawar 1)

Urmila Pawar wrote her first autobiography *Aaydan* and later it was translated as *A Weave of My Life: A Dalit Woman's Memoir*. When her work was published, it was like a discomfort in society, among men and women alike. But through her work, she projects the life of women around her. As a Dalit woman, Pawar wrote about the experiences of her life and the discrimination faced by her both within her family as well as in society. Later Pawar's work received wide readership.

The original title of Urmila Pawar's memoir is *Aaydan*, a word from the local dialect spoken in the villages that form the background of her life. *Aaydan* is the name for the cane baskets that her mother wove to sell for additional income for the family. It was translated into English as *The Weave of My Life: A Dalit Woman's Memoir*. In the foreword of translated work, Wandana Sonalkar writes that in the title of the book the 'weave' is a metaphor of the writing technique employed by Pawar, "The love of different members of her family, her husband's family, her neighbours and classmates, are woven together in a narrative that gradually reveals different aspects of the everyday life of Dalits, the manifold ways in which caste asserts itself and grind them down."

The Weave of My Life: A Dalit Women's Memoir problematises the major issues of class, caste and gender in the Indian context. It highlights the dual oppression or double marginalisation of the Dalit women on the basis of caste and gender. This is a story of three generations and transformation of growth of Dalit women who struggled to overcome the burden of their caste. This made her establish herself as a noted feminist and Dalit writer. The strongest voice of Dalit feminism has rooted her place in the history of Dalit women.

'Aaydan' means weaving of cane baskets. Weaving happens to be the central metaphor of the present memoir. The main profession of the protagonist's mother is weaving of Bamboo baskets. She belongs to low caste and very poor in the economic condition too.

So her mother wove to sell for additional income for the family. This made protagonist's mother take the work of weaving. At one point of time, Pawar declares that "My mother used to weave Aaydans. I find that her act of weaving and my act of writing are originally linked. The weave is similar. It is the weave of pain, suffering and agony that link us" (Preface ix). The original title of the novel is taken from the childhood memories of her life in the village and her mother's constant struggle to fulfill their needs. Urmila faces lot of struggles and problems. Her married life made her learn lot of things. She encounters a feminist group and later becomes a writer and organiser of Dalit women.

Dalit women face lot of hardships in their life. The hardship of Dalit women is not only due to their poverty, economical status, or lack of education, but also due to the suppression by the upper classes and above everything else, by their own husbands. "Dalit women face a triple burden of caste, class and gender." Pawar sums up the plight of Dalit women, highlighting the fact that Dalit women are a distinct social group and cannot be masked under the general categories of "Women" or "Dalits" (News Archives). They also face hardships in their own home too, which is evident in the autobiography *The Weave of My Life*. Women were exploited in their food preparation at home as separate food preparations were done for men and women and particularly the daughter-in-law is exploited up to the maximum level. Pawar states that, "When the menfolk went out and women and girls remained at home, they dined at kata. A small quantity poured in water and cooked as a soup, with chilli powder, salt and a piece of mango or maul. This was called sagar! Women ate their rice with the watery dish. The song we used to sing" (Pawar 9). She depicts the life of a wife who got beatings from her husband in front of everyone at home. She pens down the pathetic incident of beating a pregnant woman.

Dr Ambedkar, in his article titled "The Rise and Fall of Hindu Woman" brings home the point that the suffering for women in India are due to Manusmriti which divides people under caste system and promotes inequality between men and women. According to the Manusmriti, women have no rights to education, independence, or wealth, whereas in the case of Dalit women, they are treated as a sex objects and it promotes child marriage. When Pawar got married, when her husband touched her, she felt little bit upset but again the second thought came to her mind that it might be the wish of the husband himself. May be to check her being virgin, if she had taken any initiative, he would have suspected her virginity. She thought that she was aware of every move but she remained silent.

In a male dominated society, Dalit women suffered unimaginable oppression, not only through caste, but gender too, from which there was no escape. The laws in the Manusmriti and other Vedic scriptures close all economic, political, social, educational, and personal channels through which Dalit women could be uplifted. The same thing happened in the life of Urmila too. Pawar's husband objected her when she wanted to do MA degree. As a traditional husband he expects her wife to be a good housewife by taking care of the family, nurturing children's health, their education and to look after the household things as their community women do as a typical wife. He feels that wives should not be more qualified than their husbands. But when she received her first salary after her marriage, she had to give the money to her husband. It is brought down that women should be dependent on men for each and every move in their life. She states that:

> When I got my first salary, I could not believe that all that money was mine; that I could spend it the way I liked. Before my marriage, I used to hand over my salary to my mother; now I started handling it over to my husband. If this is not like deliberately offering head for the butcher's knife, what else is it? (Pawar14).

According to the National Commission for Scheduled Castes and Scheduled Tribes 2000, approximately 75% of the Dalit girls were drop out of primary school. At the bottom of it the early drop out are due to escape from humiliation, bullying and isolation by classmates, society, and even their teachers. There were many bright young Dalit girls who are punished by the upper caste teachers in the rural areas of India for daring to score good grades. Feeling rejected most girls in this situation are dropped out of school and have nowhere to turn but towards manual scavenging and other repulsive jobs. But Pawar, in her school felt humiliated in her English language class where, her teacher used to abuse her for her poor command over the subject. He used to scold her, "This is English, the milk of tigress; it is not easy, like acting in plays." But Pawar doesn't mind about it and also she doesn't quit from school. Though she faced lot of sufferings through the upper class girls in school she doesn't bother about it. She participated in drama at school as well as in her college. Later as days pass on Pawar got an opportunity to write while she was working in Mumbai. This made some changes in her life.

Pawar feels that women lack self respect both in the society as well as within her family. She says males were respected and if any man is promoted, he would become a 'Bhaushaeb' or 'Raosaheb' but a woman officer will remained only a 'Bai 'without the title of Sahib. As a Dalit writer, she felt much as it is an insult to her position and caste. Even in their own family they were treated differently. Parents of Dalit community believe that daughters have no rights to hold property. Once the daughter is married they have no rights to obtain any material advantage from their parents. When Pawar and her sisters are together Sahu's son naming ceremony and with natural expectations; they have to fight with the brother. At that time, her mother scolded the daughters that they should not expect anything from the brother since they are well versed and happily settled.

Pawar very often remembers her mother and her attempts to weave the basket, to get rid of the pain and suffering. In the same way Urmila looked upon her writing as an escape to forget the pain of lost son and to forget the sad incident she involved in writing. Once, she has asked her mother about "motherhood" and she replied in one word 'sacrifice' with intense pain on her face, "I just wanted to know how she would express the feelings behind the word' Mother'. My question made her wince with pain. She said, to be a mother is to commit sati, to immolate oneself: nothing less!" (Pawar 18)

At one point of time, Pawar decided to join in 'Matrini' club, as it was about womanhood and that also she was able to see the issues through the patriarchal eyes. She strongly believes that a woman is also just a human being like man and all rights available to man should be made available to women, all such queries were in her mind. This thought gave her new insight and she became bold enough to face realistic problems. She tried her best to provide better life for women. As an individual, she tried hard to make the Dalit women to be free from sufferings, oppressions in the society. Sharmila Rege in her afterword writes:

> Memoirs of humiliation and resistance delineate the reproduction of caste as a form of modern inequality both in the village and the city. People would first purify the Aaydan, the basket, woven by Dalits by sprinkling water on it. At school, teachers would pick on Dalit girls to clean the dung on the school verandah when it was the turn of their class to undertake the cleaning. (Pawar 26)

The Weave of My Life written in a realistic fictional mode is characterised by an honest, frank, and bold articulation of a Dalit woman's experiences. In the concluding paragraphs of her Memoir Urmila Pawar writes:

> Life has taught me many things, showed me so such. It has also lashed it me till I bled, I don't know how much longer I am going to live, nor do I know in what form life is going to confront me let it came in any form; I am ready to face it stoically. This is what my life has taught me. This is my life and that is me. (Pawar 27)

Works Cited

Aston, N.M. *Dalit Literature and African American Literature*. New Delhi: Prestige Books, 2011. Print.

Bagul, Baburao. "Dalit Shitya: Man's Greatness, Man's Freedom." *Asmitadarsh*, Vol. I, 1973. Print.

https://docplayer.net/59510626-Chapter-ii-a-socio-political-history-of-Dalit-writings-in-india-the-attempt-is-not-to-trace-the-literary-tradition-of-dahts-as-Dalits-do.html

Limbale, Sharan Kumar. *Towards an Aesthetic of Dalit Literature: History, Controversies and Considerations*. Trans. Alok Mukherjee. New Delhi: Orient Longman, 2004. Print.

Narula, S. *Broken People: Caste Violence against India's Untouchables.* London: Human Rights Watch, 1999. Print.

Pandit, Maya. "Gender and Culture: From Dalit to Ambedkarite Consciousness, the Changing Construction of Dalit Feminist Consciousness". *The Indian Express*. 27 Dec. 2017. Web. 15 Aug. 2018.

Pawar, Urmila. *Aaydan*: *The Weave of My Life: A Dalit Woman's Memoir*. Trans. Maya Pandit. Mumbai. Granthali Publication, 2003. Print.

Rege, Sharmila. *Writing Caste/Writing Gender: Narrating Dalit Women's Testimonios*. New Delhi: Zubaan, 2006. Print.

Saran, Neeti Agarwal. "Situating Dalit Consciousness with Special Reference to Bama Faustina's *Karakku* and *Sangati.*" *The Criterion: An International Journal in English*. 7.5 (0ct. 2016): 82-87. Web.

12

Journey from Marginalisation to Liberation: A Critical Appraisal of Omprakash Valmiki's *Joothan: A Dalit's Life*

— ***Sanjay Kumar***

Social stratification on the basis of people's works is as ancient as Dalit discrimination in the society. Dalits may be known from different names at different places and times such as Shudras, fifth *varna*, panchama, gandharva, untouchable, depressed class, Harijan and so on but they have been suppressed, oppressed and marginalised since time immemorial. In India, these are people who belonged to Hindu religion and do some inferior kinds of works. Some Hindu population of Pakistan, Nepal, Sri Lanka, and Bangladesh is also considered contaminated from their birth because they were either born in the fifth *varna* or the people doing the lowest kind of jobs such as scavenging, sweeping and cleansing etc. The belief of incarnation has given birth to the caste system. Early Vedic Culture depicts only four castes or *varnas* i.e. Brahmin, Kshatriya, Vaishya and Shudra but in fact, there were thousands of sub-castes and communities in Indian society. All these sub-castes and communities were based on their nature of work or the place of birth. But overall, these castes were founded mainly on the place of birth. If a person was born at a Shudra's house, he would be called a Shudra. The social division of the society should be on the basis of works only for their identity and it should never degrade or elevate one caste or class from the other. Omprakash Valmiki was born in Valmiki Community in Uttar Pradesh. The people of this community are generally called Bhangis or sweepers.

Valmiki's autobiography *Joothan: A Dalit's Life* (2003) is a realistic portrayal of the caste discrimination. Shushupna observes about the authenticity of the depiction in Dalit autobiographies, "Dalit autobiographies are realistic depiction of life of torment and anguish experienced and being felt by the Dalits. Dalits are treated either as marginal people without a history of their own or as objects rather than as subjects" (Shushupna 349). In his autobiography Omprakash depicts that he had to live at a separate place in his village and the upper caste people lived at a separate place in their village. There was a Johri or pond that separated them from them. He depicts that those people were not only segregated at the social terms, they were sidelined from the flow of money, knowledge and the fundamental human rights also because these people were treated not better than animals by the upper caste people. They had to do all kind of cheap works for the upper caste people and most of the time they were deprived of their wages also. They did not have the courage even to ask for their wages.

Another painful thing for them was the loss of respect and identity. Dalits had no social status and they had no place or identity of their own. They were considered merely as the slaves of the upper chaste people. They had to do all kind of agricultural, labour and menial works but they had no courage to ask grain or money in return. Their wages were depended at the mercy of the landlords. These people were considered lowest of the low and even the children of the upper caste either addressed them by their name or they were addressed as "Oe Chuhre or Abe Chuhre" (Valmiki 2) keeping in view their age. There was not any provision of latrines for these people. Valmiki depicts that the women of their community observed *purdah* in their homes but even the newly-wedded woman had to go to the open field to take a shit. Thus, there was not any stand of these people and they remained at the mercy of their luck.

Omprakash depicts that they lived in a big family. Five brothers, one sister, two chachas, one tau and their family lived in that community. His chachas and tau lived separately and they did one or the other kind of work to run their family. Omprakash throws light at the evil of untouchably prevalent in his village. He describes that even the stray animals of the streets such as dogs, cats, cows and buffalos could be touched by the upper caste people but a touch with the Chuhra may contaminate them and they had to take a bath to make them pure and clean again.

There was not any provision of education for the Dalit children. All the children who went to school were only from the upper caste. There was not a single child who used to get education from the Valmikis. There was a Christian named Sewak Ram Masihi. He would sit with the Dalit children and he would teach them the lessons of reading and writing because the government schools did not admit these Dalit children. Omprakash joined Sewak Ram Mashi's classes and he learnt his alphabet from this school. After an argument with Sewak Ram, Omprakash's father took Valmiki to the Basic Primary School of his village where he begged the teacher Har Phool Singh to admit his son in the school. He said, "Masterji, I will be forever in your debt if you teach this child of mine a letter or two" (Valmiki 2). The teacher told him to come the next day for the admission of his child. His father kept on going for several days until the teacher succumbed to admit Valmiki in the school. By this time, the doors of the government schools had opened for the admission of the untouchable children but there was no change in the mentality of the upper caste people including teachers. They never wanted that Dalit students may get education in government schools. Gaikwad had to face the consequences of untouchability in his school. He had to sit away from other students of his class. He was not allowed to sit at the benches but he had to sit on the floor. Sometimes he had to sit behind everybody and near the door and the letters on the blackboard were not clearly visible to him.

His school experience brings a lot of pain in his life because most of the children in the school belonged to the upper castes and they teased him and even beat him without any rhyme and reason. If he was thirsty, he had to keep standing near the hand pump but he was not allowed to touch it. He was given such treatment in his school so that he may remain at home and so the work for which he has been born. Omprakash was mocked at by the students. If he wore old and shabby clothes, the students would comment, "Abe Chuhre ke, get away from me, you stink" and if he came in neat and clean clothes, they would not spare him from their sarcastic words. They would say, "Abe Chuhre ka, he has come dressed in new dress" (Valmiki 3). Somehow he passed his three classes in his school and now he was in fourth class.

One day his headmaster, Bishambar Singh was replaced by a new headmaster, Kaliram. A new teacher also came in the school. The entry of these two new teachers brought a bad time for the three Dalit children of the school – Omprakash, Ram Singh and Sukkhan Singh. These three students became the target of new teachers. They would thrash them at the slightest mistakes. Ram Singh sometimes escaped but Sukkhan Singh and Omprakash were beaten daily. One day when Sukkhan Singh had a boil at his belly, his teacher mercilessly hits him at the boil and it bursts out. He starts crying in pain. Omprakash also starts crying to see Sukkhan in pain. The teacher starts abusing to see them crying. This new headmaster was caste sensitive and he calls Valmiki in his room and tells him to clean the school because he knew that Omprakash belonged to a sweeper class. He asks his caste also and says, "All right...See that teak tree there? Go. Climb that tree. Break some twigs and make a broom and sweep the whole school as a mirror. It is, after all, your family occupation" (Valmiki 5).

Valmiki had to clean all the rooms and verandah. After that his headmaster orders him to clean the playground also. He was the pampered child in his family and he had never done so much work in his life. He had to clean the school the next day also. The third day he went to sit in the class but the headmaster Kaliram reached the room soon and ordered him to clean the playground. He uses an abusive language to him, "Abey, Chuhre ke, motherfucker, where are you hiding... your mother...Go sweep the whole playground...Otherwise I will shove chillies up your arse and throw you out of the school" (Valmiki 5). Valmiki had to take his three-day-old broom but the every pore of his body was submerged in the abyss of pain and the tears were shedding from his eyes.

It was a coincidence that his father passed by the school at that time and he saw this spectacle. When his father called him and asked why he was doing that work, Gaikwad burst into tears and he told the whole story to his father. His father took the broom from his hand and threw it away. He was filled with anger by this time. He began to scream in the school, "Who is the teacher, that progeny of Dronacharya, who forces my son to sweep?" (Valmiki 6). But the headmaster Kaliram was also an obstinate person. He threatened Valmiki's father and started abusing him but his threats had no effect on Gaikwad's father and he faced the headmaster bravely. His father took the child at his home telling the headmaster that his son will study in the same school and other Dalit children will also follow him.

When the people of the village come to know about this incidence, the people took the favour of the headmaster and they remarked that there was no logic of sending a Valmiki child at school. According to them a crow cannot become a swan. The village women also do not take his favour and they also comment, "However much you study...you will still remain a Chuhra" (Valmiki 32). His father reaches to the village head for justice and the village head advises him to send the child to school the next day. He assures Chhotan Lal that his son will not face any difficulty in the school. After this incidence, the things became normal in the school but whenever Omprakash looked at his headmaster, he would get frightened from him. In this way Omprakash Valmiki gets his primary education.

Valmiki describes that they were forced to eat the leftover food. They had to eat the food left at the pattals in the marriage feasts. This food was generally left in the dustbin and the Chuhras would collect this food and ate it at their home. Valmiki describes, "The joothan was eaten with a relish. The bridegroom's guests who didn't leave enough scraps on the pattals were denounced as gluttons" (Valmiki 6). Omprakash Valmiki gives a narration of an event of marriage of Sukhdev Singh Tyagi's daughter. When Omprakash's mother asked for some sweets from Tyagi at the wedding, Sukhdev Singh instead of giving her any sweets points at the pattals and says, "You are having a basketful of joothan. And on the top of that you want food for your children. Don't forget your place Chuhri. Pick up your basket and get going." (Valmiki 10-11) Omprakash had also accompanies his mother and at that time he was merely a boy. He was broken from within to see the humiliation of his mother. He describes this event in his autobiography, "These words of Sukhdev Singh Tyagi's penetrated my breast like a knife. They continue to singe me to this day" (Valmiki 11).

Being a Dalit is a curse and only a Dalit can better understand the real anguish of a Dalit. Omprakash's own family and community was very poor and they had to do the work as sweepers. Valmiki's father Chhotan Lal supports him in getting education and this education brings a lot of change in their family.

Valmiki had a horrible experience at the village of his teacher Brajpal Singh Tyagi. Brajpal taught Chemistry at Tyagi Inter College. One day he tells Valmiki to go to his village. Valmiki left with Bhikhuram at bicycle early in the morning and reached his village. The boys were called for lunch. When they had taken their lunch, they were asked about their caste from an elder. When Valmiki replied that they are from Chuhra caste, the old man lifted a heavy stick and hit Bhikhuram on his back. People suggested that they should be tied with a rope and should be hung from the tree. This experience stirred Valmiki to his core.

Valmiki tells another experience of his Mathematics lecturer Narendra Kumar Tyagi. This incidence took place when he was in eleventh class. His teacher did not know his caste and he tells Valmiki to bring water. Valmiki replies that he is not allowed to bring water from the pitcher because he belongs to a Chuhra caste. He says, "I belong to the Chuhra caste." and continued, "If you still want me to get you water, I will go" (Valmiki 64- 65). The teacher does tell him to bring water and he tells Valmiki to sit down. Valmiki studied at DAV College, Dehradun and he resided at Indresh Nagar, a distant village of Dehradun and residence of sweepers and cleaners. He attended his first class at 7 A.M. and started working in the Ordnance Factory, Dehradun and abandoned his college education. Valmiki went to Jabalpur and Bombay for his training as a draftsman but his caste always followed him.

One day Valmiki meets Professor Kamble at Kulkarni's residence. He notices that Prof. Kamble was given tea in a different cup. When Valmiki interacts with Kulkarni's family, Kulkarni's daughter Savitha falls in love with him thinking that Valmiki was a Brahmin but when she comes to know that he belongs to a Chuhra caste, she starts crying bitterly. Valmiki feels the pain of being born in a low caste. He depicts, "She started crying as though my being an SC was a crime. She sobbed for a long time. Suddenly the distance between us had increased. The hatred of thousands of years had entered our hearts. What a lie culture and civilization are" (Valmiki 98). This caste brought a big ditch in their relationship and they never met again after that incidence. Caste does not humiliate him at one place. It degrades him at every place. At one occasion, Valmiki got the opportunity to deliver his lecture on "Buddhist Literature and Philosophy" at a conference. It was a public platform and people from different places have gathered there. Suddenly a member shouts, "How can a 'Valmiki' be allowed to speak on Buddhist literature and philosophy? Aren't you ashamed?" (Valmiki 131). It was Valmiki's speech that makes the public speechless and it was a slap on the mouth of that person who has raised finger on his ability.

Valmiki gives an illustration of his journey from Chandrapur in 1980. He and his wife were travelling in the Pink City Express from Jaipur. There was an affluent couple with two children near their seats. When the woman asks about them, Valmiki replies that they belong to a Bhangi caste and after that the woman had no conversion with them during the rest of the journey. Thus, Omprakash has to face many problems in his life. Thus, Dalit Literature brings forth some hidden pains to the public. Manisha Singh writes in this context, "Dalit Literature consists in many qualities which differentiate it from rest of literature. It has an authenticity, a sense of social mission, a fiery strength and vigourness" (Singh 667).

Many efforts are being made by the people to work for the upliftment and creating awareness for Dalit people. Government is also taking many steps for the betterment of Dalits but "Caste system, despite of many efforts of the government and other organisations has become a stigma on India" (Singh 84). Many Dalit writers, activists, social reformers and organisations are working for the welfare of Dalits but there is less improvement in the position of Dalits in rural areas. The real change can come from the change of the mentality of the people. Until and unless the upper caste people shed their ego and think on humanitarian ground that Dalits are also human beings like them, all the government rules will be futile. Sukhadeo Thorat writes in this context:

> Historically, India has witnessed sustained interventions by social reformers who have worked consistently towards disseminating awareness about the lack of any rational basis for discrimination on caste considerations. Such awareness led to the assertion of rights by the 'Depressed Classes' and was responsible for the signing of the Poona Pact on 16 August 1932 between Gandhi and Ambedkar. This pact provided for the equitable representation of the 'Depressed Classes' in governance and the amelioration of their socio-economic conditions. The pact was significant because it became the basis for subsequent constitutional/ legislative safeguards and other measures for the social integration of the SCs (Thorat 3).

Works Cited

Devi, Manisha. "Omprakash Valmiki's *Joothan*: A Record of Painful Experiences." *RJELAL: Research Journal of English Language and Literature*. 3.3 (2015): 667-670.

Gaijan, M.B. "Omprakash Valmiki's *Joothan: A Dalit's Life:* Interpretations from Different Perspectives." *Dalit Men's Autobiographies: A Critical Appraisal*. Ed. Bijender Singh. New Delhi: Kalpaz. 2017. 239-248. Print.

Shushupna, S.S. "From Subjugation to the Threshold of Celebration: A Study of Laxman Gaikwad's *The Branded: Uchalya* and Omprakash Valmiki's *Joothan: A Dalit's Life*." *IJELLH: International Journal of English, Language and Literature*. 3.1 (March 2015): 349-360. Print.

Singh, Bijender. "Mapping Caste-subjugation in Omprakash Valmiki's *Joothan: A Dalit's Life*." *Sangharsh/Struggle: e-Journal of Dalit Literary Studies*." 2.3 (2013): 78-84. Print.

Thorat, Sukhadeo. Dalits in India: Search for a Common Destiny. New Delhi: Sage, 2009. Print.

Valmiki, Omprakash. *Joothan: A Dalit's Life*. Kolkata: Samya, 2003. Print.

13

Picture of Motherhood in *Mother of 1084* and *Bayen* by Mahasweta Devi: A Critical Analysis

— *S. Divya Bharathi*

In accordance with the Oxford Dictionary, '*marginalise*' means to make a person or group which should be less important or less powerful. Thus, the term "marginalised" can be applied to the group of people who are not subject to their minimum rights or stance in society and even exploited. Those who are marginalised generally suffer from a crisis of identity and this perhaps leads to the rise of social negligence for that person, while women and the physically handicapped, or mentally challenged, are simply smothered and subdued into the acceptance without choice of whatever is offered to them, and views and beliefs are forced upon them. This marginalisation of mothers and motherhood can be traced in Mahasweta Devi's writings. The issues like the plight of women who are breadwinners, women who are victims of male sexual violence, dependent widows, ill-treated wives, unwanted daughters whose bodies can fetch a price and marginalised mothers are closest to her heart. She portrays the stories of mothers bearing the substance of social and political oppression, and enduring and resisting with indomitable will. *Mother of 1084* and *Bayen* highlight the plight of subaltern mothers Sujata Chatterjee, traditional apolitical upper middle class lady who loses her son Brati Chatterjee in communist Naxalite movement and Chandidasi Gangadasi, who is separated from her husband and son Bhagirath Gangaputta when she is accused of being a Bayen, a woman who breastfeeds dead children and has the ability to curse others. In the course of action they also ultimately die.

Both the plays describe the predicament of the mothers who are marginalised by the so called patriarchal society and also establish many aspects of gender subalternity practiced by the political and superstitious society. *Mother of 1084* first appeared in Bengali as *Hajar Churasshir Ma* in October 1973 in the special autumn festival issue of the periodical Prasad and in an enlarged version as a book in 1974. Devi wanted to reach to the larger portion of illiterate audience for spreading her words so in the seventies she dramatised one of her major novel, *Mother of 1084.*

The play stirs around Sujata. She is married to Dibyanath Chatterjee, a chartered accountant and a typical patriarch, her life revolves around her four children, two sons Jyothi and Brati and two daughters Neepa and Tuli. When the play opens, two of her children are already married, Jyothi to Bina and Neepa to Amit. In the eyes of the world, they are happy and settled in their lives but in reality, as Sujata later on finds out, they all are leading superficial lives. The play opens with a phone call from the government morgue asking Sujata to identify a corpse of Number 1084 – that of her own favourite son, Brati. Sujata's family belongs to 'Bhadralok,' a bourgeois family of Calcutta (now Kolkata). In this society the standards of shame and reputation are different. So as soon as Dibyanath and his elder son listen to the news of Brati's death, they try to hush the whole matter rather than rushing to the morgue. Dibyanath was much concerned for his reputation rather than his son's death. If Brati would have been ill-tempered, drunkard or characterless then these people would not have been ashamed of him. But he was different from them. That's why they are trying to hush the whole matter.

Sujata is astonished to see the pathetic behaviour of her husband, the most precise example of male dominated society who sketches out Sujata from the whole picture. Though she is also an important member of the family, he likes to consult Jyoti about the matter and not Sujata. Thus, Dibyanath fails to comprehend the state of a mother, but Sujata throws away all the pretensions of social respectability and goes to identify her son. *Bayen* relies upon superstition and demonstrates the construction of gender subalternity. Superstitions in India dominate to a large extent of people who follow the superstitious creed to such an extent that they won't even hesitate to take anyone's life.

TULI: The same thing again! You will react every time we mention Brati.

SUJATA: Yes.

TULI: Are we not worthy enough to pronounce his name?

SUJATA: The way you pronounce it! To hurt me!

TULI: Hurt?

SUJATA: To Tony and his crowd, to the others, you, your father, Jyoti, Neepa, the way

You all speak his name, as if, as if Brati was a criminal. (Bandyopadhyay 1999:8)

Sujata and Tuli's decided to be present at the engagement ceremony throughout the party, she was caught up and studied the peace that she trained from the best killing. He insists on wearing a plain white wing but his son is wrong with family members of his sense. Although she thinks she is a criminal when family members pronounce her name, "... How can you be a witch? Those who bury children turn into Bayens, when they are possessed, not witch." (Bandyopadhyay 1999: 83)

Devi is very critical of superstitious creed; she makes use of mythical figures and happenings into her writing to satirize the hypocritical society. In *Bayen*, she touches the larger space of the social forces that separate mother and son in a male dominated system. The play moves around Chandidasi Gangadasi who is separated from her husband and son after being labelled as Bayen by the superstitious society. According to the villagers, Bayen is a woman who breastfeeds dead children, raises them from the grave and has the ability to curse others. The play opens with the Bayen singing a lullaby. She is completely scruffy and tortured soul, exiled from the village. She now lives in a hovel beside the railway track and is provided minimum ration every Saturday by the villagers as they are afraid to kill a Bayen. They believe that if a Bayen is killed, it will bring bad fortune to the village. The play exhibits the transformation of a working class woman into a public scapegoat, and ultimately, a subaltern woman with no physical or communal life.

Violence is the theme on which both the plays are based. In *Mother of 1084*, violence spreads rapidly and in *Bayen*, violence grows gradually. But both the plays have serious consequences and bring to light the longing of Sujata and Chandidasi for self-determination as they struggle for freedom, justice and their identity as an individual in male dominated and superstitious society. The rendering of motherhood and woman captivate attention to debate and discuss in these plays. *Bayen* is a powerful description of woman, poverty, fate, exploitation and superstition while *Mother of 1084* has more appeal for political and social change. Moreover, the plays illustrate some kind of search and revelation of identity.

Brati, a young boy, is reduced to a number 1084 in the police morgue after his encounter. It serves as a mental blow for the mother, while the rest of the family would much rather let the skeleton rest, the mother is submerged in her search, even Sujata's daughter Tuli is indifferent to her mother's feelings for her son and feels that she is still harping on the memories of Brati. Tuli chooses Brati's birthday for her engagement unconcerned about how deeply her mother loved him. But being a mother and bound by a sense of moral responsibility. Sujata decides to remain present in Tuli's engagement celebration, but throughout the party, she maintains stiff and studied silence that she has been practicing since the day Brati was killed. She insists to wear a plain, white sari for the occasion but her feeling for her son is misinterpreted by the members of the family. She is in such a grief after Brati's death that whenever the family members pronounce his name she feels that they are referring to a criminal,

"...my mother, the late Chandidasi Gangadasi, sir. Not a Bayen. She was never a Bayen, my mother." (Bandyopadhyay 1999: 9)

Thus a child understands the plight of his mother which the so called hypocrite society failed to understand, some feminists maintain that men are only responsible for the exploitation of women. But Mahasweta Devi proclaims the bitter truth that in male dominated society men tries to maintain their ego and women, directly or indirectly, allow them to dominate. Somehow men are taught that their duty is limited to provide big house, servants, expensive clothing and luxuries of life to the women, they feel that once this duty is over, they are not supposed to answer anything to their wives. Women, in one or the other way, suppress their voice and adjust to the dominance of men and that is why men like Dibyanath and Mahindra can never understand the condition of women like Sujata and Chandidasi who are isolated from their children. They fail to value them as human beings and they can't even value them as their wives and mother of their children, when Chandidasi, thinks to throw up her job of burying the dead children, Malindar rather than helping her in coming out of her dilemma becomes angry with her. She even requests Malindar to leave the village and move to some town so that they can be free from the clutches of superstition.

The only difference between Sujata and Chandidasi is that Sujata is literate urban woman while the latter is poor and illiterate villager, though Sujata is aware of her husband extramarital affair and the family member contempt for Brati. She cannot slam the door on her husband face and leave the house. Both the women lack the guts of Ibsen's Nora who reminds her husband about her sacred duty to herself, she refuses to become a doll in the hands of Helmer and bids farewell to his doll's house, Sujata and Chandidasi become silent sufferers and witnesses injustice done to them. Interestingly, it is death that reunites the mothers with their children and permanently asserts authenticity to their lives. *Mother of 1084* ends with Sujata's breaking down at Tuli's engagement party, fervently urging the audience not to be silent sufferers but respond actively to social reality.

The children who bury the children will become demons, and when they are kept, they are not magicians. Bayen ends with the death of Bayen, regenerating identity of Chandidasi as a mother. When Chandidasi is on her way to meet Malindar to complain him about Bhagirath's sneaking out house at night, she bravely stops the train from meeting with an accident and prevents major devastation. But in doing so, she loses her life as the train swallows her, the guard of the train acknowledges her as an embodiment of courage and advocates cash reward for her, as soon as the villagers learn about the cash reward, they re-establish Bayen's identity as a dome woman, but, it is Bhagirath, dead Chandidasi's son, who steps out of the crowd and gives her a true identity of his mother.

Thus motherhood is a universal phenomenon, lose of a child to a mother is perhaps the biggest loss. As an individuals and mothers Sujata and Chandidasi's interests are natural but the interest of the community as a whole are more important than individuals, Brati is killed on his birthday and this pierces the heart of Sujata to the core as she cannot accept the reality, she is even more depressed as she doesn't know Brati's reality though he was the soul of her life.

Mahasweta Devi's *Mother of 1084* and *Bayen* are two disturbing radical plays dictating historical past, voicing self-determination, condemning violence, glorifying motherhood, demonstrating women at the centre, seeking revolution and demonstrating the exploitation of the weak and minority section of the society which is often deprived of the basic human rights. The women playwrights have concentrated on the political upheavals and unrest of their respective countries or regions and have tried to justify the reasons for revolt and agitation condemning the massacre of the innocent people that results in claiming political self-determination. It can be defined as claims of people to establish their own separate political identity. The plays share the common themes of self identity, self protection, betrayal, and tyranny of the government or police. They also share the sharp contrast in their dramatic technique and creation, thematic and theatric development. The problems that are identified in the plays remain unsolved till the end.

Mother of 1084 and *Bayen* are based on death and their plots develop gradually. They have proper beginning, middle and end. The structure of *Mother of 1084* is based on the news that Sujata, Brati's mother gets over phone to identify the corpse 1084 which is of her own beloved son Brati. Perhaps the symbol of death has been used as a mark for the revolution, protest, war cry, upheavals and unrest. The device of race, extremism, social protest and politics of representations, intersections of race and gender are few of the issues that dominate the works of Devi. Both works share a few common issues such as historical movements, violence, political self-determination, revolt, social protest, exploitation, the idea of motherhood, characterisation, and identified but unresolved problems.

In this way Devi have traced out and mastered the painful past and have vented out their experiences and emotions to build a realistic present. She attempts to human welfare and social justice seems to have mitigated the anger and suffering of the common people. The rising anger and the suffering of the people were caused by the violence and murders. Violence of any kind is harmful and unacceptable to the civilised society. It dethrones peace and harmony, togetherness and unity. As mentioned earlier that *Mother of 1084* and *Bayen* evolve around the theme of death which is caused by volcanic, unprecedented and incessant violence. The root cause for prevailing disharmony and suffering is the result of various forms of violence such as physical violence, domestic violence, psychological violence, emotional violence and communal, racial, caste-ridden violence in a civilised society.

In *Mother of 1084*, Brati, Somu and other young boys protest and plan to have their own separate region or at least they should be treated equally. The Naxalite movement though is curbed by the government but it remains meaningless for people like Nandini as she rightly remarks. Most of them wanted a political freedom and geographical space, a free state as the government was unable to care for their welfare hence the idea of political self-determination gained momentum. The exploitation of masses in every form is universal and is clearly examined in *Mother of 1084* and *Bayen*.

Mahasweta Devi is conscious of the sufferings of the people. They have tremendous sense of feeling and observation. Mahasweta Devi's other plays like *Aajir*, is based on poverty and slavery, *Water* analyses the exploitation and *Bayen* is a powerful portrayal of women, poverty, fate, exploitation, suspicion and superstition.

The portrayal of motherhood and women captivate attention to debate and discuss in *Mother of 1084* and *Bayen*. As the title *Mother of 1084* suggests that the play centres on the feeling of an ailing and heartbroken mother who has lost her beloved son. Sujata, Brati's mother is helpless and confused while tears of Somu's mother exhibit a strong bond of a mother towards her son. Motherhood is a universal phenomenon and a mother cannot forget her children. The loss of child to a mother is perhaps one of the biggest losses. Samik Bandyopadhyay considers the play as the awakening of apolitical mother. Youth's anti-government attitude and interest in the political awakening of separate state cannot be ruled out. As an individual and a mother Sujata's emotions are natural but the interest of a community as a whole is more important than an individual.

As a true writer to document the realities of the present day, Devi has written a lot of short-stories and a few plays. Her depiction of the lives of the poor, and especially about women is undoubtedly realistic. In *Mother of 1084*, Sujata's speech becomes proverbial to protect the lives of the civilians and the rights of the poor. Sujata's voice at the end becomes demagogue asking the audience to speak out, to break the silence and voice against the injustice. The injustice done to the common mass, the massacre of innocent people especially of youths a corrupt and unreliable government is held responsible for which the unrest and protest against such practices spring certain regions. Mahasweta voices such unheard cries of the people, feels for her people as they are economically not so strong and educationally backward also. She has been able to understand their psyche.

Works Cited

Devi, Mahasweta. *Bengali Books, Author Profile.* New Delhi: Ajanta, 2012. Print.

—."*Introduction*". *Bashai Tudu* . Trans. Samik Bandhopadhyay and *Gayatri* Chakravorty *Spivak*. Calcutta: Thema, 1990. vii-x. Print.

Keyssar, Helence. *Mahasweta Devi's Writing: An Evaluation.* Delhi: Book Review, 1991. Print.

Roy, Pinaki. *Mother of 1084: A Chronicle of Deadly Times*. Delhi: Seagull Books, 2012. Print.

Shah, Kalpana. *Women's Liberation and Voluntary Action.* Delhi: Ajanta, 1984. Print.

14

Projection of Dalit Womanism in Gogu Shyamala's Selected Short-Story Collection *Father May Be an Elephant and Mother Only A Small Basket, But...*: An Analysis

— *N. Kaushi Reddy*

The word 'Dalit,' a vernacular from Sanskrit language, is a term used for the castes in India that have been subjected to untouchability. 'Dalit' stands for all three genders: Masculine, Feminine and Neuter. Dalit means burst, split, broken, down-trodden, scattered, crushed, destroyed etc. It may be used in two senses: it may refer either to physical weakness or to a lower position in society. The term 'Dalit' can be used for any oppressed group or people who are marginalised and dehumanised.

Books like the Manusmriti divide the people into a socially stratified caste system which promotes inequality between men and women. According to the Manusmriti, women have no right to education, independence, and wealth. It not only justifies the treatment of Dalit women as a sex object and promotes child marriage, and violent atrocities on women are increased. Women have no rights to study the Vedas. Women have no rights to know about certain social knowledge relating to religious, political, social, educational, and personal overtones, though they are kept away from the upliftment of Dalit women. In modern times, we see the severe oppression and exploitation of Dalit women, and the opportunity of education also denied to Dalit women by 'The Laws of the Manusmriti.'

In the modern age and development of democratic values, social reforms, and certain voluntary organisations have made strong efforts to improve the lot of the Dalits. The efforts were made by Raja Ram Mohan Roy, Swami Vivekananda, Swami Dayanand Saraswati, Mahatma Gandhi, and B. R. Ambedkar to improve their social, political, economic, and educational conditions. The twentieth century has given the sound firm hope to Dalits that they are bound to become conscious about the injustice done to them. They are suppressed through the abasement and repression inflicted on them and they are becoming intolerant and experiencing dissatisfactions of the lower status assigned to them in the name of religion. In the Indian Society, the Dalits are searching for an identity and the educated Dalits have very much conscious about their past days, when an earthen pot had to be tied to their necks for the spit, a broom or a branch to their waists to sweep their own foot-prints behind, and the days when they were forbidden to hear or to recite the scriptures. The Dalits who were considered to be no-people want to assert their place in history and uphold their culture. Oppressed and marginalised so for, they want to build up a Dalit identity.

Mahatma Jyotirao Phule, a Marathi social reformer, used the term 'Dalit' to describe the outcaste untouchables as the oppressed and the broken victims of Indian Society. The word 'Dalit' denotes all sorts of oppressions, i.e., social, economic, religious, political and cultural. Then the term 'Dalit' is used broadly to refer to the scheduled caste or depressed classes of India and the outcastes, politically powerless, economically discriminated both by religious and cultural variations. The society often treated women as an object of sex and sexual exploitation. Discrimination is shown towards them in all spheres, in the disguise of tradition, and culture.

The functional relationships of several sub-castes, untouchables in Andhra Pradesh suggest a limitation or adoption of the rituals of local dominant high caste. The numerically dominant Madiga castes look like a parallel, fully fledged community within the broad framework of the society. Each caste is divided into several sub-castes like Dasari, Mastin, Pambala, Binedu, Asadi, Chindu, Dekkali, Kommuvaru, and Sangari. Social structure of the Scheduled Castes in Andhra Pradesh is based on diverse principles such as centre, incorporation in the village or caste system, participation in the village rituals, and dependency on the political and economic power of the dominant castes. These principles depend on the purity and impurity prevailing in the society.

There is a need to examine and evaluate Dalit women's historical experiences from the perspective of caste, economic class, politics, and patriarchal angles towards the transformation in work, wages, and family life. Dalit feminism must respond to the complexity of class discrimination and the differences created by the caste-ridden society. They make an attempt to emphasize the unity of caste, class, and gender and reject the efforts to bifurcate their identities. Feminist theories rejections of totalizing and universalising the frameworks of patriarchy have already paved the way for deconstruction. It is required to develop a Dalit Womanism not only to uncover the problems but also to analyze the cultural, societal specification so as to construct the Dalit woman and recover them from the oppositions. This Dalit Womanism theory aimed at social justice meted out against all sorts of exploitation and oppression towards Dalit women.

Dalit women have been misrepresented in Indian literature and Indian literature in English. Most of the upper caste male writers are biased towards Dalit women. They are portrayed as the victims of the lust of the higher caste men and never had they permitted to fight against the injustices done to them, even in the writings of the progressive writers such as Mulk Raj Anand, Premchand and so on. Dalit women are molested or raped by the upper caste men. By depicting such pictures the writers gained sympathy for the victims. They have completely ignored the fact that Dalit women can also resist and fight back like any other victim of social oppression to guard their dignity. A Dalit woman is never a fighter but always a victim.

The first generation of Dalit writers constructed Dalit women in Dalit Literature writes:

> The female characters in Dalit Literature are dynamic and not static. Dalit writers do not look upon widows, prostitutes, depraved women, as Dalit, the exploited, with compassion alone; but they make them towards radiance. In the stories and novels of Annabhau, Shankar Rao Kharat, Baburao Bagul and others, though the nature of the struggle of woman in the beginning is individual, later it becomes class conflict... As a consequence of this, Dalit female characters end the journey of deep darkness and behold dreams of sunrise...They fight for truth and for themselves. They revolt to protect their self-respect... The revolt of Dalit women is not person-centered but society-centered... That is why Dalit writers do not portray Dalit women as hollow identities, overflowing with love as embodiments of sacrifice. (Prasad 46)

Dalit women, no doubt experienced humiliation, deprivation, isolation by virtue of gender, caste, and class. In Dalit context, structures are made to break down the fixed polarities between the upper caste or lower caste and men or women. In the Indian context, caste, class, and patriarchy are the three hierarchal axes of social structure which are very essential for the understanding of caste Hindu, Shudra, and Dalit. It is caste which shapes the integral part of the gender status and identity of Dalit women. This dualistic construction of Dalit women in gender ideology legitimises the sexual subordination and subjugation of them. Caste oppression, gender subjugation, and class exploitation are interlined together. The three interlocking systems of caste, class, and patriarchy are creating a multidimensionality and intensity of oppression, which is destructive to the experiences of Dalit women.

Unlike Dalit men, only a few Dalit women have written their autobiographies and narratives of their pain which was experienced by them. Most of them have been written in regional languages and they have hardly been translated into English. The position of Dalit women is as marginalised in Dalit Literature as they are in their community. Education gave them the chance to narrate their voices of distress and sorrows in their autobiographical writings. The contribution of Dalit women writers is significant and the writings of Dalit women represent their own experiences and burning indignation.

Shyamala is a Telugu-Language writer and women's activist and a prominent Dalit. She was born in 1969 in Peddemul village in Ranga Reddy district, now part of Telangana. Her parents are agricultural workers. She was also the leader of a vetti (unpaid labour), team that worked for the local landlord. She has stated that her brother Ramachandra was found into agricultural labour, but she was the only one of her three siblings who obtained higher education. Financial constraints initially prevented her from enrolling in college; however she eventually obtained a Bachelor of Arts from the Bhimrao Ambedkar Open University.

Gogu Shyamala's writing has "an evidently oral quality" which created detailed and authentic portraits of the people. *Father May Be an Elephant and Mother Only a Small Basket, But...* which was translated into English from Telugu in 2012. Gogu Shyamala described her awakening consciousness to casteism and discrimination in India as an adult, nothing "I never realised that there was any discrimination in India as a kid. It was after growing up that I discovered it. We had a Madiga area to the east of the village where we all lived away from the upper castes".

Shyamala's concerns are about land, agriculture, Dalit politics, feminism, and oral history. In her words, "The challenge for the Dalits does not come from their community but from the Brahmanical order that actively stops them from achieving success," and adds that it's not surprising that Shyamala is one of the foremost contemporary Dalit voices in the country exploring the tribulations and aspirations of her community. Shyamala recalls with a sense of nostalgia as, "School was the one place where everyone sat together. I remember sitting with a girl who was a Reddy and neither of us had a problem. But I was never invited to her house, and she was never invited to mine" (12).

Shyamala says that the system was a continuous, practice, and attitudes passed on from one generation to another. These stories are drawn from her own life. "My book is entirely based on my experiences of things that I have seen, heard or felt. I do add a few elements here and there to brighten up the book, but the writing is largely from experience." Gogu Shyamala said:

> The society is structured in such a way that a certain sort of dress sense is considered to be immoral. Even the moral character of a woman gets questioned if they do not follow certain stereotypical notions of the traditional female. This attitude exists across all sections of the society. (10)

Gogu Shyamala's writing in Telugu has brought to light the realistic picture of Dalit and non-Dalit women's lives in their works. Shyamala addresses the caste factor very directly in her short-stories *Tataki Wins Again*, *Braveheart Badeyya*, and *Raw Wound* especially the Madiga community in Andhra Pradesh. Some of her stories are having caste names in their titles. She writes as a victim and in anger.

Gogu Shyamala's woman protagonist in her short-story *Father May Be an Elephant and Mother Only a Small Basket, But...* has devoted her whole life for her family. She starves herself but feeds her mother-in-law and her children when her husband ran away for a year from the village. When he comes back after a year, he beats his wife for not giving him money to drink. In Shyamala's short-story *Braveheart Badeyya* a woman has been continuing the traditional practices. When Dora passes by, she removes her slipper as a part of traditional practice.

In *Raw Wound*, these include access to land, education, and the role of religion in Dalit women's lives. The story's young child-narrator is destined to become a jogini or "God's wife," referring to "a lower caste woman who is declared as the sexual property of the whole village" (235). The status of jogini (also known as erpula or more generally as devadasi), an oppressive structure more commonly prevalent in the regions of Andhra, Karnataka, and Telangana is sometimes regarded as a caste in its own right.

Shyamala's short-story *Raw Wound* unveils a different kind of social problem. Shyamala's *Raw Wound* is about the jogini system prevalent in post independent Telangana and the Deccan region of Southern India. As a part of this superstitious and hideous tradition, girls born into a particular Dalit family are married to God as 'jogini's for the good of the village. Through this short-story she has projected how the rustic tradition has forcefully been imposed on the uneducated Dalits in the name of ritual or work of god. There is a girl, Syamamma, from Madiga community, who has been forced to become a jogini. Jogini is a woman who is devoted to God, who is seen as a wife of the whole village. She is good at studies and her father Balappa, though uneducated, seems to have enough ability to distinguish between good and bad. Initially the father of the girl is informed by the Patel that the present jogini is too old to carry out her practices and therefore they need to make his daughter as a new jogini. Balappa is shocked to listen, he has no other way; he is forced to follow the orders by the Patel. By disobeying the Patel he dares to send his daughter to the hostel for further studies. After some time the Patel with all the other reputed men in village takes the decision either to make the father force his daughter to become the jogini, or make him leave the village. There have always been threats to Dalit lives in the villages.

Most of the times, the upper caste people impose their decisions on the Dalits without having any concern for them. An upper caste does not want a Dalit girl to get herself educated. They are afraid if they get educated, there would be a great threat to their position. The Patel tries to convince Balappa by telling how education would be of no use to her. He mentions that her becoming jogini would solve the problem of the whole village; therefore, it is very much needed to make her as the jogini. But her father is not convinced; the Patel gets angry and beats him. He bleeds and about to die, but does not accept the Patel's decision. He is even ready to leave his house, land and village for a better future for his daughter. Though the jogini system has been banned by the government laws, it could be continued. Balappa laments that Patel is black mailing him stating, "If you don't do your duty and I mine, we are doomed. We have to follow what is written on our foreheads. Who are we to change our destiny? You know that the fingers of the hand are not equal, don't you, my man?" (721)

These lines reveal the dominant upper caste attitude that projects inequality between human beings as 'god made.' His argument that 'fingers of the hand are not equal' is symbolic of casteists discourse in which Dalits as 'Panchamas' or 'untouchables' occupy the lowest space in society. While Dalits remain untouchables, the Dalit 'jogins' are 'touchable' for free sexual pleasures of the upper caste people who forget the 'impurity and pollution' for pleasures. Patel doesn't oblige though Balappa pleads for his daughter's education as his two sons are already in bonded labour. Thus, the story envisages how caste and poverty connive to deprive of the education to Dalit women. Dalit women have to struggle against many odds to gain education. Dalit autobiographies underscore the fact that literacy and freedom is the major motif in Dalit life. Literacy for a girl is even more complicated as the story reveals. The writer emphasises the miserable family lives of Dalit:

> From now on, the red earth field will not be ours!
>
> The black clay field beside the canal will not be ours!
>
> The madiga quarter will not be ours!
>
> The home and yard we were born and brought up in will not be ours!
>
> The house we had built with lime and mortar will not be ours!
>
> We have become birds without a place to go! (731).

The writer brings out the forced alienation and exploitation of the Dalit. The Dalit history in India has many such 'raw wounds' unrecorded. Gogu Shyamala can be seen as the Dalit feminist who has given voice to these problems that women are facing at the ground level.

Shyamala does not hesitate to give the actual picture of the community. While depicting the domestic violence in *Father May Be an Elephant and Mother Only a Small Basket, But...* she clearly gives a picture of a husband beating his wife, "Father beat her like she was cattle. She said, "Oh mother, I am dead, he'll take my life" (24). Dalit women writers came forward and started narrating their experiences through life narratives and raised voices for the voiceless. Male writers have depicted such kind of violence and rarely considered for decision making. She was a kind of animal who had a tongue but had no right to talk. Dalit woman is dependent on her own labour. When she comes home, her husband will be waiting to snatch her hard-earned money which is the only source to feed the family. If the woman refuses to give the money, the husband beats her up.

In *Father May Be an Elephant And Mother Only a Small Basket But...*, Gogu Shyamala, a highly respected activist and Telugu writer from the Telangana region of Andhra Pradesh, offers glimpses into the life of the Madiga community, who is one of the most exploited, even among Dalits. In the story *Braveheart Badeyya* a son is saddened that his mother cannot wear slippers in the presence of the upper caste landlord even when walking on thorn land.

Shyamala focuses on the woman in Madiga households. She portrays them as tough, opinionated, courageous, and she makes no excuses for their hardened attitude. Indeed, it is this that constitutes their strength, the Dalit feminist stories suggest, whether evidenced in how a woman deals with her family, land or the young ones. The book titled as "Gogu Shyamala's World" has brief entries on ecology, land issues, myths and belief systems of the Madigas, including even their games and recreational activities. An interesting move is to make the readers immediately aware of the larger contexts to these stories. Shyamala does not moralize or overtly politicize grief and suffering, that is for the reader to glean. Violence is only in the subtext and Shyamala does not depict it obviously, thus marking an interesting shift within the genre of Dalit writing.

Shyamala's collection raises other issues besides language. In *Raw Wound*, she tries to exhibit struggle towards their land, education, and the role of religion in Dalit women's lives. This not only shows the specificity of women's oppression but also brings out in the open the entanglement of caste, patriarchy, and religion in the making of India's social fabric.

In the Indian context, the upper caste women sought liberty from oppressive patriarchy which entwined their lives and also Dalit women sought freedom from the stain of pollution, untouchability, and poverty. While upper caste women confront oppression in domestic realm, Dalit women have to bear it in the social, political and economic realms. Hence, as upper caste feminists are against dowry, domestic psychological violence, sexual freedom, and property rights, while the Dalit women have to fight against physical violence by upper caste men as well as their own men, basic amenities, and daily livelihood. Dalit women have to face the almost routine violence through the categories of caste, gender and class. Their voices became vibrant and struggle against poverty, the stigma of caste, and violence.

Telugu Dalit women writers expressed themselves in poetry, short-story, essays and even in critical theory and wrote to fight against varied forms of oppression: discrimination, sexual or physical exploitation and negative stereotyping of Dalit women etc. Short-stories of prominent writers like Gogu Shyamala's *Raw Wound* and Joopaka Subhadra's *A Bloody Mess in the Bathroom* are penned to analyse and understand different ways in which Dalit women face suppression of caste discrimination. They are analysed in such a way as to narrate the long journey of Dalit women from being victims of upper caste exploitation in rural areas, the struggle for education staying in government welfare hostels and finally, they had realisation over the society that even after education, they are stained under the control of caste.

The short-stories represent the three stages of Dalit women's struggle for liberation, education, and emancipation in the post independent India. Endings of these stories reveal the perpetuation of oppression and its changing colours, confirming what the Dalit women rightly pointing out that caste is a greater oppressive evil than gender and their victimisation was due to their intersectional identities of caste, class, and gender. The exploitation of women is the universal factor but the tools of exploitation are not the same all over the world. Caste becomes the major exploitative tool in the oppression of women in India.

Works Cited

Bama, Faustina. *Sangati (Events)*. New Delhi: Oxford U P, 2005. Print.

Paul, S. K. *Dalit Literature: A Critical Overview*. New Delhi: Sarup & Sons. 2008. Print.

Prasad, A.N. *Dalit Literature: A Critical Exploration*. New Delhi: Sarup & Sons. 2010. Print.

Shyamala, G. *Father May be an Elephant and Mother Only a Small Basket, But*...New Delhi: Navayana, 2012. Print.

15

The Daughters That Weren't: The Saga of Dalit Feminism

— Guni Vats

She was told
That she was dirt,
She was filth and
In this sacred land of thousands of goddesses.
She is called a Dalit.
(Aruna Gogulamanda 35-39)

In the land of Kali, Lakshmi, Saraswati and many more idols that stand decorated in the temples, mute, patriarchy thrives in the veins of the hollow men that see every woman as a body and an opportunity to become more of a man. Where women still fight to win the rights to step out alone at night, to go to the cinema at their will and to ride the city buses at all hours, there is a fragment that still fights in the ignored darkness, that screams to be heard from the corners of the civilisation who demand the right to be called but a woman! India survives on a neatly and violently carved social structure of hierarchy where the Brahmin men occupy the highest place and Shudras the lowest. But at the very depth of that social structure, there is Dalit community that has stumbled its way to the light of the day. Now when the academia is bent on recognising their existence, they unveil the ugliness of hierarchy even in their oppressed sectors. Patriarchy has successfully seeped through the crack holes of the section that should have stood together. In the hours of need of existence, Dalit men exert their egoistic rights on the Dalit women, further pushing them in an abyss that not only ditches humanity but refuses to accept the other as a human. This paper reminds us of a few women from the history that the world must never forget and tries to read in the lives of the Dalit women through the poems of Dalit women poets; the stanzas that bring the elites of the society to a shameful reconsideration of how we have always conveniently forgotten a part of us that has toiled its life in our fields and factories making our nation what it is today.

Kuyili, the commander-in-chief to Velu Nachiyar (1730-1796), waged the first war against the British in 1780, seventy-seven years before the first war of Independence was fought. Kuyili, addressed as the *Veerthalapathy* (the brave commander) or *Veeramangai* (the brave woman), was a schedule caste woman of Arunthathiyar who bravely and wittily waged a war against the British troops that had invaded her queen's fort and managed to win back the kingdom from the clutches of the foreign invasion. She gathered information about women being allowed in the fort and on the tenth day of Navaratri, when women were allowed inside to celebrate Vijaydashmi which was celebrated in the temple of Rajarajeswari Anuman, she waged a well-planned attack on the British forces that caught them off guard. She led her army dressed as civilians and swarmed inside the fort. The weapons were hidden inside the baskets carrying flowers and fruits and the war was waged that took the British army by complete surprise. Kuyili used the chaos to her advantage and made the women pour ghee and oil all over her that was kept for burning the lamps. Then she went inside the store room where the British weapons were kept and set it on fire. She destroyed the weapons and sacrificed herself to bring victory to her queen and reclaimed the fort and the kingdom. A Dalit woman burned herself to save the kingdom. The saga of Dalit women since centuries, burning metaphorically like the night lamp, are only to secure the nation that needs them but doesn't recognise them.

The margins of our nation are lined by such women who sacrifice their lives, toiling in the fields and falling prey to the lust of the upper caste men who deem it a favour to provide a pure seed to the impure castes. Dalit women are fighting tirelessly to overcome the triple marginalisation of caste, class and gender but all in vain. Dr Ruth Manorama revisits the numerous conferences in the United Nations where she somehow arranged for the Dalit women to say their piece, to exist but only on paper, merely in theory. She recollects how the Indian Constitution and the Indian law is decorated by strict promises to facilitate the existence of Dalit women but only to result in an escalation of Dalit atrocities since Independence. She blames the implementation of laws for the status of Dalits as the people responsible for the protection of Dalit come from a prejudiced upper class that still can't tolerate the Dalits to exist. In her piece on Dalit women and international advocacy she says, "Humanity for Dalits have been denied." Colonisation was a menace. We, the nation fought against for more than two centuries and once the goal was accomplished, we conveniently forged invisible colonies, the filthiest lanes of our nation where the Dalits were forced to remain and were restricted. Furthering her conversation on Dalit violence, Dr Ruth comments, "Violence is a tool to silence the Dalits." Dalit oppression has been normalised in our nation, even in the age of acute globalisation, we are not ashamed to report that we together work towards bordering a section we promised to protect when we gained freedom. The news of Dalit students being targeted or random Dalit men being tied to the trees and beaten or the hypocrisy of a system that prays to the Krishna who saved Draupadi from losing her dignity parading women in the streets, naked, fail to stir emotions in us. As the society grows, it continuously innovates the system of violence. The colony ruled by the upper caste maintains the streams that virtually abolish all recognition of the Dalits, "Untouchability was abolished by law, but still exists."

In the political quagmire, the Dalit women are inured to suffer the pain we inflict on them. They are taught at every step to bear the pain and be silent to survive and not demand the luxury of an identity. They lack voice and any involvement in the politics; even the women that do manage to find a rank in the system become mere puppets of the elitist patriarchal system and forget their roots. The existence of being a Dalit is again successfully suppressed barring them any chance of a voice that might uncover the ugly faces of a regime that denies existence to nearly eighty million women of the nation. Dalit women are systematically silenced and their vulnerability exposes them to a situation that exploits their dignity and robs them of an identity and thus a voice. The fight for their identity is not only restricted to the celebrated ranks or the decorated academia but the public spaces that are haunted by the threat of looting them of their body and their soul. Their fight for the right to exist does not only involve ending untouchability in all its forms but a true existence ending caste endogamy. Their journey to a justice that blurs the boundaries between the admission forms that declare their caste to the marriage system which accepts them as an equal contestant is a road leading to a destination that seems unclear and probably non-existent.

In the early 1800s, men and women of the lower castes, mainly Nadar and Ezhava communities were not allowed to cover their chests in front of the members of the upper caste as a sign of modesty. Clothing was a sign of prosperity and wealth and the members of lower castes were simply not entitled to it. To keep the hierarchy intact and to fuel the fire of patriarchy, the members of the upper castes would decide what the Dalits were allowed to wear and what not. In the early 1900s, women in Kerala had to pay *Mula Karam* or breast tax to be able to cover their chests with cloth. Channar Revolt or the *Channar Lahala* was a series of violent clashes in the Travancore region of South Kerala where churches and houses were burnt down and women who wore blouses were stripped in public. *Maaru Marakkal Samaram* was one of the very first struggles for women liberation in Kerala. A woman named Nangeli became symbolic of this struggle. She belonged to a place called Cherthala in the central region of Kerala. In 1803, Nangeli defied the state orders openly and decided to cover her breasts. When the news of her defiance reached the state, the *parvathiyar* or the tax collector reached her home to demand the breast tax. Instead of paying the tax money in a plaintiff leaf, Nangeli cut off her breast and gave it to the tax collector. She died of the bleeding and her husband in his grief mounted her pyre and was recorded as the first man sati of India. Following her death, the breast tax was annulled in Travancore. Although she is never mentioned in the history books or celebrated by the feminist academia, but she remains a figure as important as bell hooks was for Black Feminism. The cutting of breast was not only a symbol of the defiance of breast tax but her assertion of being a woman and having control of her body. A statement that reminds the patriarchy that Dalit women are as much women as the upper caste women are. The breast being just a part of body, a piece of flesh that could have been torn by a sickle or knife but the spirit of the woman that could not be contained by the system, the spirit that refused to parade naked and snatched her right to cover herself, not begging for it.

The paradox of the situation is not only that time has forgotten Nangeli but also that when the feminists paraded for an equal right to visit the Sabarimala temple, a campaign was launched by some women in Kerala against entering the temple named "Ready to Wait Campaign." The Nadar women in the early 1900s who fought for the breast tax were labelled *Azhinjadikal* which are translated into 'loose women' in English. The women against giving women the right to enter the temple call the women fighting the battle of equality by the same name, loose women. But they tend to forget that it was these loose women that got them the right to wear clothes and cover their breasts. The fight of Dalit women is not only against the men in and outside home but also these women who are but only the agents of patriarchy; the women who believe in their hearts that women must wait for their turn graciously standing behind the men in the queue of freedom, the women who not only believe in their lower status but also deny the Dalit women any right to exist. A Dalit woman has to fight the gender battles in her own gender, demanding the right to cover her breast and live with dignity or they would have to cut their breast and teach their elite counterparts that they are as much a woman as they are.

The world of literature provides Dalit women with the voice they have been looking for since centuries. It empowers them with the gift of words. But even this world is as ambiguous as the one that silences them with force. The academia is only interested in the voice of the privileged, someone who can afford the expenses, both monetary and social expenses, of the right to express. The words that are floated in the society are coloured with the language that the audience wants to hear, conveniently neglecting the ones that come from the most oppressed sections. Sanjeev Gumpenapalli in his article "5 Dalit women poets who remind us that caste and patriarchy are not exclusive," asserts "the community of mainstream poets denounces the poetry of the marginalised and poetry that does not fit into the mainstream...poetry that came from the oppressed sections have been othered." The organised effort to other the Dalit Literature is so precisely effective that during the research of this paper it became almost impossible to unearth the texts of many women Dalit poets. Rajni Tilak, for example, a Dalit rights activist and a leading and prolific writer instrumental in fighting for the Rightful Space of Women with two collections of poetry to her name, *Padchaap (Marching Steps*) and *Hawa Si Bechain Yuvtiya (Restless Women)* is difficult to be spotted outside a few portals dedicated to Dalit movements. The mainstream literary hierarchy has never accepted them as a part of their own. Dalit autobiographies might have made their way to the libraries and online portals as a social document of Dalit oppression but the world of poetry still remains wound around the fingers of a few elite poets. The words rhyme to tell the tales of Dalit women but the fear of academia to accept that the Dalit women could be so talented as to beat them in the convulsion of words seems insufferable. It is this fear that pushes Dalit poetry to the margins of the literary world.

Joopaka Subhadra, a Dalit woman poet from the state of Telangana paints Dalit struggles in her poems. She brings out the internal discrimination, the threads of patriarchy winding the inner sanctum of Dalit households, where a man, othered by the society comes home and suppresses his wife further to assert his manliness, to feel that he is alive and he exists. She sings the saga of rural women and uses rape as a tool used by the powerful people to oppress women.

Mallanna may be a slave to the world
But he is reputed in our *waada* (colony)
For having tied the wedlock,
I have become a slave to Mallanna.
(Leather 1-4)

She recollects how she becomes a slave even in her home to her husband, a man who is a slave to the world. Another poem, "Kongu isn't a Rag That Stands Guard over My Head," tells the tale of the free end of sari. *Kongu*, the poet's only companion through her struggle, through the times no one else would accompany her. A woman left alone in the world and at home to suffer and only her sari to witness her pain. The cultural significance of Kongu is that it is not *pallu* that the upper caste women use to cover their heads with, to maintain their status and dignity with, it is a piece of rag which might not protect the poet's dignity but would be her companion in her life through insults and hardships. The title sketches the pain of the poet accurately, *Kongu* is indeed not a rag that will guard her but her friend, her only confidant that will bear her husband's aggression and love and also nurse her children and that will wipe her tears and sweat and also keep her warm when the world turns cold. Another thing that is worthy of noticing is that the *kongu* is feminine, it is a female companion, it is she. "...when my husband reaches out in love or anger/ like a ball of butter she always gets caught before I,/ to aggression or violence, from those at home or outside,/ my kongu rag always succumbs first..." (15-18) as the poem unfolds we witness that the rag is not merely a companion anymore. It has become a part of the poet, the cloth that rinses off her bodily fluids, that soaks her menstrual blood and that licks off the dirt of her body and keeps her clean, keeps her human. The piece of rag that "rolls in my hands, sweat, bed, bones, limbs in pleasure and sorrow,/ my kongu rag that sticks to me/ in work and song, in crisis and comfort,/ like the filth that clings to my feet, the companion/ of my life path..." (44-47). The conclusion to her poem makes her one with her kongu. Her honour becomes one with the rag's:

She's not the patchy pallu that stands guard over my head
nor the hobbling stone...over my breast

how can I drag her into the bazaar
set fire to her honour and lose myself?
("Kongu isn't a Rag That Stands Guard over My Head" 50-54)

Aruna Gogulamanda, another Dalit woman poet from Telangana comes from a middle class agricultural family. Her poem, "A Dalit Woman in the Land of Goddesses" brings out the hypocrisy in the land that boasts of revering women as goddesses. "Her eyes two dry hollows bear/ silent witness/ to hundred of deaths of her mothers, daughters, sisters/ their dreams, respect and their bodies./ her calloused hands, her unkempt hair/ her cracked heels, her wrinkled hair/ tell the tales of living through fears and years/ of centuries and millennia of violations and deaths" (28-34). Through those eyes and experiences, she talks about the difficulties of working class Dalit women. Her simple and deep poetry is a metaphor for the lives of these Dalit women. Her poems are simple and deep and are wrapped in them the secrets of tortures that centuries have witnessed and are still quiet. While talking about the Dalit women, she openly claims that "none of these are Indian daughters." They are not the daughters anyone fights for or fasts for or protests for, they exist, they do not live.

She wrote an article in the Firstpost titled "A Dalit Woman in the Land of Goddesses" wherein she takes a deep look at the Indian Dalit feminism. In her column, she comments unabashedly on the inside discrimination Dalit women face from the Dalit men, how they are silenced and have to face acute criticism for voicing their plight by Dalit men. She recounts how men from the Dalit community censor the women's voice, they dictate the terms on which the women can write and the content they are allowed to write on. Then she turns to her gender partners that have turned a blind eye to their pain. The Indian feminists forget to consider Dalit women as their part; Dalit women are simply treated as the other, the mere objects who are used, exploited and then discarded. The physical body that is although untouchable is treated as a soulless object that can be used in every way and then deemed untouchable and discarded. She laments how Dalit women have found no representation in feminist literature at all.

She was told
Not to wear a blouse
To allow every male
Watch her as a device...
...she was told
To take the insults, jeers, beatings and assaults,
For being born a woman, in a cursed clan...
...she was told
That she is bad omen.
A bloody sanitary pad, useful but a disgusting topic...
(She was told! 1 - 26)

Gogulamanda recounts how women are told... how they are instructed... how they are taught who they are, what they have to do, how they have to behave, how Dalit women are trained to treat themselves as an object for the man to use...to watch...to discard. The pain of using and discarding reaches its epitome when she compares the Dalit women to used sanitary pads that are useful but too disgusting to talk about. A topic stifles between the thighs of the upper caste that deems it impure to talk about it in open space, let alone parade with it in public. Sukirtharani, a Dalit feminist poet who writes in Tamil centers her poems around caste and body and uses both to intermingle and thus, expose how caste restricts body and the freedom of women. Her collection, *Yeh Udal* (My Body) talks about how a woman's body is always seen through the eyes of a man. In her poem, *Viduthalaiyin Pathaagai*, she plays with a disturbing image of woman's body and blood to paint the pain of Dalit women. She uses the phallic imagery of 'pole' planted at the top of her vagina on which the flag of freedom will be hoisted and that flag will be painted in the colour of blood, the blood of India's daughters that are conveniently forgotten by the society, the daughters that scream to be heard and to be made a part of the struggle of mainstream, who strive to only be heard and recognised as India's daughters.

At the top of the pole
Planted in my vagina

The flag of our freedom shall fly
Painted in the colour of blood.
(Sukirtharani n.pag.)

Works Cited

Amudha, M.V. "Dr Ruth Manorama on International Dalit Women Solidarity." *Feminism in India*. n.p. 18 July 2018. Web. 1 Sept. 2018.

Angmo, Deachen. "Rajni Tilak: A Leading Dalit Feminist of Our Times." *Feminism in India*. N.p. 26 April 2018. Web. 8 Aug. 2018.

Foucault, Michel. *Discipline and Punish* 2nd ed. New York: Vintage Books, 1995. Print.

Foucault, Michel. *Power/Knowledge*. ed. by Colin Gordon. New York: Pantheon Books, 1980. Print.

Gogulamanda, Aruna. "A Dalit Woman in the Land of Goddesses." *Firstpost*. n.p.n.d. Web. 15 Sept. 2018.

Gumpenapalli, Sanjeev. "5 Dalit Women Poets Who Remind Us That Caste and Patriarchy are Not Exclusive." *Feminism in India.* n.p. 11 Jan. 2018. Web. 7 Sept. 2018.

MV, Amudha. "Kuyili: The Dalit Commander Whose Sacrifice Remains an Unsung Tale." *Feminism in India*. n.p. 31 July 2018. Web. 5 Aug. 2018.

Subhadra, Jupaka. "Kongu isn't a Rag That Stands Guard over My Head." *Dalitweb.org.* n.p. 3 Mar. 2012. Web. 11 Aug. 2018.

16

A Threefold Oppression in Bama's *Karukku* and P. Sivakami's *The Taming of Women*

— *Disha Sharma*

Human beings are capable of living and working together for the upliftment of society as a whole. But contrary to this, human beings also have got the potential to suppress other and step ahead of him. This suppression would demand some means to get hold of higher position and keep dominating; they are the power, the wealth, the gender, the race, knowledge and class. There are plenty of theories fabricated to interpret the working of such ideologies. But above all, there exist a tool that abates any sort of rebellion and that is – religion. Similar suppression has been established in *Sanatan Dharma* as postulated by the Brahmins of the religion, that caused the rise of a lower cast termed, Dalit that eventually outlaid Dalit Literature. According to the Vedas as Brahmins tangibly state that it was the Brahmin who was born out from the mouth of Lord Brahma, followed by Kshatriya who was born out of Lord's shoulders, then came the Vaisya from His thighs and lastly the lowest of all, Shudras from His feet.

For as in the title of the paper has mentioned oppression as its main keyword, Kimberle Crenshaw in 1989 while coining the term 'Intersectionality' for women describes oppression as, "Cultural patterns of oppression are not only interrelated, but are bound together and influenced by the intersectional systems of society" (Crenshaw 18). Oppression is that manipulation of one section of society that discriminates and segregates a group of community on any basis of caste, race, gender, religion, nationality etc. This paper tends to explore the circumstances of thrice oppressed women in the society through religion, gender and race.

As such the term 'Dalit' has been long ago finds its roots in one religion of Sanatan Dharm and under the implications of the Hindu *varnas*, people are identified and divided within a structure. They are segregated into four main sections i.e. Brahmans, Kshatriyas, Vaishyas and Shudras. These four major sections are not only divided but are imparted their specific roles in the society to perform as mentioned in the Manusmriti – the Brahmans as are born out of Lord Brahma's forehead are the supreme of the four castes and shall do the work of interpreting Vedas and can become priests for studying scriptures; Kshatriyas are born through the limbs of God are expected to work as warriors of the state; Vaishyas, are born from Lord's belly shall involve themselves in business and Shudras, as the last and the meanest of all, are born out of Lord's feet shall live to serve the upper three castes of the society. And hence, the Dalits are not even majorly divided by God Himself rather those who could not find place in the *varnas*. They are treated as untouchables and are expected to do the lowest chores.

Dalits have been mistreated as untouchables, and are subjected to malice and injustice. Under the pretext of religion, some communities have taken control over every resource of nature and impose their will as the will of God on other communities. This parallels Karl Marx views on religion and its functioning in the society. Marx's theory of religion is a complex one where Marx's most famous statement about religion comes from a critique of *Hegel's Philosophy of Law:*

> Religious distress is at the same time the expression of real distress and the protest against real distress. Religion is the sigh of the oppressed creature, the heart of a heartless world, just as it is the spirit of a spiritless situation. It is the opium of the people. (145)

Marx's this statement about religion is mistakenly taken negative altogether when not considered in full phrases. Religion indeed is fabricated by the upper class people who hold the capital to legitimise their status of 'haves' and miserable conditions of 'have nots.' But by saying this, he does not advocate to eradicate religion altogether from the society because religion is only a tool, a drug, that induces forgetfulness about the misery of working people and curbing the tool only will never help in improving the conditions of the society. This provides the foundation of this paper that traces out this religion and its use as weapon in the hands of other people.

The paper takes up two works – one autobiography by Bama and other novel by P. Sivakami. As a Dalit woman, Bama writes about Dalit women in her novels. Being a Dalit, she voices out her experiences from the margin. In her writings, she dominantly demands change in the lives of Dalit women.

Through her work *Karukku*, Bama portrays the life of a Dalit Christian woman. Before the publication of *Karukku*, it was evident that only Hindu religion has divided people into castes but Bama's path breaking work explicates Christianity as practicing this hierarchal structure. The Dalits hoping to transform their fate and troubled by this caste system in Hindus, started converting to other religions, but their castes have been fixed on them as birthmark, consequently, forming more sections like, Dalit Christians, neo-Buddhists, Dalit Muslims and so on.

Thus, Dalit Literature is a form of activism that projects to unhook Dalits from the orthodox ideology of casteism in society. Similar to B.R. Ambedkar's opinions, Bama's work argues for the empowerment of Dalits and women in particular in her town. She was aware of the power of education and believes that "reading and writing are political practice," for which Dalits have always been kept away from formal education under bindings of ideological paradigms. For ages, Dalits have not been permitted to study Vedas or other scriptures and even today, not much has been altered.

During the publication of *Karukku* in 1992, India was experiencing mass conversions that were sparked by Ambedkar's words. It was during this period, a revolution in Dalit community surged against

Hindu orthodoxy which eventually saw the rise of Dalit Literature coming from Dalit publishing houses, and budding writers proudly affirming their Dalit identity.

The pathetic condition of the Dalit folks remains to the fact that people are changing their religion and shifting to other faith that allows them at least to live as a human. And this seems so relevant that even Marx affirms of it. Marx says, "Religion is the sigh of the oppressed creature ..." and "Religious distress is at the same time the expression of real distress and also the protest against real distress" (Marx and Engels 1975: 39). This suggests the concrete happening that a man turns to religion only when the circumstances of his life are not favourable to him anymore and in the scope of betterment of his miserable conditions, he seeks to the almighty God for his sustenance. In his manifestations of religion Marx says that religion in turn provides a relief. Conversion by Dalits has always been undertaken with the desire for social transformation. To get rid of demeaning labels and condemned status, Dalits have converted to such religions which promise the possibility of a casteless community on the outer face of it. They have hoped to be accepted and treated as human beings rather than sub-human creatures.

In her work *Karukku*, Bama emphatically sketches the position of Dalit girls even at their homes as subordinate to their male siblings. In Pariayar village the boys play act as Naickers that is, upper caste landlords and the girls as Pannaiyaals that is, workers at farms. Their games would always place the male at superior levels to girls such as, the boys would play a shopkeeper and the girls would become customer; the boys act as drunken husbands returning home and the girls as submissive wives that should be beaten. Thus, girls in Dalit homes encounter oppression when they have no one to take care for themselves. The poor status spurs them to dig and eat earthworms, net fishes from the ponds and relish their taste unless they are caught by some upper caste guard roaming nearby. The guard would not only take their baits but intimidates them by breaking their fishing rods. Though boys and girls would play along the streets but for certain pleasures boys are permitted only like riding on buffaloes' backs or going for hunting water snakes.

Education for Dalit girls has never been less than a milestone in their lives. Those girls who get a chance to get educated, like the author Bama herself, often experience casteist discrimination in their school life. As she recounts in *Karukku* when she was in third standard, she came to realise, recognise and felt humiliated to be born in a lower untouchable caste. Despite the fact, Bama usually enjoyed her school days with her friends of the same caste while returning home from school but it was only the tag of untouchable and the consequential discrimination that spotted her childhood memories of love and laughter. The cruelty imposed on the lower castes is depicted when the narrator watches an adult Dalit male carrying a packet of *pakoras* for his upper caste boss. The fritters were wrapped in a banana leaf, and again rolled in a newspaper. The adult man held the packet from a long string with which it was tied up. He handed over the packet to his boss with bent backbone and lower voice. This incident amused the girl child but later on she is informed by her elder brother that Dalits are expected to behave towards the upper castes exactly the same way because their touch is supposed to pollute everything. This makes the young girl offended and she wishes to retaliate the misbehaviour by holding that snack in her bare hands. This is the first instance where Dalit consciousness sprang up through the girl of third standard. She questions, "Aren't we human beings? Our men should not run errands for those fellows. We should simply collect our wages for our labour rendered in their fields and go our ways." (*Karukku*12).

Another instance of discrimination is observed when the young girl narrator becomes a witness to a caste-riot. There the police despite of solving the issue, bluntly sides away with the aggressor and intimidates the Dalits. The skirmish breaks out between two communities of the village: Saliyar and Paraiyar community. The Saliyars took life of a Paraiyan during the riots. The reason of riots was the burial land of Dalit Christians where Saliyars claim their right since it was near the school Saliyars own. The futility of the riots parallels the matter behind its rise that is, the occupation of burial land, people believe in reserving lands for their after lives. The fact that reveals itself here is the disputed land occupied and used by

Dalits for burial rituals; Dalits have no grounds to fix their feet at. The Saliyars used their upper caste hegemony to grab this land for their vested interest of extending their school building and for this they resort to violence over the Paraiyars. They also harass young Paraiyar girls on their way to school.

A significant aspect of *Karukku* relates to the fact that Dalit Christian girls are further subjected to a strict regimen of Rosary classes in the mornings and evenings, learn hymns and japams, and attend sessions of regular, weekly confessions and so on. It is an enforced rather than a devout exercise. Early in the morning, before sunrise, they are made to run to the church to attend the morning mass. If they ever skipped the mass, they were severely punished at the school assembly the following day. The interaction between the girl-child and the church takes place in an unmistakable atmosphere of fear, superstition and violence, physical as well as psychological. The sisters at the church feed the girls fear of ghosts, demons and, black devils, tails, nails and teeth who kept a record of the evil deeds committed by the girls and pounced upon them when the notebook overflowed with their 'sins.' The narrator recalls that as soon as she entered the church, visions of terror would come before her and she would rush to do every single directive of the sisters to escape the devil's net. She would recite mantras frequently, run for every errand set by the sisters without delay and attend confession sessions every week. The authoritative and self-belittling nature of religion that attributes the qualities of strength and goodness to Supreme Being, God is laid bare, when the narrator confesses:

> Prayers to the omnipotent. I am a sinner. Kindly bless me. It has been a week since I offered confession. I lied four times; I stole five times; I did not obey my elders; I stared here and there at the temple (church). I confess and regret these and all those sins I forget to recall. (*Karukku* 69)

As the narrator grows up and reaches college, she wonders at the deception practiced by the sisters and the priests towards poor Dalit devotees. She questions the dictum of daily visits to the church and the routine of japam classes and periodic communions.

> I felt that the sisters and priests had deceived me a lot. I was made to believe that god could reach me only through them. But I recognize now that god is nowhere near them. They are the most ungodly creatures. I fought with them. I questioned them. Oh! How fraudulent are these people? Cheats, hypocrites, actors – I hated them. (*Karukku* 83)

While all Dalits are ill-treated and discriminated against, Christian Dalits face more specific forms of discrimination. Dalits who had converted to Christianity or born in Christian families experience caste discrimination within church and its various official organisations. Christianity and Islam, theoretically, do not practice untouchability. But a separate category of Dalit Christians or Dalit Muslims has emerged in our country underlining the hegemonic structure of caste that permeates every layer of our society. No area of social experience is immune to operation of caste ethics. When the narrator in *Karukku* enters a nunnery, she is appalled to discover that this profession too is not untouched by caste hatred. Teachers, disseminators of knowledge and ethical conduct also practice untouchability. They enjoin upon Dalit students to sweep and mop the classrooms and clean the toilets. The narrator laments, "Is there no space without the presence of caste?" (*Karukku* 21)

Dalit Christians, especially the women among them look up to the church to resolve their problems, both domestic and social. The church, however, is shown to be utterly callous and insensitive towards their plight. Moreover, the institution like church aggravates the plight of such people fighting for their circumstances to get transform in any way.

The novel *The Taming of Women* (2012) is P. Sivakami's second novel translated in English by Pritham Chakravarthy. Sivakami remained a political figure for a span of thirty years. She has worked as a Dalit woman IAS officer. Her novel reveals the first-hand experience of the society. In this novel, Sivakami sketches the trials and the miserable plight of women and how they are subjugated by men in patriarchal Indian society. Through the novel, Sivakami straightaway explains about women of all ages and generations who are made to suffer physical assault and gender discrimination. The novel depicts the crude remark on the male dominated society that forces the beautiful women to end her colourful life. Women have to suffer manifold trials and tribulations in the course of their lives in a small village. The main protagonist Anandhayi is married to a womaniser, Periyannan, an unsatisfied contractor who is not content with the wealth that his farms bring him. He is after power that money can bring, and amassing wealth, treats women as sub-creatures serving the only purpose of satiating the hunger of physical needs of men. He treats his wife, his concubine, his old and ailing mother, his daughters the same way. The novel also details in the way women have been made to think about one another under the power of men. One such instance in the novel is, when Periyannan brings his concubine, Lakshmi to his home after the demise of his young son, where his wife already struggles with the labour pain. There Anandhayi prays to her God calling Lakshmi a 'slut' and wishes she comes down so that she would get it from her. This portrays the misdirected hatred women reserve for each other, a social and cultural interpellation where the worst discrimination and judgement comes from other women. Despite blaming her husband, Anandhayi's anger finds its source in the women he sleeps with. Anandhayi's pathetic condition becomes apparent when she finds it difficult to raise three daughters Dhanam, Arul, and Kala.

Periyannan brings Lakshmi home as his second wife. Lakshmi reaffirms the image of a destitute woman ending up as a concubine. Before Periyannan married Lakshmi, she was a childless widow and her youth was exploited by numerous men, the last of whom abandons her at a lodge. She is happy to live with Periyannan. In this novel, at many places, the wife emerges as the "other woman." While Periyannan keeps himself busy with numerous liaisons, either be with professional prostitutes, or with distant relatives, he even had a relation with the mid-wife Muthakka who visits to help his wife deliver his fifth child. Aanandhayi is held always a captive by repeated pregnancies domestic chores, and going for work at distant family land and is constantly subjected to severe violence by her husband. In fact, during her labour, Periyannan pushes her on the floor, give blows to her and mounts the stairs to sleep with another woman.

Though he is captivated by Lakshmi's beauty, he denied to give her money for abortion. He commanded her to keep the baby. On her recounting that she is weak and cannot bear another life inside, he overlooked the matter and ultimately, she had to sell her nose stud to get the money needed. Laxmi, instead of being Periyannan's longing, is tormented and almost butchered by Periyannan physically and sexually. Women, in the novel, irrespective of age, are tortured and humiliated by males. Periyannan stays away from the house for days and each time he returns home he questions Aanandhayi of her loyalty and chastity, scolds her for being a careless housewife. He charges Anandhayi for every minor lapse of any of their children but never took responsibility of his children. He terrified almost every member of the family whenever he visits for short span. For all his preferred love, Periyannan tortures Laxmi's body almost every night and often has sex with her violently. His insecurity has risen to the extent that he does not allow her to talk to anybody and imprisoned her in one single room. Imprisoning a woman's body, causing psychological torment is a strategy used by Periyannan of the society to wield power and authority over women. Many a time Laxmi tried to get away with her conditions and elopes, first with a lorry driver plying to her hometown and later with Manickam a young, rich, philandering son Kangani. For finding out Laxmi, Periyannan hires a taxi, spends tremendous money to bring her back. Each time after her return, violence and sexual abuse increased. Periyannan also grows more suspicious and insecure about her. He held her captive within fourwalls of the room. Laxmi craved for the freedom she earlier had. Aanandhayi felt helpless and was tied down to motherhood which never let her think of the freedom she requires. But Laxmi as a concubine is expected to serve at her best to her master. When he brings her home after her first elopement, he along with his son, Mani, drags Laxmi from the gate to the room, beating her up viciously. Mani assaults her violently and she is numbed with shock. After all, she had treated him like a son. The ageing Periyannan needs Mani's physical prowess and thus, he never scold him over his failure in studies and drinking habits. Mani shows his patriarchal authority in the household by exercising physical violence on women. Both the father and the son beat up the unmarried daughters/sisters and resent the visits of the married ones to their natal home. Laxmi unable to fight with her circumstances, finally, consumes poison to free herself of ceaseless torture. Periyannan was shattered but soon turns to Aanandhayi with vengeful violence. Laxmi finds freedom only at death, and freed her body of the assaults. Through her suicide, she affirms her claim to an identity beyond the body. Aanandhayi is left to face viciousness of a husband. His desperation for no longer getting Laxmi has resulted in the worst situation made for Aanandhayi whom he started to consider below a maid. For only Aanandhayi has put up with Periyannan's brutality or his ill-treatment, she even made her children to fear only father and look down upon their mother as powerless. In the lives of all the three daughters, Periyannan's intolerance of a woman's attempt at self-articulation or her interrogation of male injustice precipitates enormous violence against them. Periyannan is very cruel towards his daughters. Kala, the eldest of the three daughters is a studious girl and a voracious reader of fiction. She borrows books from her friend's brother and devours them after school hours, reading up a novel a day. Her father, during one of his rare visits to home catches a glimpse of her reading. He quickly snatches the book and interrogates, "From where did you procure this?" The younger siblings report from Dingumalli Annan. Dingumalli is the mentally retarded brother of Kala's classmate Maariayee. Periyannan flares up, "How dare you bring books over from a male fellow? Has your mother let you loose on the streets?" and thrashes her, hitting her hard on her head with the book gnashing his teeth like "a wrathful dog" (48). The price paid by the daughters to get educated becomes apparent in the lines above. Though the daughters have always been shown beaten up for no faults of their, the two sons are never shown to be beaten up, even for their grave lapses. Moreover, the sons are not allowed to go against the father and if they raise a whisper, they would get no share in the property. Thus, all the children are controlled treated harshly by the father and are molded by him in such a manner that they perceive their mother as someone who deserves the violence she receives from her husband.

They are not equipped with education or sensitivity to perceive the two women as fellow victims. Although abused by their father, they are in awe of his authority and power. As economic power and social prestige rest with their father and their mother is reduced to a domestic drudge and a child-bearer, the daughters fear the former while feeling ashamed of the latter.

Both the works, Bama's work *Karukku* and P. Sivakami's *The Taming of Women* project reality of Dalit women in the society, where Bama's work exhibits the condition of Dalit community as a whole in the society and their struggles with the upper caste communities. Sivakami's novel vividly picturises the sad reality of Dalit women within their household as captives and suppressed creatures no matter what age they belong to in the household. But the overall oppression is presented through the language of the works only which is a kind of rebellion towards the set norms of the society. Bama most distinguishly writes words from her Dalit culture and incorporates in her work. The works proved landmarks in the revolution of Dalit culture and community and somehow unleashes Dalits pathetic circumstances for a better future.

Works Cited

Bama. *Karukku*. Trans. Lakshmi Holmstrong. Oxford U P, 2012. Print.

Lockhart, Lettie L. and Frans S. Danis, Eds. *Domestic Violence: Intersectionality and Culturally Competent Practice*. Columbia U P, 2010. Print.

Marx, Karl. *A Contribution to the Critique of Hegel's Philosophy of Right*. Cambridge U P, 1843. Print.

Sivakami. *The Taming of Women*. Trans. Pritham K. Chakravarthy. New Delhi: Penguin Books, 2012. Print.

17

Subaltern Voices and Dalit Issues in Bama's *Karukku*: A Critical Analysis

— *S. F. Filomine White Sheela*

There's really no such thing as 'voiceless.' There are only the deliberately silenced, or the preferably unheard.

– Arundhati Roy

India is growing fast at the map of the world and but in spite of its journey of development, there are still many unsolved problems. Caste discrimination is still one of the major hindrances in the social development of India. Such kind of development shows the narrow-minded mentality of the people. The discrimination at the name of caste, religion, sect or ethnicity is derogatory and such people, who advocate such kind of mentality, are inhumane and despicable.

So far as the growth of Indian civilisation is seen at the pages of history, the advent of Aryanas and the Hindu scriptures have played a vital role. Due to division of the people on the basis of their works, the society was divided into four parts: Brahmins, Kshatriyas, Vaisyas and Shudras. These Shudras were placed at the basement at the ladder of status and respect. They were assigned menial works to do and their duty was to serve the people standing at the top of the ladder of the society. They were labelled as untouchables because they had to do remove the dirt and their bodies were smeared with that and that bad smell became the cause of their social ostracisation. They were deprived of their right of getting education. Many social reformers and Dalit activists worked for them to improve their social standard and to provide them equal respects and rights.

Indian society was constructed around Varnasrama Dharma, a labour based division of castes in India that inevitably brought about racial prejudices. The Brahmins were the topmost in the pecking order. The Sudras were destined to serve the three upper ladders, namely. They remain the "untouchables" in society. They have been accepted as Scheduled Castes in the Indian constitution after the British use of the phrase. Gandhiji and Ambedkar used two different terms to name them- Harijan and Dalit. Their efforts have brought about an upliftment in their social status. They also encouraged education of the Dalits that ultimately led to a new writing.

Indian Dalit Literature began as a concerted movement in the 1960s, though clannish elements were visible as early in the 11th century. It began in Marathi literature and later on infiltrated to Hindi, Kannada, Telugu, Malayalam and Tamil literatures. Dalit writers initiated a realistic experience based on authentic literature which threatened the upper class hegemony in society and in literature. The anger, sorrow and the indomitable will and hope of Dalit protagonists were offered in a tongue which is often denigrated as vulgar. The writers of different states in India share a collective relationship to a common cause, a common identity and a common political stance.

Dalit Literature in India is not of whole community but of an individual. Many writers, thinkers, social reformers and political figures gave their contribution in the Dalit Literary Movement like B.R. Ambedkar, M.K. Gandhi, Rettaimalai Srinivasan etc. Exploitation or oppression to the weaker by the stronger is as old as mankind itself. The Indian history has been a vibrant record of conflict and dialectic between two opposite forces like exploiters and exploited, coloniser and colonised, powerful and powerless. Dalit Literature is always marked by revolt and a great struggle of lower caste, against the high class people commonly known as Savarna.

Southern India has witnessed organised attacks against Dalits through Panchami Land issue, Chengara struggle and Muthanga issue. Dalit caste organisations like "Dalit Panthers of India" in Maharashtra, "Dalit Mahasabha" in Andhra Pradesh, "Dalit Sangharsha Samiti" in Karnataka, and "Arundhatiyar" in Tamil Nadu were formed in response to mainstream atrocities. They demand for equitable shares in opportunities and reservation. Most of the activists are good writers as well.

Caste and gender are the two important identity building mechanisms that create a Dalit feminist perspective. Dalit feminism redefines women from the socio-political perspective of a Dalit, taking into account the caste and gender oppression. This paper focuses on the sufferings of Dalit women in two aspects: first, being a woman second, belongs to the lowest community. Therefore they are double oppressed.

From the time they are born, girls are discriminated against just by their sex. A girl-child is neglected at infancy in favour of the boy. The girls play gender-games like cooking or getting married. The women of Tamil Dalit community are on their feet doing back-breaking work from morning till night, all just to make ends meet. The men never do their share of the work. Dalit women participate in productive works, earn wages and participate in the economic chain. But they are paid less. They are also constantly under the threat of sexual harassments in the field of work. Family, Church and Caste-Courts are usually male-led.

In Tamil Nadu, a laudable attempt to couple "Penniyam" (feminism) and "Dalityam (Dalit Studies) has been recorded by Bama whose *Karukku* speaks of the hitherto unheard annals of Dalit women. While going through all this caste system, some important questions arise in the mind: Who are Dalits? What is feminism? What is women's identity focused in Bama's *Karukku*? What are the solutions suggested in Bama's *Karukku*? These are some important questions which pressurise us to go through the text. It is mainly concerned with women's movement in India. Literature also contributes to the Dalit movement and to the women's movement in India especially in Tamil

Nadu. Movement of 1960s may be noted as the starting point of Feminism. But of course, before this there already occurred various struggles against male oppression, the privilege systems and inequality. As an exponent of Dalit feminism, Bama has found in *Karukku* the right way to explore the sufferings of Dalit women. The conditions of Dalits were very bad as they were not allowed to enter into the temple, for worship and schools for education. This form of discrimination was based on identity akin to racism. Thus, Dalit Literature is an umbrella term, which may be substituted by subaltern studies. "The Dalit movement has emerged in response to the numerous injustices suffered, mostly in silence by Dalits for centuries" (Randhawa 2013:39). Dalit women are always victimised at home as well as outside. Their songs, dances, community cooking at weddings bring out their innate talent. Dalit women's sexuality is an important domain of creative or critical concern in Tamil Dalit Literature. Partha Chatterjee quoted in his essay "Caste, Subaltern and Consciousness" that "Common sense is not something rigid and immobile, but is continually transforming itself, enriching itself with scientific ideas, and with philosophical opinions which have entered ordinary life" (Guha 2010:171 Vol. VI). Bama's very ordinary life depicted in *Karukku* has made her a woman of high importance. The efforts of Bama in presenting her autobiography are the product of her experiences as a Dalit-Christian woman. In her essay "Subaltern Studies: Deconstructing Historiography" Spivak says, subalterneity has to be taken "...in relation to histories of domination and exploitation rather than within the great modes of production narrative..." (Guha 2010: 330 Vol. VI). Caste dominance and caste exploitation have been working gravely in the Indian society. Dalit Literature describes the factual life of Dalits. Hence the primary motive of Dalit Literature is the liberation of Dalits who have been the victims of caste system in India for ages. Sharankumar Limbale (2010: 25) says, "Dalit writers persisted in writing and making every possible effort to be heard." Although Dalits found inspiration from the movement of Blacks in the distant land of North America, Dalit Literature and Black Literature cannot be compared, asserts Gangdhar Pantawane, a well-known litterateur and critics in Dalit Literature. On caste and Dalit Literature, Randhawa says:

> Dalits have been a part of the Hindu society and yet were outside it in the sense in which they were marginalised and inescapably reduced to servitude. This gives the Dalit an opportune position to question and critique caste Hindu and Indian aesthetics. The origin of all art can be located in religion and it was religion that was responsible for the most inhuman exploitation of the Dalits (2013: 40).

As Bamanego-feministicly voices out the grievances of the Paraiyya women, there is, in the first place, the question of economic inequality. Women are presented as wage earners as much as men are; they work equally as men as agricultural and building-site labourers, but they are given less wages which throws light on the gender discrimination. Not only this, they become the target of the landlords, zamindars or the contractors wherever they work.

The characters often break into a song or a chant when the situation demands and there is a song for every occasion. But what is thought provoking is Bama's sketching a positive identity for the Dalit woman. An alternate of her story as opposed to the mainstream is drawn with vivid descriptions of a marriage ceremony, attaining of puberty ceremony, joy of togetherness, singing songs, cooking and sharing food. In most of the rural homes, the Dalit woman is an earning member, widow re-marriages are possible and tali or the sacred thread worn as a chain during the marriage is not this binding symbol as in other communities. It is interesting that the Dalit woman cannot be suppressed in spite of caste or gender oppression.

Bama is a Tamil Dalit woman writer who has contributed many literary works to Dalit Literature such as novels, short-stories, poems etc in her autobiography *Karukku*. She has written about the gender and caste discrimination faced by them even if they attain good education. Bama's expectation and desperation regarding religiosity and the persistence of caste discrimination in her life deserve mention here.

Bama belongs to Christian religion and goes to Catholic Church from her childhood. She has got impressed by the Christian scripture which is teaching about love and about the intimate relationship with

God. She decides to become a nun and to serve God. After joining the nunnery, she comes to know that there is a separate training centre for Dalit Catholics and she has to go there. The way how Dalits are treated on the basis of their caste makes one feel that she has taken a wrong decision. She gives up her wish to become a nun.

Through this part of life of Bama, we can clearly understand that the caste discrimination occupies a major role even in the religious places and whom Dalits believe as highly spiritual are disappointing and humiliating them without reasons.

Bama has bitter experiences on caste discrimination in her village. She wants to go to a new environment which gives her peace and to prove her identity. She has studied the Holy Bible which says about the love and scarification. After the completion of her studies, Bama joins a catholic Christian school as a teacher. She finds many Dalit children studying there and she likes to serve them with devotion as her primary duty. When she observes the behaviour of other teachers and nuns towards the children, she gets angry and keeps on arguing with them for the sake of poor children. This experience pushes her to think about becoming nun and says:

> It struck me overwhelmingly that these nuns collectively oppressed Dalit children and teachers so very much; why should I not become a nun too and truly help these people who are humiliated so much and kept under such strict control? (Bama 23)

Amidst the strong opposition from the family members and friends, she prepares herself to go to convent. All her relatives and friends advise her that she could not find the peace in nunnery and nuns will never follow the truth of gospel in real life but Bama could not accept it. Moreover, before joining the convent, she has learned about a nun who lived and sacrificed her life for the sake of downtrodden and poor. Bama wants to live like her and believes wholeheartedly that her wish will never put her in shame, "They said I could do far more useful work as a layperson than I would do as nun. They said that caste-difference counted for a great deal within convents" (Bama 23).

After entering into the Convent, very soon, she finds that the atmosphere is not up to her expectation. She feels that the environment and life style of nuns are against the God's call. She has seen how she is discriminated in front of other trainees without consideration. The Sister who supervises the training has asked Bama about the change of her date of birth from christening certificate and school certificate. Whatever the explanation she gives, the Sister could not agree to it and she tells that the Tamil people will cheat the school administration to get admission with wrong date of birth, "What a nuisance this is turning out to be; thus far they made us hang our heads in humiliation because of our caste; in this order being a Tamil seems to be equivalent to being a Paraya" (Bama 25).

At the time of British colonisation, many Christian missionaries came to India and helped poor people through some charities and by prayers. By seeing the Dalit community and their sufferings, they introduced Jesus (who gives eternal peace) and Christianity to them. Due to their preachings of God many Dalits got converted to Christianity. Those people are called Dalit Christians. Bama has strong belief on Jesus and on the teachings of Holy Bible. So she has expected the same good qualities from the nuns who claim that they are the followers of Bible.

The other experience that she shares about caste-discrimination removes the curtain of the order (convent). In a particular class at the time of completion of her training, a Sister says that there are certain orders which do not agree to see Harijan (Dalit) women as prospective nuns and they have got separate nunnery somewhere. Bama could not digest it and tries to find out about her position. When she has enquired, she is completely disturbed with the reply of the Sister.

> At once she asked me whether any other order had invited me to join them. I said yes, while I was working in a convent school earlier, the Sisters had invited me to enter their order. Our sister said, 'Well, they asked you too, did they? Don't worry about it. You may join us.' I wished I could have disappeared from the spot and vanished then and there. (Bama 25)

In the Convent, she watches that many rich children happily come, study and go but the Dalit pupils are used to look after the jobs like sweeping the premises, swabbing and washing the classrooms and cleaning the lavatories even though they are not given respect. They are all insulted by other children and by the nuns too as low-caste people who do not have moral discipline, neither cleanliness nor culture. Bama could not show her anger because she is afraid that if they come to know her caste, they may not give same respect or they may stop talking with her.

Karukku is a unique autobiography published in Tamil. The reasons for its uniqueness are many which make is different from the other Dalit autobiographies. The events of Bama's life have been beautifully narrated by her in lucid, linear or chronological order. *Karukku*, the title stands for palmyra leaves and the serrated edges of the leaves on both sides give a look of double-edged swords. It is a Tamil word which means embryo or seed which is a symbol of new birth, new life or freshness. Bama has written about it in her foreword and it gives the reference of Hebrews (New Testament) in these words: "For the word of God is living and active, sharper than any two-edged sword, piercing to the division of soul and spirit, of joints and marrow, and discerning the thoughts and intentions of the heart" (Hebrews 4:10).

In *Karukku*, the main philosophy of human life is clearly revealed. It does not mean in which religion the person is born, it means that in which way he is grown. The society is having a blind eye on Dalits. Bama became doubly depressed after joining Convent school. Being a poor Dalit Christian woman, she has learnt the Gospel and possesses the wish of helping and serving poor as they have learnt that Jesus himself was born in cattle-shed and died for the poor, ugly, and disgusting sinners. We are surprised to hear about nuns through Bama who could not possess such love in them. How the truth of Bible is hidden to their eyes? Bama raises many questions to society, she asks, "Are Dalits not human beings? Do they not have common sense? Do they not have such attributes as a sense of honour and self-respect? Are they without any wisdom, beauty, dignity? What do we lack?" (Bama 27)

As a part of this society, we have to answer this question by understanding and uplifting Dalits. According to some critics, it is stated that the Dalit Christians are completely forbidden by the government and by the upper class. Due to the class discrimination, upper class could not accept them. Due to the conversion from Hinduism to Christianity, the government could not recognise them as low-castes. The Dalit Christians are much depressed when compared with other Dalits. *Karukku* proves that even in religious places, they are not treated with respect, "Those who commit atrocities against Dalits do not differentiate between Christian Dalits and non-Christian Dalits. For an Indian, a Dalit is a Dalit, whether Christian or not" (Arulraja 9.)

Bama decides to come out of the Convent. She has refused to listen to anybody's words and has joined in Nunnery as a full time teacher. With the same speed, she wants to come out of it. She is giving many reasons for her emotional action and reaction. Not only the caste-discrimination matters her, she points out the way how the order runs too. She complains that there is no presence of God. Bama stays in Convent, gets a good and nutritious food, nice bed to sleep and a comfortable life with all facilities inside the compound. She says that the Convent schools are admitting wealthy children compared to the poor. When she asks about that she has got a reply that their parents are the sponsors for their sophisticated life, for their building constructions and there is no use of serving only the poor who could not give or do anything to the order. So it is important to help, obey and honour the rich pupils.

The other thing which disturbs her is, in the convent is the rich children who act as the owners of the order. Whatever they do, nuns keep quiet, accept all their mistakes and admit them as innocent in the class, act only on their demands but Dalit children are punished severely even for small mistakes. They have to suffer for the mistakes of wealthy children also. Bama could not bear such an injustice and unkindness. She says:

> All those people who had taught us, had taught us only that God is loving, kind, gentle, one who forgives sinners, patient, tender,

> humble, obedient. Nobody had ever insisted that God is just, righteous, is angered by injustices, opposes falsehood, never countenances inequality. There is a great deal of difference between this Jesus and the Jesus who is made known through daily pieties. (Bama 104)

Before joining in the order, Bama has got freedom to say what she likes and dislikes and at least to raise her voice but it has become so pathetic to her and feels as if she has become a slave to the order by losing all her birth rights and human rights. She is insisted only to shut her mouth, eat, pray, work and sleep. Nothing more than these things she can do from there. She can do these things from outside also. It is not needed to wear a mask as nun. Her aim to serve and help poor Dalit children in school has become a dream. At last she finds clearly without any doubt that there is no godliness but worldliness, respecting only the wealthy. She feels shame to be a nun thereafter and tries to run away from the place.

> But there is something ugly in saying one thing and doing another. How long can one play-act in this way?......And I don't know if they have become so habituated to their play-acting that they can no longer distinguish between the role and the reality. (Bama 107)

When she has decided to leave the Convent, she faces many obstacles and restrictions from the Sisters. Bama's religiosity has taught her a bitter and an unforgettable experience. According to Bama, religiosity is gentle love, equality, honour, politeness, kindness and true devotion but she has seen the negative form of religiosity which speaks about inequality, selfishness, greediness, partiality, enslavement and control. Each coin has two sides, she has found the other side of it but she could not digest it and did not want to live with unrighteous and injustice nature in the sight of the true God, Jesus Christ. Finally, she concludes her journey as nun and says:

> Today I realise what an extremely foolish thing I did. But at that time I didn't understand in the least what I was doing. I was like one who was falling into a well, blindfolded. (Bama 105)

With fear and humiliation, Bama travels to her native place. She could not control her tears when she rewinds the past incidents in mind especially when she travels to Jammu to take up the job in convent, how the nuns send her in an unreserved compartment and deceive her as if some of their person will climb the train with ticket and how she has thrown by TC to sit near toilet for not having the ticket.

In conclusion, the person who has gone to nunnery very actively and happily, the same person comes back to her native place sadly and shamefully by showing the traces of failure in all over her face. Bama is an educated and a bold woman. So she faces struggles and comes out of them very bravely without losing her confidence. The expectation what Bama has on religiosity has given the scars of everlasting and ever forgotten desperation in her heart.

Everywhere people believe that if a person appears to be religious, surely they will be having all religious oriented qualities and a good attitude. When it comes to reality, everyone will have their own reasons. When a group of members takes up a congregation or an organisation, they should have rules and regulations. It is mandatory for them to follow those rules by themselves and to live according to the doctrine what they preach truthfully otherwise they will lead the innocent people to unnecessary sufferings. Bama proves through her activity of coming out from the Convent the Christianity is not to survive, it is to serve the poor and it is not the way to gain but to give.

Work Cited

Arulraja, M.R. *Jesus: The Dalit*. Secunderabad: Jeevan Institute of Printing, 1996. Print.

Faustina, Bama. *Karukku*: Trans. Laxmi Holmstrom. New Delhi: Oxford U P, 2012. Print.

Guha, Ranjit. *Subaltern Studies I & VI: Writing on South Asian History and Society*. New Delhi: Oxford U P, 2010. Print.

Guru, Gopal. "Dalit Woman Talk Differently" *Economic and Political Weekly*. (Oct. 2013):14-21. Print.

Randhawa, Habir Singh. *Dalit Literature.* New Delhi: Sarup & Sons, 2013. Print.

Rege, Sharmila. *Writing Caste / Writing Gender: Narrating Dalit Women's Testimonios*. New Delhi: Zubaan. 2006. Print.

Rode, Sonali. "A Brief Study of Dalit Literature after 1960s." *International Research Journal*, 2010. Print.

Webster, C.B John. *Religion and Dalit Liberation: An Examination of Perspectives*. New Delhi: Manohar, 1999. Print.

18

Malayalam Dalit Poetry: A Reflection of Cultural Marginality

— Dr S. Chelliah and Dr Kishore Ram

The Dalit poets of Kerala are considered as leading poets of the state. Their contribution to the Malayalam poetry is recognised by the fact that awards initiated by many literary forums were given to poets belonging to backward community. The Dalit movements of Kerala are headed by young poets like Renukumar and Manoj, both doctorate degree holders and mainstream poets and their poetry along with that of their predecessors and contemporaries have succeeded in supporting the Dalit uprising and in giving it an intellectual pedestal to rise up as a new caste group and to affirm their presence in social and political institutions. The present essay tries to examine the growth of Dalit poetry in Malayalam.

Existence itself is a trauma for the Dalits. Conversion, education and employment the three options before the Dalits to improve their social status have failed and this failure is a major theme in most of the poems written by Dalit writers. "Identity Card" by S. Joseph (Translation by K. Sachidananda) shows how the poet – a Dalit converted to Christianity – fails to achieve success in a love affair because of his identity card – the official record of his scheduled caste stipend.

In my student days
A girl came laughing

Our hands met mixing
her rice and fish curry
On a bench we became
a Hindu-Christian family
I whiled away my time
reading Neruda's poetry;
and meanwhile I misplaced
my Identity Card. (Tharu 454).

Jospeh's poem opens up layers of thoughts regarding the Dalit issue. Susie Tharu and Satyanarayana feel that "for the one who assumes that a secular modernity may be taken at its face value, that he can be a world citizen, aspire to poetry and to love, the real betrayal is not singular or by an individual; it is a many-layered betrayal by politics, a government, an era" (3). It is rather ironic that the only escape route before Dalit education, reservation and stipend – further adds to their misery. These supportive endeavours from the government paradoxically stigmatize the Dalit and mock the aspirations of the Dalit lover in the poem and "returns him to his place, exposed, humiliated, externed from the world of those 'normal' others who can love and unite" (Tharu 3). What could have been a thrilling Hindu-Christian love story ends up in disaster with the lover doomed to grope his way in search of his identity in the dark valleys of discrimination. Conversion to Christianity did not help the Dalits as expected. *Poikayil Yohannan the leader of the PRDS depicts the struggles of Dalits seeking their self in the met narratives of the Bible:*

I haven't seen God
I haven't seen Jesus
My eyes haven't seen
The spirit and the angels
I haven't seen Moses

In another poem he writes:
Church after church has come up in a line
I find distinctions still not removed

The master has a church
The serf has another
A church for pulaya,
A church for paraya
A church for Marakkan. (www.Dalitindia.com)

Christianity, though it appeared as a gateway to freedom from social outcast, in fact, complicated the situation of the Dalits. After conversion they had a dual identity like paraya christiyani and kurava christiyani. Prakash in *//Dalitindia.com//* notes that the Dalits were "second rate members in the church." *Joseph's My Sister's Bible thematises the inefficacy of the Bible alias proselytised Christian identity in earning them a social span and dignity.*

These are what my sister's Bible doesn't have:
Preface,
The Old Testament and the New,
Maps,
The red cover. (Tharu 458)

The Bible for the Dalit is just a book /an alternative space that constantly reminds the Dalits that things haven't changed. The upper caste converts continued the same hostility towards the Dalit-coverts. This dilemma is well pictured by M.B. Manoj in his poem "The Children of the Forest Talk to Yesu" (Trans. Sachidanandan)

Here, on this churchyard,
your devotees screamed with the same tongue
that had offered you prayers:
"This man is a tribal.
Throw him to the police."
Yesu,
For which side did you pray for then? (Tharu 529)

R. Prakash notes in // *Dalitindia.com//*

Large Scale conversions took place in the lower class among Ezhavas, Pulayas, Parayas and Kuravas....But the convert from

> Ezhava had no social contacts with the converted Pulayas. In 1870 and in 1880, they did not look upon conversion as an uplift to the level of Syrian Christians, but as a lowering to the level of the pulayas. But they had used conversion as a means to claim superiority from the upper caste Hindus....But conversion of Christianity among the Dalits acted in a different perspective and manner. It seemed a temporary relief from oppression and castism from the upper castes. But conversion did not help them to advance to the level of the upper classes. In addition, they had to face severe opposition from Syrian Christians. The church discriminated them. (n.pag)

The poets of the past and present emphasize that conversion is not an effective way of escaping from the social segregation that the Dalits had to undergo. It has left them in a twilight identity zone without being able to locate a space for them.

Education too did not help the Dalits to find a new identity in the caste dominated world. They were not accepted even in the educational institutions. In *University Oru Padam* M.B. Manoj pictures the painful experience of a Dalit university student who is described as "black short fellow" and the one who comes to college "dressed like a labourer". Joseph pictures the distressing existence of a Dalit in a college:

> Tomorrow is social and group photo
> Don't be absent
> I have given the money
> We'll stand together for the snap
> Says one girl.
> She showed me the photo
> Standing by her side was one who used to follow her always.
> Same caste
> It was because he had the illness mentioned above that he stood touching her.
> Could have deleted him and pasted my photo there.
> Time has changed.

Still not doing it.

Some Malayalees are there, suffering alone a dammed life.

The poem reveals how the Dalit compares himself with his fellow students and suffers silently. In contrast to "Identity Card," in this poem the girl is willing to cross the limits but the Dalit boy who is aware of the intricacies of the social system does not desire such a change. It also projects the sufferings of Dalits in society. Education and employment cannot help a Dalit to erase his Dalit identity.

The sufferings of the Dalits are similar to those of the segregated all over the world. Suffering, discrimination and segregation are universal themes. Joseph sympathies with the destitute who are packed off from their dwelling places in cities in the name of development. He feels that it is not something that can be pictured or penned in poetic terms. Reality cannot be pictured using poetic words but it will come out in plain words only.

A leaf in which an ant was marooned was plucked by me and placed in flowing water.
This can be written poetically as
Deserting a penniless friend in a lonely town.

And the girl who came to live with me was
Packed off in a bus with a lie to her houseless house.
And this can be read poetically as
Leaving a kitten in the shoreline.

Yet, those who are thrown out or their houses, towns and villages and to where they can go
Can only be written and read like that only.

Dalit poets stress that the Dalit identity cannot be deleted through education or employment. It can never be deleted and will always remain. It is as futile as the father's attempt to scrub of the black colour of his son in Renukumar's poem:

I remember how father used to scrub me
With a stone while washing me so that
I might become fair. "Anonymous"

The only alternative before the Dalits is to be contented with their present existence and to project the positive sides of being a Dalit: their folk songs, their simple ways of living the complicated life, the little happiness that they can carve out from their problematical existence. Poetry is a powerful medium to express the Dalit identity and to project their problems before the world. K. P. Karuppan succeeds to give a new identity to the Dalit in his poem "Pulayar" (Trans. Pratap)

> Haven't the people of the world
> struck with wonder
> at the glory of fame
> spread from this hard-working folk
> who are blended ever
> with Indraneelam splendour ?
>
> They are not children of darkness
> but only got dark-skinned
> as they are sun-tanned.
> Or, they may be the incarnations
> of the Dark Lord of Vrindavan,
> of black-cloud grade —
> the sweet son of Devi Yasoda. (JLA 297)

Karuppan stresses the importance of the pulayas engaged "tirelessly in toil so enterprisingly alert" and he warns the world of the importance of the pulayas:

> Don't be generous, Oh Mankind,
> to abuse and intimidate
> these Valluva group of workers!
> How can one cut off the roots
> of the trees which are useful! (JLA 298)

Renukumar succeeds in presenting Dalit issues by using simple themes, images and language. "Small is beautiful" is the right expression for Renukumar's poems. His poems are made up of simple words, set in a small world and they talk about small things. He has mastered the craft of leading the reader through small words and images to a world of the Dalits clubbing it with the world of simple creatures like grasshoppers, earthworms, ants, and dogs. The reader who enters through the small entrance to the world of Renukumar leaves it with a big heart, for the message that Renukumar has to communicate through his lucid simple style is surprisingly serious. The Dalit existence is pictured comparing it to the world of unimportant creatures. In "*Urumpukalude School*" (The School of Ants) Renukumar is concerned with the little world of ants. Though small insects, ants too have desires: the desire to stand on the edge of a leaf and stretch up and touch the sky, to cross the river on top of seaweed, to stare at the orgies of a couple vigorously engaged in lovemaking amongst the dry leaves. Renukumar is trying to picturise the importance of the ant-world thereby indirectly indicating that the marginalised is insignificant like the ants, yet have their own world, feelings and aspirations. By picturising the cravings of the ant-world, Renukumar is communicating the message that Dalit dreams are similar to those of the ants. They cannot dream big dreams but they can in their little ways gain importance and can do small things in the best way possible.

Renukumar is concerned with the little world of nature in the poem "Bhumiye Pande Kelkendi Irunnu" (Should Have Listened to Earth Earlier.) He observes like a small boy the little world of nature: "The wings budding on small insects," "the reflection of the world on the eyes of the ant," "the footprints of the birds," "the itch worm's itch," and "the velvetiness of the earthworm." After his preoccupation with the little things of nature Renukumar communicates his serious message:

Only after death
We tend to listen
To Earth
We listen not just with our ears
Pressed on the ground but
With our whole body closely pressing the earth.
Then we feel
We should have listened to Earth earlier. (29-36)

Renukumar indicates that the world should listen to nature. The Dalits and aborigines are the ones close to earth and if mankind fails to give them importance and to learn from the ways of the people closely associated with earth, they will have to pay the prize which will even lead to the extinct of mankind. Here Renukumar's Dalit tone transcends its usual domain and sets foot on eco-philosophy.

"Aniyagraha Vrithantham" (News from Another World) portrays the non-existence of the Dalits. It is a poem about traditional utensils – symbolically representing the Dalits – now sidelined by electronic items. Renukumar personifies these utensils and pictures their non-existence in the fast world. The knife-without-handle desires to rust in the soil beneath the wash-stone. The aged coconut cruncher wishes to be axed and levelled into firewood. The wooden grinder that gets filled only with rain water craves for an end to this useless existence. Clay pots and vessels long for death. The aged *Korandi* (stool,) that crawled on its three legs to the door, hurried back to its hiding place, hopeless. The old household utensils symbolically stand for the tradition and customs of the Dalits that get rejected in the high-tech world.

"Mozhi" (Deposition) is a simple poem. It deals with the age old theme – molestation of the men of weaker section by the men of the upper caste.

When you came out of the woods
Carrying dry leaf bundles on your head.
Your whimpering deposition:
the blood drops dripping on your lips
Were from the wound
Made by the dry branches. (1-6)

The simple but communicative way in which this overused theme is presented makes it exceptional. The Dalit woman's condition is like that of the dumb animal/ slave. She cannot even speak out the violence loosed on her.

Chodyakadalas (Question Paper) directly pictures the problematic existence of the Dalit. It is in the form of questions. The "question paper" is filled with the little doubts of a school boy seeking explanations of various issues concerning his daily life like why his book has no cover page, why his buttonless shirt and bottomless knickers are not suiting his body, why mother cries when she smoothens soiled rupee notes, why father smiles when he shaves off sorrow from his face, why his sister has to go in the dark to borrow fire from the neighbour and why mother said that for each questions he would get answers when he grew up. The simple versification of these daily horrors that the Dalits have to suffer disturbs the readers' mind and stresses on the theme of this paper that poetry is the powerful medium for communicating the miseries of Dalits.

Dalit issues and life can be best brought to the notice of his "social betters" people effectively through poetry. Poetry is a powerful tool in the hands of the Dalit poets. Contrasting the purity of the Dalit life with that of the tainted outer world is a technique employed to project Dalit issues. In "Nomads and House Dwellers" Joseph uses the technique of contrast to picture the dilemmas of the wandering aboriginal tribes:

> The home dwellers stay in the houses that they built
> Nomads stay in the very large house that no one had built.
> Home dwellers sit in wooden chairs with spiders underneath.
> Nomads sit on grass with worms crawling underneath
>
> In the moonlit night the home dweller husband and his wife sleeps
> The moon doesn't see them
> In the moonlit night the nomad and his woman sleeps
> The moon sees them.
> The same sun rises and the same sun sets.
>
> Housewife bathes her son
> The rain bathes the nomad son
> Housewife sends her son to school protected with an umbrella
> The nomad mother sends her son stained by the sun into life.

The home dwelling girl marries a home dwelling boy and goes with him into a house

The nomad girl marries a nomad boy and goes with him.

But where can they go to?

Homelessness is a major issue faced by the Dalits. Government polices to house the aborigines and the Dalits have not attained complete success and the rootless Dalits in the cosmopolitan system often have to seek over bridges and shop floors to rest. "Kali" by Joseph pictures a tribal family eagerly waiting for a shop to close and the people to leave so that they can make the shop floor their home. Shibu C.M. pictures this further in "Cinema Poster" (Trans. Manoj):

Our home
Is filed with cinema posters
Nevertheless,
The Theatre isn't our home.

If Mammotty, Mohanlal and Suresh Gopi
Brandished guns and pointing their fingers,
Point their fingers to us
We just don't care!
We have been living –
Amidst pointed fingers all the while.

This is the only blame-
Because there are no windows
We use *you* as a cover. (JLA 345)

Dalit Revolutionary messages are also transmitted powerfully and effectively through poetry. G. Sasi in "Ambavaade" (Trans. Ajir Kutty) asks the Dalits to

Roar in unison:
Liberation,
the liberation of man
That alone is the
armour of the black. (JLA 338)

Dalit Literature according to R.K. Naik is the "verbal and imaginative expression of the Dalit movement" and many poets maintain similar tones like that of Sasi" (JLA 243). Balachandran Inchakkad in his poem "To Return? Where?" questions the pseudo scholars who implore people to return to good old age. He says that there is nothing called good old age for the Dalits: "Which is the age of virtue that you talk of?"(Trans. by S. Sreenivasan). If the society is to return to old times the life of the Dalits will be much worse than the present one:

> Shall we hide on hearing the cry?
> Keep off! Keep off!
> Shall we lose our head for drawing
> Drinking water?
> Shall we go to be bartered as cattle
> In the slave market? (JLA 334)

Resistance is a way station and not a final solution for the Dalits. In following the path of resistance the Dalits should always uphold the methods of Gandhi and poetry verbally gives great momentum to non violent resistance. Poetry has acted as a powerful tool in the hands of the Dalit poets: to picture their dilemmas, to project their identity and to strengthen their resistance. Lamentation alone can bring them no good; they have to rise and fight and suffer and gain the social space that is their dream and that is their right. It is apt to quote Hindi Dalit poet Harpal Singh Arush to conclude this paper sharing the awakened sentiments of the Dalits:

> Come forward,
> Strike, strike this stone wall,
> Let fearless TRUTH step in . . .
> Tramp. . . Tramp . . . Tramp . . . (JLA 201)

Works Cited

Joseph, S. *Uppante Kooval Varakkunnu* . Kottayam: D.C. Books, 2009. Print.

Manoj, M.B. *Koottanthathayude Ezhupathu Varshangal*. Kotttayam: D.C. Books, 2004. Print.

—. *Kannunilla oru Aksharavum*. Kotttayam: D.C. Books, 2007. Print.

Prakash, R. "Dalit Consciousness and Its Perspective on the Basis of PRDS History in Kerala." *www.Dalitindia.com/guest/RP_DConscious. Web 29 August 2018.*

Renumumar, M.R. *Vishakkaya*. Kottayam : D.C. Books , 2007. Print.

Sreenivasan, ed. *Journal of Literature and Aesthetics.* Jan-Dec 2008. Print.

Tharu, Susie and K. Satyanarayana, ed. *No Alphabet in Sight: New Dalit Writing from South* India. New Delhi: Penguin, 2011. Print.

19

Dalit Marginalisation and Caste Atrocities in Sheoraj Singh Bechain's *My Childhood on My Shoulders*

— Dr Kusum Kanger

Manusmriti's Churvarna system has germinated many riddles in our minds about the past view of the ancient society. The people of fourth *varna* i.e. Shudras have been at the target of society. Later the fifth *varna* or the untouchable people came to be seen in the society. These people were expected to do all kind of inferior works. All those people who are supressed or opressed are known as Dalits these days. Earlier the Shudras were considered untouchable. Dr B.R. Ambedkar writes about the existence of Shudras:

> Under the system of Chaturvarnya, the Shudra is not only placed at the bottom, the Shudra is not only placed at the bottom of the gradation but he is subjected to innumerable ignominies and disabilities so as to prevent him from rising above the condition fixed for him by law. Indeed until the fifth Varna of the Untouchables came into being, the Shudras were in the eyes of Hindus the lowest of the low (Ambedkar: *Who were the Shudras*)

Sheoraj Singh Bechain is a well-known name in Dalit Literature. He was born at the contour of the fringe line of the society. It was a very backward village Nadrauli of Budaun district in Uttar Pradesh.

He was born in a skinner or tanner caste. His ancestors and relatives also were engaged in the same work. They used to carry the dead animals and took off their leather. Many incidences of his life have given him tragic experience. His parents were uneducated and he had seen the days of crisis in his life. When he was only five or six-year-old, his father went to heavenly abode. There was the problem of livelihood in his family after his father's death. It was the phase of his life which made him tough to face every kind of adversity of life. He had to take the help of other people. Sheoraj Singh was born as a poet. He started writing poetry even when he was merely a child. He had not taken any training or formal education for it. He started writing just seeing the things happing around him. His surroundings inspired him to write a lot and it provided him much material to write.

He came to Delhi when he was merely a child. He had to do some petty jobs like selling the lemons and eggs to earn some money. He started writing in Hindi. Sheoraj Singh presently works as a senior Professor in the Department of Hindi in the University of Delhi. He has been awarded by the President of India for his contribution in creative writing. His autobiography *My Childhood on My Shoulders* helped him to earn international fame. His autobiography was published in Hindi entitled *Mera Bachpan Mere Kandhon Par* and this autobiography has been published in 2018 by Oxford University Press in English. It has been translated by Deeba Zafir and Tapan Basu. He has written many books on different genres but it is his autobiography which brought him to the limelight. He has been criticised also for his ideology on dalit aesthetics. He was much influenced by Urdu and found that he has been less affected by Hindi.

Sheoraj Singh writes in the beginning of his autobiography regarding his background that the men of his family would carry carcasses and it was their family profession. He writes that his family lived in the mud house which was built by his forefathers. The opening lines of the autobiography reveal it clearly, "It has been almost thirty years since my paternal uncles, Beedhe Phupha and Gangawasi, earned their livelihood through petty business in scavenging, skinning carcasses of cattle, and trading in the remains of dead beasts" (Bechain 1).

He describes that the Jats had big houses in his village. His uncles brought the skin of the dead animals properly hidden because the Hindus had objection in bringing the skin in the village. That's why they would scatter salt on the skin so that it might not stink. They would put it on the acacia tree for drying. Bechain describes that the people of his caste who had stopped carrying out the carcasses considered themselves superiors to the other people but financially they were also very weak. People of the upper caste like Jats and Brahmins did not do this kind of paltry work and that's why now Chamars were also looking for a change in their work.

Bechain describes how his father, Radhe had to take Bechain also to see his tantrums in the wedding by putting him on his shoulders at his Chhoti Bua's village. Pyarelal, his uncle was also with his father. When he was going there his mother was much worried. He was named Sheoraj by his Bua. It was a much strenuous journey and they had to reach after taking rest at many places and drinking water from many wells. He finds that his Bua's in-laws were uneducated and none of the children from her family went to school. His *nanad* and *nandoi* did the same work of carrying the dead animals. They lived in an ostracised, alienated and a mortified world. There was no any place of wine, gambling and the other addictions. They performed all the rituals like fast, worship and *gangasnan* according to their clans. He writes how the superstition and untouchability were prevalent in the society. His father did not drink wine but some people insisted on him to drink at the wedding and consequently, he become ill. He started vomiting. Sheoraj Singh becomes very restless to see his father dehydrated. He was not given any medical treatment. By the evening, his health was deteriorated. *Ojhas* or the wise men tried their exorcism and he was tormented by them:

> Three exorcists, in unison, had invoked the spirits upon themselves. Swaying wildly and with strange gesticulations, they swept their arms through the air to plant the soundest of slaps on my father's cheeks. (Bechain 5)

When his health got badly deteriorated, he was taken off his bed and he was slapped and whipped by the wise men. They thought that some evil spirit had entered his body. The wise men convinced the people that they would remove the evil spirit out of his body for ever. Radhe would cry in pain and say that no any spirit had entered his body and he requested them to bring a doctor for him but nobody paid any attention to his appeal. The wise men kept him beating and whipping for the whole three days. Radhe opened his eyes in some hope but the whips made them tearful. Many people came to see this scene but the high caste people had no concerns what was being happened in this uneducated and untouchable world.

Sheoraj Singh was very listless to see the pathetic condition of his father. His mother, great uncle and uncle were called from the village. Sheoraj had a ray of hope to see them. When he did not see his mother, he came to know that she was also coming. She had given birth to a baby around one or two weeks back, and her second child was in her lap. His Tau and his Gangi uncle were blind and his Bidhe uncle was lame. They were not in the position to travel and had no money to own a bull-cart. By the evening the wise men had disappeared after taking their money and knowing that Radhe's life was in danger. When Sheoraj's mother entered the home at night, Sheoraj's father took his last breathe. The house was sunk into wailing now. Sheoraj had never seen such wailing in his life. His life was filled with double darkness now. When he came to Bua's house, he was happy but when he was returning he was without his father and his childhood had come on his shoulders.

His father's pyre was prepared and a bull-cart was arranged from an upper caste man. The crematorium of Gangaghat was five kilometres away from Dhurra Premnagar and six kilometres from Nandrauli. Radhe's pyre was being carried by four people and Sheoraj, his mother Mukhi and Rambhrose were sitting at the burning material used for the cremation. Sheoraj grandfather was also sitting at the back of the bull-cart and he was also weeping. When Sheoraj's mother was wailing saying that how she would bring up the children without her husband, he soothes her saying that he is also the unfortunate one who has seen the death of his son by his eyes. His grandfather consoles Sheoraj's mother when she was wailing:

> 'Mukhi Beta, you need to steel your heart. My son has left behind three miniatures of himself. It is your responsibility to safeguard

their interests. There s lifetime ahead of you to shed your tears. Think of your children instead.' (Sheoraj 10)

Sheoraj could not forget this horrific incidence in his life. He started crying too see the scene of wise men slapping his father and he would start crying and requested them in his somniloquy not to kill his father. Now there were his grandfathers Bhagirath, Gangi and his Tau Baburam, all were blind. His grandmother, Vidharam was lame. His home was filled with the handicapped and helpless people. For his mother, it was impossible to run the family without the help of any man. Her age was only twenty-five-year old. There was little material in the home. When all the guests who had come to express their sympathy left Sheoraj's house, there was nothing left at the home to eat. Nobody came to help them.

His father was the only man in their family who was healthy. He was married at the age of eleven or twelve and he died at the age of twenty-two or twenty-three. After his death, Sheoraj, his Tau and grandfather would sit in front of the house so that somebody may come and take them for work. They were ready to do any work even in the field or to do any other kind of labour. Sheoraj also started learning the art of removing the skin from the dead animals. It was very difficult to carry the animal to the jungle. They could not drag the animal as the skin could get damaged and the price of the leather would have been the half. Sheoraj Singh writes that a doctor is respected for doing operation but a chamar remains humiliated and untouched for this work.

Sheoraj's maternal grandfather married Sheoraj's mother with Ramlal who was from Naura-Baura village. He was very poor man and he would collect the horns of the animals and sold them in Sambhal. No any advice was taken from Sheoraj's grandfather. When he came to know that Surajmukhi, Sheoraj, Maya and Rambharose have been sent to Naura-Baura, he reached at Sheoraj's grand maternal uncle's home. The latter lived in the city and he hated the village people. He tells the grandmother that he and his two handicapped brothers are depended at others for food and how they would feed a widow and four children. He says:

> 'My daughter is but in her early twenties. What has she seen of life? We are not Brahmins or Banias that we can afford to keep our widowed daughters unmarried, nor are we Chaudhuriss whose daughters can feed off the fat of their lands. We are Chamars. This is our custom. On whose support can we keep our daughters home? Is there any prospect of sustenance to be provided from your end?' (Sheoraj 19)

The poor old man had no answer of these questions and he returned silently. He was in rags and when he was asking the address of Ramlal, Sheoraj's mother recognised her and took him to home. Ramlal was not at home at that time. Sheoraj's mother started crying to see his pathetic condition. Both started weeping. He requests her to go with him at his village but she refuses politely. He gives *jalebis* to his grandchildren and they ate them with relish. It was Sheoraj's last meeting with his grandfather. The latter caught cot after reaching his village and he left this cot only after his death. They did not attend his funeral but they came to know that their condition was very miserable.

There were conflicts with Ramlal and Sheoraj's mother only after six months of their marriage. His earning was not good and he was not able to feed her children. He wanted that her children might remain at their grand material's home but Sheoraj's mother was against it. After some time, her mother separated from Ramlal.

This autobiography depicts how Sheoraj's Jeeja Gangawasi's death became a big problem in the family. They had no money at that time. Ultimately, the people of their neighbourhood came forward for their help. There was an emancipated man named Bande who helped them at that time. All the people of the slum areas took it as a collective responsibility and did all the arrangements for a dignified cremation. Sheoraj writes, "How affable these people were! The women had tears in their eyes when we left. These jhuggis were inhibited by Dalits who were rich in the emotion of love" (Sheoraj 81). These people were living an accursed life and their penury tormented them bit by bit. Even at the death of Sheoraj's Jeeja, Bechain's mother says:

> You are dead, son! And we could do nothing about it! You must forgive us. You must convey our helplessness to God in Heaven. We are praying for you with our heart and soul that in your next birth you are born in a more fortunate home. (Sheoraj 82)

Sheoraj depicts that there were no any restrictions on the widow marriage or remarriage like Brahmins and Jats. They were free to take their own decisions. After this, his mother gets married with Bhikari. He was the step son and he felt insulted and isolated everywhere. Her mother also warned him that now his father would not come back and he will have to learn some work to fill his stomach. She advises him to fix the cycle puncture at least. Balbir Madhopuri also writes in his autobiography *Changia Rukh: Against the Night* how they were reprimanded and insulted by the upper caste people, "'Haven't I told you "again and again" you low castes, to sit patiently in one place!'Yet we contrived to stand stretching out our small hands cupped together, to receive the Prasad" (Madhopuri 12).

D.R. Jatav's *A Silent Soldier: An Autobiography* also describes his struggle of life but he had not experiences such pain of caste discrimination in his life like other dalit writers. Harish Trivedi writes about this autobiography:

> It narrates a seemingly artless tale of Dalit life in all its misery and humiliation, and it shows the child-protagonist striving to pull himself out of poverty and inequality. This book is also a nuanced depiction of the infinitely intricate web of caste equations in which the exploited lose no opportunity to turn into exploiters. It is not the Brahmins or Thakurs but the Yadavs who perpetrate the worst atrocities here. (Trivedi n. pag.)

Sheoraj's father was a skilled cobbler and he could make shoes according to the demands of people. One day a customer comes to him with his peculiar problem that he could not find the shoes for his feet. He gave the advance for this work and his father made a pair of customised shoes for him. He becomes famous in the village but his skill puts him into trouble also. He started making shoes according to the demands of people. For a man he had made shoes with two big toes and crooked feet. There was an incident of thievery in Raipur village and when the villagers woke up, the dacoits ran away but one of them left a shoe behind. It was a special shoe made by Sheoraj's father. The police inspector summoned his father and asked his father for whom he had made such shoes. There was no any record with him for this work. The inspector got angry and Sheoraj's father had to pay its price:

> As the blows of the rod fell on his body, he groaned with pain. When they rained kicks and pounded him, he cried for help but to no avail. Finally, Chacha had to pay a fine of one rupee and fifty paise in addition to being beaten up. (Sheoraj 58)

Sheoraj has to face many difficulties in getting his education. He had to go from pillar to post for his studies and food. In the last few pages of his autobiography Sheoraj writes about an incidence. He was in tenth class and board exams were going on. It was his Sanskrit paper that day and he leaves for school early in the morning with his Massaab. When they had travelled around twenty kilometres past Narora, they found their art teacher Thakur Ramvir Singh Raghav. Massaab requests him to drop the child to school. But after going just few kilometres, the chain of the motorcycle came off. Sheoraj puts in back on but after some time it came off again. Instead of reaching early he was getting late by pushing the motorcycle for the rest of the way. Ultimately, the teacher advises him to run to the school without him. He was around one hour late and the invigilator did not allow him to give the examination. He sat for the exam only after the principal's permission. Students were laughing at him because of his present condition:

> ...as I began my paper and looked around, I found all the students laughing at me. I soon divined the reason for it....the repeated attempts at putting the chains of the motorcycle had blackened my hands with grease and i had been wiping the sweat off my face with the result that it was completely black. The students found that funny.... (Sheoraj 249-50)

Thus, Sheoraj Singh Bechain's autobiography is an endless account of his inner throes. All Dalit autobiographies depict such hidden pains of their own life and the whole dalit community. These autobiographies have been written in different Indian languages. Om Prakash Valmiki's *Joothan*, Laxman Gaikwad's *Uchalya: The Branded*, Suraj Pal Chauhan's *Triskrit*, Urmila Pawar's *The Weave of My Life*, Bama's *Karukku*, Mohandas Naimshrai's *Apne Apne Pinjre*, Dharamvir's *Meri Patni aur Bheria* and Tulsi Ram's *Murdaiya* and many more autobiographies are the strong testimonials of dalit oppression. Sheoraj Singh Bechain's autobiography has added a new chapter in this context. He has shed light on the unheard agonies of his family and his caste. In fact, he has been successful in his efforts also and now enjoys a good status today being a reputed Dalit writer as well as a university professor.

Works Cited

Bechain, Sheoraj Singh. *My Childhood on My Shoulders*. Trans. Deeba Zafir and Tapan Basu. New Delhi: Oxford U P, 2017. Print.

Madhopuri, Balbir. *Changia Rukh: Against the Night*. New Delhi: Oxford U P, 2010. Print.

Trivedi, Harish. "Weapon of Choice." *The Indian Express*. July 21, 2018.

https://indianexpress.com/article/lifestyle/books/weapon-of-choice-my-childhood-on-my-shoulders-5268431/

20

Looking at Caste, Gender and Dissent in Baburao Bagul's "Mother"

— ***Dr Prachi Priyanka***

> Dalit Literature is a journey from mainstream literature to marginal literature, from grand narrative to little narrative, from individual identity to group identity, from ideal to real, from vertical literature to spiral literature, from self-justification to self-affirmation. (Trivedi 7)

The rigid Indian caste system did not provide opportunity to Dalits to read, write or share their experiences in written form. Hence, it is mostly through oral narratives or stories about them expressed in writings of others that we come to know about the miseries of their lives. When Dr Ambedkar pushed the people of his community to maintain written records of their thoughts and give shape to their struggle through literature, Dalits slowly started writing about how they had been denied even basic human rights and treated as outcast in society. Poems, stories and autobiographies were produced that transformed the social scenario through the power of the written word. *As this movement of literary assertion by Dalits grew stronger, the unseen side of India – the side that is brutal and inhumane – came to the surface and became visible to the world. Maharashtra was at the forefront of this revolution that has, over the last six decades, helped transform the worldview about Dalit lives. Almost all of the writers who shaped the early theoretical discourse of Dalit Literature were from Maharashtra and Baburao Bagul holds a prominent place in the impact of Dalit consciousness on the literary world.*

Baburao Bagul was born in Nasik on 17 July 1930. It was the period during which Babasaheb Ambedkar's anti-caste movement was gaining momentum. It was the same year in which Ambedkar led a famous protest in Nasik in front of the Kalaram Temple. Bagul's magnum-opus *Jevva Mi Jaat Chorali* was published in 1963, and it turned out to be very different from the popular stories written by his contemporaries like Shankarrao Kharat, Anna Bhau Sathe and Bandhu Madhav. Contrary to their writing styles and narrative approaches, Bagul's depiction of people in his stories was harsh, passionate, vigorous, and full of hope to persuade the Dalit community to rebel against the atrocities of life.

Baburao Bagul was influenced by the works of Marx, Phule and Ambedkar. He has been a major inspiration to the younger generation of Marathi Dalit writers. He was also actively involved in the discussions that would lead to the founding of the Dalit Panthers. *According to Baburao Bagul:*

> Dalit Sahitya is not a literature of vengeance. Dalit Sahitya is not a literature which spreads hatred. Dalit Sahitya first promotes man's greatness and man's freedom and for that reason it is an historic necessity. At a Dalit conference held in Nagpur in 1976, Baburao emphasized his point that anguish, waiting, pronouncements of sorrow alone do not define Dalit Literature. We want literature heroically full of life for the creation of a [new] society. (Maloney 86)

Most of the stories of Baburao Bagul explore 'lumpen' characters and the ethical implications of their actions as they fight to survive the unrelenting misery and poverty of urban modernity. The inhabitants of these stories are mostly uneducated lot who lack any kind of sophistication. They live in a world full of sufferings and fight for survival. When we delve into his stories, we can see that a major chunk of his writings reflects on the brutality of the caste system. It is not surprising if he deals with violence and sex predominantly in his literature but this is not done to stimulate the baser instincts of readers. This is the stark reality of the life he portrays. He brings out very powerfully the woes, miseries and economic inequality which are based on his own experience. His perverted, violent and imbalanced individuals are the victims of the social system in which casteism is a dominant factor. Baburao picks up the dramatic situations from the loathsome reality and represents them in rather gaudy colours. His style is full of activation and his idiom is rough but rigorous (Datta 1823). His characters are ones who survive in situations of hunger and criminality, in dwellings without any civic amenities, and often exploit or violate other characters in similar circumstances. This was probably because Baburao Bagul's purpose was to present the world of the lowly in all its harshness in order to make the middle class understand. Heroism and hope come in facing and acknowledging what is, in order that something better may be created (Maloney 86). In his story "Kalokhache Kaidi," Bagul brings out the feelings of revenge prevailing in a section of the society in general and the young son of a rich man in particular against a beautiful widow. In another story "Waterwarchi," he brings forth the issues concerning a woman who is forced to accept prostitution. Similar fate is met by the woman in "Spradha" who is sexually exploited and forced to allure workers in the mill.

The greatest strength of Baburao's stories was that his protagonists always had an identity, and the ability to rebel. And Bagul's gift to the world of literature – especially Dalit Literature – was that he provided the theory to their anger, rage, restlessness, compassion, hope and vision of life, caught amid the inhumane, chaotic circumstances of the caste system. In the poem "You Who Have Made the Mistake" we see how he incites Dalits to question their predicament and protest against the injustices done towards them:

What will you say if someone asked you –
What is untouchability?
Is it eternal like god?
What's an untouchable like? What does he look like?

Does he look like the very image of leprosy?
Or like the prophet's enemy?
Does he look like a heretic, a sinner, a profligate, or an atheist?
Tell me,
What will your answer be?
Will you reply without hesitation:
'Untouchable – that's me?'
That's why I say –
You who have made the mistake of being born in this country
must now rectify it: either leave the country,
or make war! (*Poisoned Bread* 70)

Caste stigma is a running theme in many Dalit writings – the offending touch, the association with dirt, labour, 'unclean' occupations, and finally the quality of being polluting that is ever present in Dalit writing is from access to the otherwise common resource of water, the very basis of life without which the possession of land itself would be rendered meaningless (Chaturvedi136). Literature on caste from a feminist perspective began to appear when questions of caste surfaced in the 80s and 90s after the Mandal agitation. Dalit feminist consciousness became a force to reckon with. For Dalit women were the worst affected in the social pyramid and faced violence on multiple levels. Verbal abuse, physical assault, sexual assault, rape, and forced prostitution are examples of abuses inflicted upon them.

But why is this discrimination and resentment towards the Dalit women? The answer to this lies in the distilled impact of centuries-long alienation generated by both – the ingrained patriarchal and Brahminical values at all levels in society, which in turn causes the high level of exclusion, invisibility and structural and domestic violence which is the everyday experience of Dalit women. Uma Chakravorty in her book *Gendering Caste* summarises it in a nutshell that the "women's movement was also critiqued by Dalit feminists for not paying attention to the specific and more extreme forms of oppression experienced by Dalit women who bore a triple burden: as Dalits from the upper castes, as labourers from the landlords, and as women from men of their own families and caste" (Chakravorty 4).

Indeed, a Dalit woman bears the triple burden of discrimination on her shoulders. Their marginalisation is three-fold due to class, gender and caste. She is subjugated to violence on the name of family norms and tradition. The Dalit male goes out and gets thrashed everywhere in society, and finds it the easiest way to assert his masculine power on the women at home, the right of domestic tyranny. Ironically, it is not just that the Dalit men and the men of higher caste assert their patriarchal power on the Dalit women – for they are deliberately alienated and abused by the high caste women as well. Even the mainstream women's movement consists of high class urban-bred women and there is rarely a voice that speaks for the Dalit women's ordeals.

Susie Tharu observes that the widow is a figure whose very life is marked by a specific death. She is 'vidhava' – without husband – and consequently in need of sympathy and protection, but also of regulation and governance. The rules and regulations set out for Hindu widows are mentioned in the Manusmriti and Reena Patel aptly quotes from it in her book *Hindu Women's Property Rights in Rural India: Law, Labour and Culture in Action*:

> Let her rather emaciate her body by living upon pure flowers, roots and fruits, but let her not, when her husband is dead, even to pronounce the name of another man ... let her live a life of austerity, strictly observing the rules of continence, and foregoing all sensual pleasures until she dies. (Patel 84)

Thus, the upper class widow is instructed to strictly live in deprivation of all worldly pleasures and temptations and connect to her husband in a transcendental way even after his death. But the life of Dalit widows turns out to be worse as they do not have time and luxury to moan their dead husbands. As they struggle to survive and feed their families, they are devoured by men who lust after them. Sharankumar Limbale's experience regarding his mother subscribes to this practice of the Dalit society that at the same time uses and abuses their women. In *Outcaste*, Limbale narrates how his mother had to succumb to different men in order to survive:

> To be born beautiful among Dalits is a curse.... Masamai was beautiful and she suffered for it. She was divorced by her husband, after which Hanmanta enjoyed her and then deserted her ... how long would she go on being a woman without a man? People who enjoy high-caste privileges, authority sanctioned by religion, and inherit property, have exploited the Dalits of this land. (Limbale 37-38)

Pandu's mother meets with a similar plight in the story. She is described as beautiful and attractive, which makes her husband suspicious of her when he was bed-ridden, and an object of lust for the male neighbours, when he was dead. The women in the neigbourhood could not take easy that she could obtain the little luxuries of new clothes for her son or enough food to feed the two, and hence, condemned her as a whore. They treat her as a fallen woman who fails to perform her maternal duties and instead engages in sexual pleasures. The story, at some point raises the question if Pandu's mother fails as a 'good mother'?

Adrienne Rich in "Of Woman Born" distinguishes between the "potential relationship" of a woman to her powers of reproduction and to children" and the "institution" that ensures that the "potential – and all women – shall remain under male-control" (Rich 13). This patriarchy-imposed institution 'motherhood' predicates the role of a 'good' mother on "unconditional love ... as a single-minded identity" in relation to one's child. A 'good' mother is "beneficent, sacred, pure, asexual, nourishing" woman. Rich argues that patriarchal cultures across the world define motherhood in such terms. Hence, mothers feel compelled to evaluate themselves against these standards and often feel guilty for not being able to conform to them. Rich argues that "the glorified ideals of motherhood are not applicable in circumstances in which mothers can only reproduce children but cannot mother or nourish them" (7). The institution of slavery that prevailed in many parts of the world did not allow slave-mothers to have any legal claim on their children. The children were often sold off and hence the high ideals of motherhood did not extend to these slave women, who later, after emancipation, found these notions of personal ownership and claims on their children to be new and unfamiliar.

In the Indian context, the Dalit women had always been contributing economically to the family's needs. While they worked in fields in rural areas; in semi-urban location, they were pushed to work at construction sites for meager wages. Life for these Dalit women working in small factories and construction sites made them vulnerable to exploitation by high caste factory owners and lust of contractors. To make things worse, Dalit men internalised the upper caste notions of repressing women by imposing restrictions upon them, and the low caste women were not safe even in their own domestic spheres. With so much violence, abuse and mental torture to deal with, they struggled to fulfill their duties as wives and mothers.

The life of Pandu and his mother too was brought in a turmoil because their mutual understanding was breached and also because the upper caste people exploit the innocence of the child by poisoning his mind against his own mother. When Pandu's teacher recites a poem on motherhood, where a mother is referred to Vatsalya Sindhu (a river of mother love), Pandu wonders about his own mother and tries to fit her in that idealised image of woman; however, his thoughts are interrupted by the loose remarks of a few upper class boys of his class who make fun of his mother stating *"Don't touch Pandu, any of you. My mother says Pandu's mother sleeps with the Mukadam"* (Ramakrishna 411). The Dalit children are prone to become victims of discrimination and ridicule. When Pandu is told that his mother is a slut and sleeps with the overseer, Pandu feels enraged and humiliated. Bagul's description of this moment is quite poignant:

> Pandu's face burned with shame and anger. He felt a demonic, murderous rage rising within him. He could have killed them, murder them all in cold blood. It was good to think them lying together in a pool of blood. It was short-lived joy, however. He remembered he was an orphan, now that his father was dead, and his mother an unprotected widow. He was afraid that Dagdu, their neighbor would pick fight with his mother, try to strip her

> sari ... Rage gave way to infinite helplessness and he felt spent. (Ramakrishna 412)

Life for Pandu's mother wasn't easy ever. Her brother-in-law lusted after her and Pandu's father was diagnosed with tuberculosis. Things got worse when he started to abuse verbally and physically and accuse her of infidelity, making attempts to make her unattractive and undesirable. Such a narrative reflects the deeply engrained patriarchal mindset in Pandu's father, where he feels a strong sense of entitlement over '*his*' woman's body. This need to conquer, control, and confine a woman's body is a way of asserting male privilege on women. He would burn with jealousy and greet her with comments like "your sari looks as if you've worn it in a hurry, your hair's coming loose, where were you, slut?" Furthermore, he would assert his rights of being a husband over her and "would strip her and examine her feet, her thighs, her breasts, her sari and blouse, and would carefully scrutinise her lips and cheeks." When her husband died, she had no any choice but to stay outside to work longer hours so that she may fill the stomach of Pandu and herself. Consequently, all this does not allow her to stay outside in the personal realm of the household mostly, thereby, not allowing her to foster her child. So does that imply that Pandu's mother is a '*bad*' mother? No, the cultural demonstration of ladies as mothers is so unidimensional. Mothers having distinctive experiences of maternity appear as an incongruity in the paradigm of motherhood altogether. With a constant struggle to earn money, feed, educate and survive amidst severe circumstances, Pandu's mother is unable to find any time for mutual understanding between the mother and the child. Bagul demonstrates how Pandu's 'bad mother' status emanates from her perseverance on parenting her child on her own conditions. Initially, she does not succumb to community pressures, but she suffers defeat when her own son fails to understand her endeavours and walks out of the house, leaving her alone. The torrent of abuse of community hurls at her and her rejection by Pandu makes her fill with guilt and her sacrifices seem to go in vain.

This story also focuses on the marginalisation of Dalit children at school who are continuously discriminated and ill-treated by the upper caste classmates. With so much inner mayhem to bear with, they are left with little space to understand and value their individualistic experiences. Upper caste boys label Pandu's mother as a prostitute. Pandu too begins to scrutinise her whereabouts. Caught in the midst of patriarchy and casteist mindset, the sacrifices of Pandu's mother, to provide her son with a better life, are ultimately overshadowed. The story ends on a quagmire, pushing readers to think and reflect on better possibilities for mother and child:

> 'Come son, forgive this old sinner'
>
> The door opened and the overseer stood in the doorway. His massive frame seemed to dwarf everything else in the room.
>
> 'What's happened? Why do you look so scared? You're sweating'. He hugged her, pretended to wipe the sweat off her face, and started caressing her arms and breasts. She slowly responded, and out of the hunger of the past ten years of widowhood, flared an uncontrollable desire. And that was why she failed to hear the timid knock at the door, the faint hesitant cry, 'Mother!' He saw them, his mother and the towering figure of the overseer in a tight embrace. His last hopes seemed to crash about his head; broken hearted, he wildly rushed towards the door. She saw him then, ran after him calling his name but the overseer , already blinded with lust, refused to let her go; he was pulling her into the room with his strong brown arms
>
> Pandu was running away at great speed; his fast falling tears had almost blinded him, the stray dogs ran at his heels, snapped at him, and now he was screaming, shouting with terror, afraid of the dogs...
>
> She was trying desperately to escape from the bear-like hug of the overseer. But like a person stuck fast in a quagmire, she found release impossible. (420)

Bagul's story thus, raises several questions on the social fabric and its destructive influence on individuals and relationships. It also attempts to blur the line between the personal and the political, by giving women a voice from the margins. Through the story of a mother, Bagul brings to light the dual discrimination faced by Dalit women along the lines of gender and caste, thereby exposing realistic experiences of the Dalit community. Filled with feelings of pain and loss, the author attempts to provoke readers with questions such as – whose experience of motherhood is universalised? Does motherhood differ along the lines of caste? Can the voice of a subaltern mother be heard? If so, is there any form of emancipation possible for her? Trapped in a cycle of eternal oppression, not only from society but also by her family members, the quest for emancipation for Dalit women becomes difficult to obtain. It is only when perspectives of people who face instances of political inequality and oppression are incorporated in everyday discourse that the reader is brought closer to the subaltern lifestyle. To conclude, we may say that in recreating a Dalit mother's story, Bagul attempts to make the subaltern's agency 'speak'.

Works Cited

Bagul, Baburao. "Mother." *Poisoned Bread: Translations from Modern Marathi Dalit Literature*. Ed. Arjun Dangle. Bombay: Orient Blackswan, 1992. Print

Bhagwat, Vidyut. "Marathi Literature as a Source for Contemporary Feminism." *Economic and Political Weekly* 30.17 29 April 1995. 24-29. Print.

Chakraborty, Sayanika "Understanding Dalit Women: A Reading of Baburao Bagul's *Mother*" in *Lapiz Lazuli: An International Journal*. 5.2 Autumn 2015. Web.

Chakravorty, Uma. *Gendering Caste: Through a Feminist Lens*. Calcutta. Stree, 2003. Print.

Datta, Amresh. *Encyclopedia of Indian Literature*: Devraj to Jyoti. Vol. 2. New Delhi: Sahitya Akademi, 1988. Print.

Guru, Gopal. "Dalit Women Talk Differently." *Economic and Political Weekly* 14-21 Oct. 1995. 48-50.

Limbale, Sharankumar. *Outcaste*. Trans. Santosh Bhoomkar. New Delhi: Oxford U P, 2013. Print.

Maloney, Clarence (ed.) *Language and Civilization: Change in South Asia*. Leiden: Brill Academic Publishers, 1978. Print

Misir, Prem, (ed.). *The Subaltern Indian Woman: Domination and Social Degradation*. New Delhi: Palgrave Macmillan, 2018. Print.

Patel, Reena. *Hindu Women's Property Rights in Rural India: Law, Labour and Culture in Action*. Farnham: Ashgate Publishing, 2007. Print.

Prasad, Amar Nath and M.B. Gajjan (ed.) *Dalit Literature: A Critical Exploration*. New Delhi: Sarup & Sons, 2007. Print.

Ramakrishnan, E.V. and I.V. Ramakrishnan. *Indian Short-Stories 1900-2000*. New Delhi: Sahitya Akademi, 2009. Print

Rege, Sharmila. *Writing Caste/ Writing Gender: Narrating Dalit Women's Testimonios*. New Delhi: Zubaan, 2006. Print.

Rich, Adrienne. *Of Woman Born: Motherhood as Experience and Institution.* New York: W.W. Norton, 1996. Print.

Singh, Bijender (ed.) *Dalit Men's Autobiographies: A Critical Appraisal*. New Delhi: Kalpaz Publications. 2017. Print.

Tharu, Susie. "The Impossible Subject" in *Sign Posts: Gender Issues in Post Independence India*. R. S. Rajan (ed.) New Jersey: Rutgers U P, 2001. Print.

21

Juxtaposition of Dalit Narratives with Afro-American Slave Narratives in the Vicinity of Emancipation: A Brief Comparative Note

— A.P. Pavithra Bhuvaneshwari

> Before diving deep into Dalit Literature, it would be worthwhile to give a demarcation of Dalit Literature and to know the poignant position of Dalits and socio-political and cultural-religious backgrounds of Indian Dalits....Due to the existence of unjust social order, Dalits were deprived of their fundamental rights and thus, they stood at the tassel in the social order and thus, remained marginalised at every walk of life. As a result, Dalits had no option except serving upper caste people in order to cater to the needs of their children. – (Singh 20)

Under the roof of the world, the mortal beings are all ingenerated in the identical way as humans and therefore all human beings, in the eyes of God, are all equal and fitted with suitable appropriateness of identical rights and integration. Human beings heed according to the laws and respect the norms to protect and survive themselves. However, throughout the former times of history, human beings were predominated by the ego-centric world where the established sets of human kind are set in the position of injustice because of a specific race, skin colour and culture. According to the Supreme Being, each and every creature which God has created is equally supplied with food for thrice a day. There is no superior and inferior in Supremes' dictionary. This is unveiled through the verses from Old Testament, Galatians verse 3:28 admits the following:

> There is neither Jew nor Greek;
> there is neither slave nor free;
> there is no male or female;
> for you are all one in Christ Jesus. (Galatians 3.28)

and also the verse 3 from chapter Colossians rightly observes the following;

> Under the roof of Christ, here there is not
> Greek and Jew, Circumcised, Uncircumcised,
> Barbarians, Scythian, slave, free; but for Christ
> is all and in all. (Colossians 3:11)

The philosophy of universal equality is dehumidified in the heart, soul and mind of the human race. Humans brood, ponder and contemplate more on the materialistic facets, since there is no space for universal equality and they addict and float in the world of ego-centricism where they found and accept everything in the entirety. This unsecure and precarious possessiveness foster their gluttonous ravening mind to dissect their own human race into masters and slaves; superiors and inferiors on the basis of occupation, skin colour and race. In words of Lord Krishna through the Bhagawad Gita uncovers the intrinsic truth of universal equality as follows:

> Where in the Universe, there is no
> Differentiate between Bhramin, Kshatriya
> Vaishya and Shudra; I treats everyone
> equal and resides in every heart in the
> form of soul; the fourfold caste has been
> created by me according to the GUNA and KARMA. (Bhagwad Gita)

Thus, the Bhagwad Gita admits that human race is split as claimed by their "Guna" that is attitude which provokes the thought of contemplating goodness in their life and also their abilities, capabilities and mental strength in surviving their life and by "Karma" which provokes the doing of goodness to variants. Lord Krishna insists that the human race is dissected only by their attitude not by their birth. This *varna* philosophy of fourfold division is not only a useful pragmatic expedient to Indian people but also for the other distinct people in the universe. However mankind without a hitch and on a cruise control pretermits the philosophy of universal equality and with their material gain and with their mortal fading physical vigour they hegemonise their own kind for their gluttonous ravening attitude.

This philosophy of universal equality is spurned to the Dalit peoples in India and synchronously to the peoples of Afro-American in the United States who were afflicted to the identical predomination. Both Indian Dalits and Afro-Americans are two idiosyncratic classes existing as analogous downtrodden stances in their relevant civilization and community. Indian Dalits as well as Afro-Americans were the children of dark world which encircle their livelihood with exploiting casteism, slavery, disintegrating racism and inelastic attitude towards skin colour voyaging in the ship of iniquity through the myriad storm of grieving and agonising despair. Both Dalit Literature and Afro-American Literature focused upon the boosting ideas of universal equality, justice for their masses and opposition to their suppression, marginalisation, discrimination and exploitation in economic, social and academic background. Thus, the masses of Dalits and Afro-American are very much alike. There are parallelisms in their desolating pains; their rebellions and revolutions; their trust and aspirations; their expectations and desires. Though both Dalits and Afro-Americans are with unassociated resemblance both in language speaking and physical appearance, their mental predicaments and sensational vehemence revealed through literatures are corresponding to each other.

Both Dalit narratives and Afro-American narratives are considered as slave narratives which proclaim the unique ideas and themes. The slave narrative generally refers to the subjective account written by a slave or a downtrodden expressing and describing his or her own life experiences. Both the narratives put on question on the mainstream ideologies of the upper caste system and the whites predomination. Dalit and Afro-American Literature are the experience based literature. Humiliation, acrimonious wrath and aspirations are the authentic mark of both the literatures. The silenced anger against the oppression, subjugation and enslavement makes the writers of Dalit and Afro-American Literature express their emotions in the tone of anger through their narratives which explore them to pave the way for their emancipation.

Autobiographical narratives by Dalits and Afro-Americans are the narratives which encounter the disdainful circumstances by the writers in their own life as a representation of a Dalit and an Afro-American. Om Prakash Valmiki's *Joothan* is an autobiographical narrative of his untouchable life. Om Prakash Valmiki in his autobiographical narrative describes his own life growing up as an untouchable in a village in Uttar Pradesh in the newly independent India of the 1950's. Valmiki's early life begins in an account of the individual struggle by a Dalit boy from the sweeper caste Chuhra. The word 'joothan' literally means left over from meal and also in another sense it also means unsuitable/unfit for consumption by another person. Thus, the Dalits have been mandatorily kept under control to eat 'joothan' for their livelihood.

The title *Joothan* conveys the shame and painful suffering as a Dalit and because of his community; he has been treated like 'joothan' be used and thrown away in the dustbins. His own struggle as a downtrodden made him realise the circumstances of Dalits and became one of the revolutionary voices for the voiceless Dalits under the influence of Dr B.R. Ambedkar, not only Valmiki but also other writers extracted the Dalit consciousness from their agonising experiences and tried to build up this Dalit consciousness in their writings that allows for their budding of intellectual pride, self-respect and a vision for future emancipation. Valmiki in his *Joothan* concretely unmasks the abstract emotions of a downtrodden born as a child of Chuhra caste, a sweeper marginalised group. The first and foremost inflicting experience by Valmiki is that Tyagi Brahmins of the upper caste will not address them by their names. This Brahmin insults them by saying, "It was alright to touch cows and stray dogs but touching a Chuhra inflicted instant "pollution" on the Tyagis" (Valmiki 12).

Valmiki's family worked hard for managing to get two decent meals a day for the entire family. As a downtrodden caste, these Chuhra's were not paid for their labour instead; they were beaten up and brutally abused.

The oppressed childhood days of Valmiki were like a bad dream for him. He was born in the sweeper caste that his oppressed masses were forced to live outside the village. The high wall and a pond segregated their clay houses in the village. Upper caste men and women of all ages came out and used the edge of the pond as an open-air lavatory, squatting across from the Chuhra homes. The pigs wandered in narrow lanes in front of his houses. Naked children, dog's daily fights and these circumstances were found to be the environment of Valmiki's childhood. His Chuhra caste became like a stigma to him, "The children of the Tyagis would tease me by calling me "Chuhre Ka." Sometimes they beat me for no reason. This was absurd, tormented life that me introverted and irritable" (Valmiki 18).

During rainy season, the narrow lanes in front of the houses of the Chuhra caste filled up with muddy water mixed with pig's excrement; flies and mosquitoes thrived. There was one drinking well in their area which becomes full of long worms during this rainy season. They had no other choices but to drink that water as they were not permitted to use the well of upper caste folks. Valmiki admits in his narratives, "The days of the rainy season were hellish. The lanes filled up with mud, making walking difficult. The mud was full of pig's excrement, which would begin to stink after the rain stopped" (Valmiki 21).

Valmiki was more interested in his studies and his parents wanted him to be a literate in order to prevent him from the future oppression and enslavement. His father had a hard time getting his admission into a primary school. When Valmiki finally got admission, he was not allowed to sit on the benches but on the floor away from the upper caste boys from where he could not see the black board properly. Even the teachers looked for the excuses to punish him, so that he could run away from the school and took up the kind of work for which he was born. The words of Valmiki hold, "If I got thirsty in school, I had to stand near the hand pump. The boys beat me in any case, but the teachers also punished me. They tried all sorts of strategies so that I could run away from school" (Valmiki 27).

One fruitful day of realising his talent emerged out by his father's action. In the fourth grade, Valmiki was heavily thrashed almost daily by the newly arrived headmaster and he assigned to sweep all the classrooms and the playground in the school. The hapless Valmiki spent two days in sweeping hoping that soon it will be over. This was seen by his father, little Valmiki sobbed and told all the happenings to him. His enraged father directly moved to the headmaster and raised his voice against the torments given to his son. Suddenly the headmaster bombarded against his father and roared, "Take him away from here otherwise I will have your bones broken" (Valmiki 30).

On his way out; his father declared in a loud voice that not only this Chuhra kid would study right this school but also there will be more coming after him. That day and that moment was a great day in the life of Valmiki. His father's courage and fortitude left a deep and decisive scar on the boy's personality. In the midst of prolonged subjugation and enslavement, Om Prakash Valmiki burst out with colours and became the gallant voice for the voiceless downtrodden. In the words of Valmiki himself:

> The school had a library where books were gathering dust. There I first became acquainted with books. By the time I had read Saratchandra, Premchand, Rabindranath Tagore. Their characters touched my child's heart very deeply. Reading was my main passion. (Valmiki 36)

In addition to Om Prakash Valmiki, there are outstanding noteworthy Dalit writers like Narendra Jadhav, Baby Kamble, Kashi Ram, Kancha Ilaiah, Mukta Sarvagod, Shantabai Kamble, Urmila Prawer, Sheoraj Singh Bechain, Balbir Madhopuri, Janabai Girhe, and many existing budding writers to unveil their Dalit consciousness which paves way for their liberalisations. Valmiki intimately states, "The deeper I was getting into Literature, the more articulate my rage became. I began to debate with my college friends and put my doubts before my teachers. This literature gave me a courage" (Valmiki 43).

The identical themes of Dalit Literature and its consciousness coincide with the literature of Afro- American society encircled with the hardships of racism, slavery and inequality. Slave narratives of Afro-American conjoin with the narratives of Dalit Literature with a parallel basis of journey towards freedom with equal rights and independent living. Afro-American narratives describe the slavery torment experiences of an apartheid group. In India Dalits are considered as untouchables. Likewise in the United States, Afro-Americans are considered as slaves. Slaves and untouchables mean the same that they are neglected, oppressed, unfit and subjugated downtrodden.

Om Prakash Valmiki is homogeneously cognated with Olaudah Equiano. His autobiographical slave narrative chronicled his encountered confrontations in slavery. Equiano's account is considered as an originator of slave narratives. Olaudah Equiano is given a new name; he is named after Gustavus Vassa, a Swedish freedom fighter. In *"The Interesting Narrative of the Life of Olaudah Equiano or Gustavus Vassa*, he shares out one of the first major slave autobiographies. In this autobiography, he remarkably writes his slavery agonising circumstance and painful sufferings as he is kidnapped from his homeland Africa, when Equiano was eleven years old and sold into slavery first in Africa.

Incredibly, it is to take into account that Equiano first served as a slave for other African tribes and this noteworthy point which manifests that in their culture Africa was also involved with the white European slave dealers. At one point, Equiano was later transported from Africa and placed in slave ship which possessed by the European slave dealers. As Equiano admits himself in his narratives:

> The first object which saluted my eyes when I arrived in the coast was sea, and a slave ship, which was then riding at anchor and

> waiting for its Cargo. The filled me with astonishment, which was soon connected with terror, when I was soon carried on the board. I was now persuaded that I had gotten into the world of bad spirits, and they were going to kill me. (Equiano 48)

Equiano assimilated, afflicted the hardships and the terrors of being packed and cramped into a slave ship. Equiano tolerated, sustained and subjected to severe terrors and whippings in the slave ship where countless Africans tightly packed in this journeying to a life of cruel servitude. On the ship Equiano and his masses experienced starvation and cruel treatment by the European slave traders. The word of Equiano holds:

> This produced the copious perspirations, so that the air soon became unfit for respiration, from a variety of loathsome smells, and brought on a sickness among slaves, of which many died, thus falling victims to the improvident avarice, as I may call it, of their purchasers. This wretched situation was again aggravated by the galling of chains, now become insupportable; and the filth of the necessary tubs, into which the children often fall and almost all were suffocated. The shrikes of women, and the groans of the dying, rendered the whole scene of horror almost inconceivable" (Equiano 58).

This terrible ordeal nightmare is ineradicably made a haunting mark upon the mind of young slave Equiano who stood as an evidence for the numerable men and women of Africa tightly packed in the suffocating hold of the ship where they underwent and experienced filthiness, stench, diseases, tortures, sexual abuse and severe starvation. Equiano unambiguously wrote the truth of his haunting and horrible mental and physical sufferings. As a young slave, he was encompassed in a threatening fear looking at the European trade dealers as though there are the flesh eaters. After the horrible experiences in the ship, he was sent to Virginia. A British Royal Navy Captain purchased him. He was whipped almost all enough for all things what he does. For several years, he sustained and survived in the grip of harsh indictment of slavery. Later Equiano learns to read and write since he was placed in a trading ship by his master Navy Captain. He was introduced to a new religion and thus, he becomes a Christian. Equiano continues to work in the trading ship and saves enough money to buy his liberty. Then he becomes the part of the crusade to abolish slavery and decides to write his autobiography to bring forth the pains and sufferings that he has undergone associated with the slave trade as an Afro-American slave.

Indubitably, Equiano influenced and paved way for other Afro-American slaves to write their own slave autobiographies which stood as a tool for abolishing slavery and urged the people to protest against slavery. Following Olaudah Equiano, there aroused some magnificent sensational writers. Fredrick Douglas, W.E.B. Dubois, Charles Waddell Chestnut, Solomon Northup, Harriet Beecher Stowe, Harriet Jacobs, William Wells Brown, Richard Wright, Johnson etc are the exclusive writers of Afro-American slave narratives who used only pen as their weapon in abolishing slavery and as a tool through which they expressed their sufferings, agony, anguish and anonymous identity.

Though Om Prakash Valmiki and Olaudah Equiano belong to two different countries and speak different language, their background as a Dalit and Negro and also their disdainful pains, torment undergone by them as untouchables and downtrodden and as slaves unite them. Not only do these sufferings unite them but also their intellectuality in using their pens for making a revolutionary scar in the mind and heart of both Dalit and Afro-American people, unites them. Both Valmiki and Equiano are sandwiched by discrimination and inequality right from their young age. The sense of slavery and downtrodden encircled their living atmosphere. Among these scorching slavery circumstances and unsympathetic consequences, they both sprouted like a seed which sprouts really in dire straits. The sprouted seed grows into a huge tree which gives shelter and it is responsible for other new saplings that grow around it. Likewise Om Prakash Valmiki and Olaudah Equiano grew as a huge tree in penning their slave narratives not in a desire but in a need of emancipation where they influenced other budding writers paving way towards the freedom.

Dalit narratives and Afro-American narratives are juxtaposed by the concept of sufferings, pains, torments, agony, anguish, sense of alienation, shame, anger, searching for true identity which is expressed in the writings of Dalit Literature and Afro-American Literature. These literary works are not written in the mood of desire and happiness. These are written in the basic need to fight and struggle and get liberty. Since both the Dalit and Afro-American writers are suppressed and marginalised, they used the pen and urged the people of both cultures to protest against the unjust treatment meted out to them and urge them to proceed their journey towards emancipation.

Thus, it can be concluded that the philosophy of universal equality is deprived in the heart and mind of human race since ancient time. There is no superior or inferior position in the universe for human beings. Human kinds are dissected only by their attitude and not by their birth. The man with great ambition; great wealth; the man of the higher caste and the man of lower caste; everybody goes asleep beneath their grounds counting worms. During that specific time no more ambition, wealth, position of superiority and inferiority will not save them and reside with them beneath their grounds. Human race is born without anything and dies without anything. In this respect, the literature of Dalits and Afro-American is parallel with their writings focused in the vicinity of emancipation.

Works Cited

Aston, N. M. *Dalit Literature and African Literature.* New Delhi: Prestige Books, 2001. Print.

Equiano, Olaudah. *The Interesting Narrative of the Life of Olaudah Equiano or Gustavass Vassa, African.* Peterborough: Broadview Press, 2001. Print.

Singh, Bijender, Ed. *Dalit Men's Autobiographies: A Critical Appraisal.* New Delhi: Kalpaz. 2017. Print.

Valmiki, Om Prakash. *Joothan: A Dalit's Life.* New Delhi: Columbia U P, 2003. Print.

22

Pariah or Harijan: The Struggle of a Lifetime

— Dr Jayashree Hazarika

In India, despite 72 years of Independence and the reservation system the problem of untouchability still exists. Simply speaking, untouchability is seen as the practice of alienating a person or a whole caste on the basis of their being born in a caste which deals with menial jobs like cleaning of public toilets among others. The discrimination can happen as a result of physically or socially boycotting the person or the whole caste from the society. Instances of untouchability can be seen when people from the higher castes like Brahmins or Kshatriyas refuse to dine or interact with people from the castes which are seen as untouchables like the Bhangi caste. There was a belief that if people from higher castes came in contact with an untouchable person they would become impure. Even the shadow of an untouchable person could make one impure was the belief that led to the shunning of the people from lower castes caste like the sweepwers. To re-gain purity a person had to then take a dip into the holy waters of the Ganga.

In the traditional Hindu 'Varna System,' there were four classes that a person was born into and it was based on the person's karma and 'purity'. The priests and teachers belonged to the Brahman caste; the rulers and soldiers formed the Kshatriya caste; merchants and traders were part of the Vaishya caste; and Shudras were those that worked as labourers. But the untouchables did not figure into any of the traditional 'Varna System' of Hindus and were literally the outcastes. According to Dr B.R. Ambedkar, untouchables form an entirely new class i.e. the fifth varna apart from the existing four varnas. Hence we see how even the caste system of Hindus failed to recognise untouchables. In the Hindu society untouchables were those people who did menial jobs, were criminals, or those persons who suffered from contagious diseases. Even tribals who did not follow the Hindu caste system were considered as untouchables. These people were considered to be impure and harmful and hence were ostracised in civilized societies. Untouchability was also used as a form of punishment to the people who broke laws or were criminals. These people were boycotted socially because of their actions.

The untouchables were known as 'achhoot' or 'pariah' which means they were not welcomed in civilised society. Mahatma Gandhi gave them the name 'Harijan' which means the 'children of God' to create a place for them in society. Today the untouchables are referred to as 'Dalits.' In the Indian society members of Schedule Castes and Schedule Tribes (SC/ST) are also considered as Dalits as they too face different forms of prejudice in the society. Persons doing menial jobs such as tanning, skinning, work on leather goods, sweeping, scavenging etc are seen as untouchables in today's age. Despite so many years of independence, India has still a long way to go in the case of uplifting the life of the Dalits especially their women. The focus of this chapter will be more on society's treatment of Dalit women. I shall also compare the two monumental works on the life of Dalits: Mulk Raj Anand's *Untouchable* and Viramma, Josiane Racine and Jean-Luc Racine's *Viramma: Life of an Untouchable*.

Dalit women have been facing many problems in the Indian society which are more than a normal woman faces due to the stigma attached to their caste. Their problems are rarely discussed by the political leaders and it is only recently that scholars have started looking into their lives. The cause might be due to the lack of social and political awareness among the Dalit women and their constant fear of society which makes them seem voiceless. The society rarely sees a Dalit women as a threat to their social structure as people rarely hear a united voice from them and hence they do not find any political representation in India. There have been attempts in recent years to bring forth their problems by different political and socio-cultural groups but still there is no common platform where Dalit women's voices could be heard in the national level. There have been formation of groups like the National Dalit Women Federation which help the Dalit women but a common unified front is yet to be presented by these women as they still have to breach their different cultural, linguistic and geographical barriers. But one of the advancements is the coming of Dalit women's literature as well as Dalit women's autobiographies where the voice of the Dalit women can be heard and their problems may be highlighted. In the autobiography *Viramma: Life of an Untouchable*, Viramma gives the readers a glimpse of her fascinating life. Viramma's style of storytelling is unsentimental, humorous and dramatic. She talks about her carefree childhood, her marriage before puberty, and giving birth to twelve children while working as an agricultural worker. *Viramma: Life of an Untouchable* is a deeply personal and moving portrait of the extremely hard life of Viramma which was told over ten years to Josiane and Jean-Luc Racine. The autobiography also traces the social change in contemporary India. Viramma's life can been seen from many angles: as a Dalit, one of the oppressed; to Gandhians she is a Harijan, a daughter of God; in her village she is still treated as an untouchable, a Pariah. The book highlights the life of an extraordinary woman who spent the life at the very margins of the Indian society. Mulk Raj Anand's *Untouchable* too deals with the problems of the Dalit and their manhandling by the civilized society. Although more focus is given on the main character Bakha but we do find mention about the problems that his sister Sohini faces as a Dalit woman.

Mainstream feminist discourses mostly overlook the problems unique to Dalit women. Dalit women are rarely mentioned by Indian feminist writers and their representation is minimal. Due to insignificant representation of the Dalit female writers, there are also cases of misrepresenting. As Gopal Guru argues, "Social location which determines the perception of reality is a major factor that makes the representation of Dalit women's issues by non-Dalit women less valid and less authentic" (81). In India feminist critics have examined mostly the relation between class and gender but the relationship between caste and gender has been overlooked by them and it is only recently that studies have been undertaken in that direction. According to Uma Chakravarti "Class, caste and gender are inextricably linked, they interact with and shape each other, the structure of marriage, sexuality and reproduction is the fundamental basis of caste system" (*Gendering Caste* 39). For example Anand's *Untouchable* is a tale about class struggle. The narrative shows how Bakha's day is shaped due to the different class struggles he faces. In every interaction of Bakha, class and caste play a very important role which is highlighted in the course of his day. When Bakha's hero Singh promises to give Bakha a hockey stick, Singh highlights the "trait of servility" that Bakha is embedded with that he has inherited from his forefathers. Bakha is "queerly humble" and passively content like a "bottom dog" (Anand 31). This shows how caste has been internalised and it reflects in the personality and demeanor of a person and how the society takes advantage of it.

Socio-cultural categories of caste and gender are so inseparable in their material manifestation that they cannot be analysed separately in the specific Indian context. The older approaches, which isolate caste and gender inequalities, have already been questioned (Tharu and Poduval 33). Anupama Rao notes that the new approach of Dalit Bahujan feminists and theoreticians demand the exploration of their shared histories and cultural contexts (1-47). The rules relating to sex and marriage are controlled by the ideology of caste and these are used as tools to control women. Women's sexual freedom is contained to preserve the identity of caste. Inter-caste marriages are prohibited to safeguard the purity of caste as a result of which the caste system becomes unyielding and autocratic. In this regard, Uma Chakravarti observes:

> The structure of marriage, sexuality and reproduction is the fundamental basis of caste system. It is also fundamental to the way inequality is sustained; the structure of marriage reproduces

both class and caste inequality and thus the entire production system through its tightly controlled system of reproduction. (*Gendering Caste* 68)

According to Uma Chakravarti, Brahminical patriarchy consists of a set of rules and institutions in which caste and gender are linked with each other. Here women are given the crucial role of maintaining the purity of the caste. The caste system is reproduced through endogamous marriages to uphold the patriarchal codes. In the hierarchy of caste, Brahminical codes for women differ according to the status of caste group. Here a lower-caste man cannot marry a high-caste woman. Both will be punished if there is any violation. But a high-caste man can keep a low caste woman. Uma Chakravarti argues that Brahminical patriarchy evolved as a mechanism to preserve land, women and the quality of caste (*Gendering Caste* 37-40). These three are linked structurally. Without controlling female sexuality it is difficult to maintain all the three. Without guarding women who constitute the core of the structure of the caste system neither land nor purity of caste can be ensured. Hence, women's sexual subordination was institutionalised by patriarchal Hindu texts and enforced by law and authority. Anand in *Untouchable* exposed the double standards of society through the Sohini incident. Just moments ago Bakha was publically beaten and humiliated for mistakenly touching a priest. But on the other hand the priest in the temple was obsessed with the beautiful Dalit girl Sohini who was Bakha's sister and did not hesitate touching her forcefully. On one hand it is shown that people are polluted by the shadow of untouchable and on the other hand they don't hesitate to try to molest the untouchable girl. Through the character of the priest Anand unmasks the face of patriarchy. The priest tries to control female sexuality by forcing himself on the innocent Sohini and when the incident of the molestation comes out, the priest blames Sohini of polluting him. Here we see the highest levels of subjugation where the men from the untouchable class are excluded from society but the females are seen as sexual objects to be used for one's pleasure. There is no voice that can be heard from the female. Anand shows that Sohini is scared but we do not find any mention of her inner turmoil in the novel. Anand does mention Bakha's anger and frustration and seeking revenge for his sister's humiliation but the voice of the sister is not brought forward by the writer. This was the type of representation of the Dalit women where the women were expected to remain silent and bear their ill treatment by not just their own class but higher classes also.

The caste issue is usually overlooked in woman's movements. To strike a sense of unity among all the women, the feminists in India are inclined to consider all women as identical victims of patriarchal oppression, irrespective of their class and caste differences. There is a false assumption that all other forms of oppression will fade if patriarchy is tackled. It is assumed that since patriarchy and caste are jointly accommodating institutions of capitalism, then if patriarchy is destroyed, caste will have a normal death. Feminist see an association between control of women and control of lower-caste people. Hence, the problems of Dalit women are not seen from the point of caste by the propagators of the women's movement. But the fact is that Dalit women are doubly oppressed by both patriarchy and caste. Dalit girls do not have a right to choose their life partners as their families decide their fate and the higher caste men too think that Dalit women are their free property. This fact is amply reiterated in the autobiography *Viramma: Life of an Untouchable*. Here the narrator Viramma tells how she is married off as a child. For her own marriage her consent was never sought. She was just married off to a person of her father's choice. The narrator was a mere child and did not have the ability to understand what her family was doing. She becomes a victim of patriarchy. Even her husband is the typical symbol of patriarchy. Despite Viramma'a refusal to get physically intimacy, her husband forces himself upon her. Viramma narrates how in the initial days of her marriage, she used to hate her husband because of the pain he caused her at night. Her husband physically forced her when she was merely a child. Viramma sees not just the ugly face of patriarchy but also faces humiliation due to her status as a Dalit woman.Viramma narrates how she was being abused by the Civil Servant. "...what did I see when I raised my eyes? His dick! A fat dick! He was holding it in one hand and he had money in the other. I screamed. I was trembling all over and I didn't know how to get out of the situation" (52). She tells her readers how due to her low caste people from the higher caste assumed that they were easy women. According to Viramma, "We Paratchi have the reputation of being easy women who'll jump into bed with anyone if they whistle... But we're not whores" (52). This is the common plight of a Dalit woman where she is seen only as a sex object by people from the higher classes. This is the problem which feminists fail to see and bring forth. The same view is also highlighted by Anand in the *Untouchable*. Dalit women face not just patriarchy but also discrimination based on their class and hence is doubly oppressed.

A separate framework is needed for "caste" and not just "class" to understand the oppression of Dalit women. The way women experience issues like violence which is universal depends on the circumstances in which they face it and such issues are common in all caste and class. So although subjugation of women by males is a universal problem but the extent and form of subjugation is conditioned by socio-economic factors. For example, crimes related to dowry are common among the middle class and upper class women in India. But such crimes are not seen much amongst the Dalit classes. Also the upper and middle class women have to uphold the image of prime and proper women with proper 'sanskar.' But such expectations are not held for a Dalit woman. Hindu patriarchy upholds the myths of Savitri, Sita, Radha, Draupadi and other such models of womanly virtues who would surrender and endure everything for the sake of their husband and children's happiness. But Dalit women are not expected to internalise such patriarchal ideology. Therefore, they are not obliged to be devoted to their husband. In the Dalit community women are seen to have an independence and uniqueness which is separate from their husband and children. The narrator Viramma in *Viramma: Life of an Untouchable* describes how she openly insults her husband with sexual innuendoes. Even in front of her children she is boisterous and is not ashamed of using vulgar language. In fact, it is the children who close their ears while she keeps scolding her husband with different types of sexual references. Dalit women assert their sexual freedom to a certain extent. Dalit activists like

Ilaiah argue that women in Dalit community have more socio-economic independence:

> The Dalit Bahujans of India are the only people on the globe who, while living in a civil society, have lived outside the defined structures of all religions. Take, for example, their marriage contract. It is a human contract. It is governed by the rights guaranteed to women within the broad system of patriarchy. A situation of disrespect to each other's rights can result in breaking that contract and will result in divorce. If after the divorce the man or woman comes across another possible partner, either by way of parental arrangement or because of his or her own initiative, such individuals have the right to enter to another contract. Because of these inherently assured rights, a wife does not have to treat her husband as a God. A Dalit Bahujan woman does not have to perform Padapuja (worshiping the husband's feet) to her husband either in the morning or in the evening. She does not have to address her husband in a way she would address a superior. In a situation of dispute, word in response to word, abuse for abuse is the socially visible norm. Patriarchy as system does exist among Dalit Bahujans, yet in this sense it is considerably more democratic. (*Why I am not a Hindu* 34).

Viramma too is seen to enjoy a sense of freedom which is not common to contemporary upper class women of her time. Feminist writers fail to see this differentiation among women of the upper and lower classes. Only in recent days, scholars have started taking up the issues of the Dalit women and placing their problems differently.

Hence, we see that the issues of Dalit women although seem similar to all the problems of middle class and upper class women yet they are different too. In some cases Dalit women face greater freedom to exercise their rights but on the other hand, they also face a lot of restraint. Their lower status attracts unwanted attention from upper classes which almost disregard their basic choice. Dalit women are seen more as sex objects rather than breathing, feeling human beings. To help the Dalit women, feminists in India need to see their different socio-economic and cultural conditions and not put them in the same chambers as middle and upper caste women. Dalit Literature has started coming where female's voices can be heard but the need of the time is to make these voices more mainstream.

India Today's article titled "Untouchability in India: Some facts on the oldest social hierarchy still being practiced in India" (2015), mentions a shocking survey conducted by the National Council of Applied Economic Research and claims that untouchability is still prevalent in India and "every hour two Dalits are assaulted; every day two Dalits are murdered, and two Dalit homes are torched." More than 160 million are still treated as 'Harijans' and shockingly every 3rd Hindu person practices untouchability. Literature only presents the face of it and words only express in miniscule the actual atrocities incited on millions of these Hindus.

Works Cited

Ambedkar, B. R. *Dr Babasaheb Ambedkar: Writings and Speeches.* Vol-18, Part. I. Print.

Anand, Mulk Raj. *Untouchable.* London: Wishart, 1935. Print.

Chakravarti, Uma. *Gendering Caste through a Feminist Lens***.** Stree: Calcutta, 2003. Print.

Dasgupta, Susmita. "Another Song of the Road." *Economic and Political Weekly,* Volume XXXV, No.24, June 10, 2000. Web

Guru, Gopal. "Dalit Women Talk Differently." *Economic and Political Weekly*, vol. 30, no. 41/42, 1995, pp. 2548–2550. *JSTOR.* <www.jstor.org/stable/ 4403327>. Web

Ilaiah, Kancha. *Why I am not a Hindu*. Kolkata, Samya, 2005. Print.

Rao, Anupama. *Gender and Caste: Issues in Contemporary Indian Feminism*. New Delhi: Kali for Women, 2003. Print.

Tharu, Susie and Satish Poduval. "Obscure Subjects of Desire: Gender, Conjugality and the Remaking of Class in 1970s Hindi Cinema". Vol. 52, Issue No. 39, 30 Sep, 2017

<http://www.cla.temple.edu/chat/india/documents/Poduval.pdf> Web

Viramma, Josiane Racine, Jean-Luc Racine. *Viramma: Life of an Untouchable*. Trans. Will Hobson. London: UNESCO Publishing: 1997. Print.

"Untouchability in India: Some Facts on the Oldest Social Hierarchy Still Being Practiced in India." *India Today*. 28-09-2015.

https://www.indiatoday.in/education-today/gk-current-affairs/story/ untouchability-in-india-265233-2015-09-28

23

Ventriloquising Dalit Repression in Aravind Adiga's *The White Tiger*

— *Dr Pallavi Saxena*

Aravind Adiga is an acclaimed winner of 'Man Booker Prize' and his debut novel *The White Tiger* has presented an unflattering portrait of India as a society racked by corruption, servitude and caste discrimination. Some of the nationalists have even lambasted it as a western conspiracy to deny the country's economic progress. However, in an interview with Stuart Jeffries, Adiga justifies himself saying:

> At a time when India is going through great changes, and when China is likely to inherit the world from the west, it is important that writers like me try to highlight the brutal injustices of society. That's what writers like Flaubert, Balzac and Dickens did in the 19th century and, as a result, England and France are better societies. That's what I'm trying to do – it's not an attack on the country, it's about the greater process of self-examination. (Adiga n.pag.)

Discrimination on the grounds of caste, creed and colour is one of the major problems which have become endemic throughout the world. Most of the marginalised groups all over the world have a system of oppression. In India, it was under the pretext of the 'caste' and in the western world it was under the name of the 'race.' Racial problem is only one of the many problems that not only America but many parts of the western world also are grappling with at the present time. Inequality may be accounted one of the main sources of this marginality which led to insecurity, injustice and exploitation. Marginalised sections have always remained on the periphery and distanced from the power centers.

For several thousand years, the caste system has been a prevalent institution in Indian society. Manusmriti described 'varna' system of the society based upon the occupation. It is a four-pronged 'varna' system comprising four kinds of people of the society borne out of the body of Lord Vishnu. According to this myth, Brahmin was born out of head, Kshatriya was born out of arms, Vaishya was born out of abdomen and Shudra was born out of feet. Brahmins were at the top of the hierarchy. They were the priests and teachers who served the functions of learning, teaching, and performing sacrifices. Kshatriyas were the warriors, skilled in the martial arts and educated to be leaders whose task was to protect the people and fight their enemies. Vaisyas were the merchant class. Shudras were the labourers and were not entitled to get any education. They generally served as servants to the other three classes.

There was a fifth category of Indian society which was considered either the lowest of the varnas or outside the varna structure entirely. This was the 'untouchable' or 'Dalit' category. They were typically associated with activities such as removing faeces or dead animals, and their 'untouchability' stemmed from a cultural notion of pollution. They were denied basic civil rights and were often subjected to tragedies. Although, in modern democratic India, anyone can choose a profession irrespective of the class he has been born in, yet the caste archetypes are still strongly implanted in the minds of people. Balram Halwai finds it very difficult to come out of the clutches of the caste system and make a foray in the domain of drivers:

> The old driver asked, 'What caste are you?' 'Halwai.' 'Sweet-makers,' the old driver said, shaking his head. 'That's what you people do. You make sweets. How can you learn to drive?' He pointed his hookah at the live coals. 'That's like getting coals to

> make ice for you. Mastering a car – he moved the stick of an invisible gearbox – 'it's like taming a wild Stallion – only a boy from the warrior castes can manage that. You need to have aggression in your blood. Muslims, Rajputs, Sikhs – they are the fighters, they can become drivers. You think sweet-makers can last long in fourth gear? (Adiga 56).

Etymologically speaking, the term 'Dalit' has originated from Sanskrit word 'Dalita' meaning 'oppressed.' In 1935 the word 'Dalit' took an interesting turn when the British Government used its English translation as 'depressed classes' to mean downtrodden people of India who were till date referred to as 'Harijan' by Mahatma Gandhi.

However, Dr Ambedkar sensed the multiple nuances the word could exude and gave it a more respectable identity by calling them 'Dalit.' In the post-Ambedkar era, it became a part of political activism and led to the inclusion of all those deprived people who have remained historical victims of both class and caste exploitation.

Dalit Literature is a saga of the anguish and injustice experienced by Dalits since times immemorial. Dr Ambedkar was the main source behind the progressive and radical thoughts portrayed in Dalit Literature. It artistically portrays the sorrows and sufferings, trials and tribulations, ridicule and poverty endured by Dalits. Arjun Dangle defines 'Dalit Literature' as: "one which acquaints people with the caste system and untouchability in India... It matures with a sociological point of view and is related to the principles of negativity, rebellion and loyalty to science, thus finally ending as revolutionary" (Dangle 319). Recognising the centrality of human being, this literature is thoroughly saturated with humanity's joys and sorrows. It regards human beings as supreme, and leads them towards total revolution. Dr M.N. Wankhede states, "The pens of the Dalit writers are ready as lever, to lift the people's democracy out of the mud of anarchy" (Wankhede 53). The objective of Dalit Literature is exclusively to awaken an ideological revolution in the Dalit community.

At the prima facie level, Dalit Literature may appear to be protest literature but it also shows the cultural values of Dalits. It talks about their art forms as well as their oppression and helps the reader to understand their way of life. Lalmingthani rightly observes, "We can see from reading Dalit Literature that spans several decades, that the suffering of the untouchables is a never ending chain" (Lalmingthani 11). The dispossession and deprivation, neglect and estrangement, subjugation and subordination, the resignation and silence mark the lives of subalterns. Even when they resist and rise-up, they feel bounded and defeated in their respective positions. They have virtually no representative or spokesperson in the society they live in. They suffer precariously and get a marginal place or no place at all in the history and culture of which they are the essential part as human beings. The established literature of India is Hindu literature. But it is Dalit Literature which has the revolutionary power to accept new science and technology and bring about a total transformation. Dalit is the name of a total revolution; it is revolution incarnate.

Aravind Adiga's *The White Tiger* presents a brutal view of India's class struggle. It shows the dark underside of India and flaunts the suffering of poor people, Dalits and the lower caste people. This novel has been woven around the socio-political life of India and shows the glaring vices prevailing in the country. *The White Tiger* revolves around Balram Halwai, the son of a poor rickshaw puller, Vikram Halwai. He is the strong voice of Dalit community in which the subalterns, landless labourers, unemployed youths, poor auto-drivers, servants, prostitutes, beggars and unprivileged figure prominently. The victims of this corrupt system called the underclass society constitute 'dark India'. The caste that one is born into affects the past, present, and future of most Hindus. However, it becomes an obstacle in the path of the people belonging to subaltern class and they have to overcome it in order to become successful.

In the present novel, Adiga satirically compares the ancient Indian segregationist system to a systematic zoo wherein all the animals were kept systematically in the cages in accordance with their respective status and professions, "See, this country (India), in its days of greatness, when it was the richest nation on earth, was like a zoo. A clean, well-kept, orderly zoo. Everyone in his place, everyone happy. Goldsmiths here. Cowherds here. Landlords here. The man called a Halwai made sweets. The man called a cowherd tended cows. The untouchables cleaned faeces. Landlords were kind to their serfs. Women covered their heads with a veil and turned their eyes to the ground when talking to strange men" (Adiga 63).

The Dalits and the underclass have been subjected to perennial discrimination and exploitation at the hands of the feudal and colonising class. In *Between the Assassinations* Aravind Adiga depicts the problems of untouchables. Dalits have always been assigned menial jobs. He presents it through the story of a Dalit book-seller known as 'Xerox." He narrates his own father's story humorously to bring out the pathetic and deplorable conditions of Dalits in society. The story of what his father did all his life for a living–taking the crap out of the houses of the rich landlords, the traditional occupation of people of his caste:

> All day long, the old man would hang around the back wall of the landlord's house, waiting for the smell of human faeces; as soon as he smelled that smell, he came close to the house, and waited, with bent knees, like a wicketkeeper waits for the ball in cricket. (Xerox bent his knees and showed how) then, as soon as he heard the, 'thud' of the boom box closing, he had to run to the wall, pull out the retractable potty through a hole in the wall, empty it into the rose-plants, wipe it clean with his loincloth and insert it back into the wall before the next person came to use the toilet. That was the job he did, his whole life, can you believe it! (Adiga 44-45)

The White Tiger is an enthralling black comedy. During the progression of seven nights, Balram Halwai tells us the comical story of how he became a success. He starts his life as a poor boy in the rural village of Laxmangarh and aspires to become an entrepreneur in the city. Despite his success as a driver, Balram realises that he is still a servant in the "darkness" with innumerable disadvantages. In the city of Delhi, Balram becomes exposed to the wide-ranging corruption of Indian society. He grasps the separation between the rich and the poor, and desires to become affluent. Pinky, one of Balram's masters, decides to drive the car drunk and assumes that she has hit a child. The family agrees to frame Balram for the hit and run. After Pinky and his other master Ashok split-up their marriage, infuriated Balram kills Ashok and flees to Bangalore with his nephew. Balram rationalises his actions at the end of the novel by stating that his freedom was worth the slaying and transforms himself into a very successful business entrepreneur.

The White Tiger is an eye-opening cultural experience that addresses some pressing human rights issues. A lot of subjects like caste system, wealth divide, pollution, disease, globalisation, education, and family traditions have been explored in the novel with a sprinkling of comedy here and there. The whole novel revolves around the life of high profile society and underclass society and creates a veritable difference between the life of rural and urban society. Balram's journey from Laxmangarh to Dhanbad, Dhanbad to Delhi, Delhi to Bangalore, tells us the difference between the life of rural and urban, rich and poor society. Adiga strongly believes that "in India the disparity in the rich and poor is just a fact of life, which has been there since ages" (Nimsarkar and Mishra 18).

There exists a bizarre dichotomy between the rich and the poor in Indian society. In urban society, the rich people are very fat. They have lost their health and suffer from a number of ailments due to their life style and excessive eating. Their only tension is to reduce the weight and look like the poor i.e. thin and physically fit. As Balram says, "See, with all these late-night parties, all that drinking and munching, the rich tend to get fat in Delhi. So they walk to lose weight" (Adiga 225). Their only tension is to remain physically fit but they can't keep it up. Balram says, "Every evening, the compound around Buckingham Tower B-Block becomes an exercise ground. Plump, paunchy man and even plumper, paunchier women with big circle of sweat below their arms, are doing their evening walking." (Adiga 225)

On the other hand, the poor people lead a life of abject poverty and can't afford to get good clothes and meals in their life. The brutal irony is that they get good clothes only once in their life when they die, Balram says, "My mother's body had been wrapped from head to toe in a saffron silk cloth, which was covered in rose petals and jasmine garlands. I don't think she had ever had such a fine thing to wear in life. Her death was so grand that I knew, all at once, that her life must have been miserable. My family was guilty about something" (Adiga 16).

It is extreme poverty which creates darkness in the life of the Dalits and subaltern class in the rural as well as in urban society. Underclass and subaltern have no place in society, they are always deprived of their rights and have to suffer and remain silent. Balram asserts, "The dreams of the rich, and the dreams of the poor – they never overlap, do they? See, the poor dream all their lives of getting enough to eat and looking like the rich. And what do the rich dream of? Losing weight and looking like the poor" (Adiga 225).

In *The White Tiger*, Aravind Adiga depicts the deplorable condition of Dalits in the society. They are so poor that they can't provide for the proper education and schooling of their children. Due to ignorance, they give birth to a number of children and sometimes even forget to name them properly. For instance, Balram's parents are not bothered about giving a proper name to their child; they simply called him 'Munna.' Balram feels humiliated when he is asked his name by the school teacher and says:

> When I told him what my name was, he gaped at me: Munna? That's not a real name'. He was right: it just means 'boy'. That's all I've got sir, I said. It was true. I'd never been given a name. Didn't your mother name you? She's very ill sir. She lies in bed and spews blood. She's got no time to name me. And your father? He's a rickshaw-puller, sir. He's got no time to name me (Adiga 13).

It was the school teacher who named him 'Balram' and marked his age in the school. His parents didn't know his correct age even.

Dalits have long been oppressed with an iron hand by *Zamindars* in rural India. In this novel, the four landlords have been very interestingly named 'Buffalo, Stork, Wild Boar and Raven' on the basis of appetite detected in them. Pratibha Nagpal says, "Together they form a mafia that controls everything – the river, the agriculture land, the roads and the hillside" (Adiga 153). The Buffalo was one of the greediest landlords of Laxmangarh who extracted one-third of the earning from the person using his roads. The Stork was a fat man who owned the rivers that flowed outside the village. He took a toll from every catch of fish caught by every fisherman. His brother 'Wild Boar' was also a landlord who owned all the good agricultural land around Laxmangarh. "If you wanted to work on those lands, you had to bow down to his feet, and touch the dust under his slippers, and agree to swallow his day wages" (Adiga 25). The Raven owned the unfertile and rocky land and demanded money from the goat herders that used his land. If they didn't give their money, he liked to dip his beak into their backside, so they called him the Raven.

These fabulously rich landlords lived in high-walled mansions, having their own wells, ponds and temples and never ventured to come out into the village. They also supported political parties for their selfish motives. They paid loans to poor people and charged a whooping amount as interest. Even Balram's family had to take loan from Stork on the lavish marriage of his cousin, Reena. In lieu of that, all the members of the family had to work for him. Balram was also pulled out of the school and forced to work at tea shop.

The author calls them animals due to their exploitative tendencies. He takes us directly into the jungle that is contemporary India. Savita is of the opinion that "Animals and their sights, sounds, activities, characteristics and qualities fill up the novel making it a veritable zoo of animals: dogs buffaloes, the creepy crawlies, the nocturnal, and the white tiger" (Adiga 149).

In *The White Tiger* Adiga decries the pathetic condition of the poor Dalits who migrate to big cities in search of employment but are not able to get it. They have to sleep on the roads and footpath. Their filthy appearance and dirty clothes give them the appearance of animals. In order to famish their hunger, they have to pick up food from garbage and consume it. In fact, they not only look like animals but live like animals too. They come to cities in search of light but they remain in darkness always. Sudhir rightly says, "The financially weaker people who fail even to get employment in the village come to the cities in the hope of better opportunities that will bring light into their lives but unfortunately they are more exploited than ever and are left in darkness amidst light" (Adiga 129). This is the miserable condition of the Dalits, particularly economically weaker ones who do not have even enough to earn bread for their livelihood.

Balram believes that 'humans should live like humans, and animals should live like animals'. In the later part of the novel, when he visits the zoo, he sees a tiger pacing back and forth inside a cage and passes out. He feels that he too has been treated like an animal for the majority of his life. Balram addresses the human rights issues that all humans should be treated fairly, and be able to move freely as they please. At the end of the novel, he finally feels that he is being treated like a human when he becomes an entrepreneur.

The White Tiger has exposed the miserable condition of the underclass and servants who have to suffer at every step of life. They get exploited everywhere. In villages, they are ruled over by the landlords whereas in cities, they have to remain under the oppression of their employers. Dashrath rightly asserts, "The high-class Indians have no respect for their service-providers – cooks, drivers, sweepers – whatever the nature of their job may be, they just fit into one class-servants or slaves" (Adiga 238). They are appointed as drivers but have to do all the works of household. Balram was a driver but he was forced to do all the works, "Are you a sweet-maker? Can you cook for us while you're not driving? Certainly, sir. I cook very well. Very tasty sweets. Gulab-Jamun, laddoos, anything you desire," I said. I worked at a tea shop for many years. Mr Ashok seemed to find this amusing. Only in India," he said. "Your driver can also make sweets for you. Only in India" (Adiga 65).

Aravind Adiga vicariously feels the anguish of the servants and reveals their pain through this novel. Indian servants do all sorts of work but are invariably humiliated and tortured by their employers. They are regarded merely as commodities which the employers have purchased. The drivers have to do all the works like cooking the food, mopping the floor, and washing the clothes in their free time. Their employers never pay them proper wages, yet they remain silent and never ask for money. Balram gives vent to his anguish saying, "I had to heat water on the stove, carry it into the courtyard, and then lift the old man's feet up one after the other and immerse them in the hot water and then massage them both gently." (Adiga 70)

The condition of the poor Dalits is so pathetic that in spite of their exploitation, they can't dare to raise their voice against the masters and landlords for fear of losing their jobs. The irony is that though they are treated like slaves yet, they are satisfied with their position of having two times meal and shelter on their head. Balram says, "I had a covered room to sleep in. True, I had to share it with the other driver, a grim-looking fellow named Ram Prasad, and he had the nice big bed, while I had to sleep on the floor-still a covered room's and much nicer than sleeping on the road, as Kishan and I had been doing all the time we were in Dhanbad" (Adiga 67). These helpless classes have no alternative to earn money, so they remain silent and satisfied with their job-providers and bear the oppression of their masters. So, the rich take benefit of their helplessness and use them like multipurpose machines.

Adiga asserts that despite financial poverty, the underclass is morally and ethically very rich. These underclass people like servants and drivers come from rural areas and remain honest for a long time but city's corruption makes them corrupt. The rich confine the bag of money to their drivers and servants. They never embezzle a coin from it. This reveals the honesty of Indian servants. Balram says, "Don't test your chauffeur with a rupee coin or two- he may well steal that much. But leave a million dollars in front of a servant and he won't touch a penny. Try it: leave a black bag with a million dollars in Mumbai Taxi. The taxi driver will call the police and return the money by the day's end. I guarantee it whether the police will give it to you or not is another story" (Adiga 177). Adiga feels that in India, servants remain very faithful to their masters, but in return, they get nothing but humiliation. Often, when their masters impose their own crime on them, they don't try to run away rather, confess it silently. Balram says, "I was to go to jail for a killing I had not. Running away never crossed my mind. Not once did the thought, I'll tell the judge the truth, cross my mind" (Adiga 111). This is the dark face of Indian-urban society. These servants and drivers remain honest for some time but can't retain their honesty for a long time because the corruption of cities makes them corrupt. As Beena Agarwal asserts, "Not only is Balram corrupted, but his master is also corrupted in the mysterious life of Delhi" (Agrawal 172).

Despite prevailing oppression and suppression of the Dalits in the novel, there are occasional silver linings too. Vijay, the first entrepreneur from Laxmangarh is Balram's personal hero. Vijay is Balram's childhood role model who has improved his station in life by forging his own identity. The son of a pig herder, Vijay's first success came with becoming a bus conductor. Balram and the other village boys admire his prestigious job and his uniform. Later, Vijay enters politics and quickly rises in the ranks and becomes a prominent official in the Great Socialist's Party. By the end of the narrative, Vijay is a powerful politician, just as corrupt and power-hungry as any of the rich elites in the novel. The case of Vijay unravels the prevailing reality of democracy that one can rise above his caste. Balram observes this stance of wonder at the bungalow of the Stork, "I waited by the gate and watched. The stork himself came out to see Vijay, and bowed down before him – a landlord bowing before a pig herd's son! The marvels of democracy" (Adiga 103).

To sum up, Aravind Adiga's novel *The White Tiger* happens to be one of the most entertaining and enlightening sources of information about the Dalit underclass. Through Balram's eyes, Adiga has exposed the glaring social evils in India. One of the basic ideas promulgated in the novel is that there is an element of domination and control that seems to be a part of the Indian historical DNA. However, the two instances of Balram and Vijay, rising high in life from the perennial abysmal state, ensure that a person can achieve anything in life if he does not allow anything to stop him.

Both Vijay and Balram attain success in their life but their path to success passes through foul means. There is much talk in this novel of revolution and insurrection. Balram even justifies his employer's murder as an act of class warfare. Balram's successful rises as an entrepreneur from age-old fated miseries through foul means amply bring forth the politics of the novel as being an onslaught on the age-old feudal system. Balram Halwai is indeed a modern Indian hero. He is a successful entrepreneur, a self-made man who has risen on his own. In a nation proudly shedding a history of poverty and underdevelopment, he represents, as he himself says, "tomorrow."

Works Cited

Adiga, Aravind. *Between the Assassinations*. New Delhi: Picador, 2008. Print.

—. *The White Tiger*. New Delhi: HarperCollins. 2008 Print.

—-. "Roars of Anger". Interview by Stuart Jeffries. *The Guardian*. 16 Oct., 2008.

Agarwal, Beena. "Delhi as a Metaphor of Post-Industrial India in *The White Tiger*." *Aravind Adiga's The White Tiger: A Symposium of Critical Response*. Ed. R. K. Dhawan. New Delhi: Prestige, 2011. Print.

Arora, Sudhir K. *Aravind Adiga's The White Tiger: A Freakish Booker*. New Delhi: Authorspress, 2011. Print.

Bagul, Baburao. 'Mother' in Dangle Arjun, ed. *Poisoned Bread*. Bombay: Orient Longman, 1992. Print.

Dangle, Arjun, ed. *Poisoned Bread*: *Translation from Modern Marathi Literature*. Mumbai: Orient Longman, 1992. Print.

Dhawan, R.K., ed. *Adiga's The White Tiger: A Symposium of Critical Response*. New Delhi: Prestige, 2011. Print.

Lalmungthani, Melody. "From Oppression to Liberation through Education." *Critical Essays on Dalit Literature*. Ed. D. Murali Manohar. New Delhi: Atlantic, 2013. Print.

Nagpal, Pratibha. "Aravind Adiga's *The White Tiger*: A Critical Response." *Four Indian Novelists*. Ed. R. K. Dhawan. New Delhi: Prestige, 2009. Print.

Nimsarkar, P. D., and Shubha Mishra. Eds. "Aravind Adiga: An Introduction." *Aravind Adiga: An Anthology of Critical Essays*. New Delhi: Creative, 2010. Print.

Singh, Savita. "Animality in Aravind Adiga's *The White Tiger*." *Aravind Adiga: An Anthology of Critical Essays*. Eds. P. D. Nimsarkar and Shubha Mishra. New Delhi: Creative, 2010. Print.

Wankhede, M.N. "Dalit Literature: A Historical Background." *Dalit Literature and African-American Literature*. Ed. N.M. Aston. New Delhi: Prestige, 2001. Print.

24

Unheard Agonies: An Analysis of Balbir Madhopuri's *Changiya Rukh: Against the Night*

— Dr Sumitra Singh

Only ash knows the experience of burning.
– Dr Jai Prakash Kardam

Many Dalit autobiographies have been written by the men and women writers and they have depicted their unheard agonies in them. There is a distinctive difference in their autobiographies before they have different pains. Shweta Singh writes, "Men and women have different stories to tell and also sometimes different modes of narration. This essay tries to highlight the way Dalit women have been represented very differently in autobiographies of Dalit men and Dalit women" (Singh 39). Balbir Madhopuri is well-acclaimed figure in Punjabi Dalit Literature. He is best known for his autobiography *Changiya Rukh: Against the Night*. Changiya Rukh means lopped tree. After lopping the tree, the growth of a tree gets stopped; likewise Balbir Madhopuri also could not a fertile environment in his small village Madhopur in Punjab. He started the journey of his life as a child labourer and an agriculture worker but now he is an established Punjabi writer who has written fourteen books in Punjabi. He has translated thirty books and he has edited forty anthologies in Punjabi till date. His autobiography *Changiya Rukh* has been translated into many languages. Himanshu Sharma writes about this autobiography "*Changiya Rukh* is a powerful autobiography that shows the story of silence, suppression, anger, agitation and resistance of the leather workers called Chamars. A boy is seen planting a mango sapling which is snatched by his father just because he thinks that this little boy knows less about the caste" (Sharma 221). He retired as the Deputy Director, All India Radio (News), New Delhi on 31 July, 2015 and he had served as the editor of *Yojana* (Punjabi), Publications Davison, Ministry of Information and Broadcasting. He presently works as the Director of Punjabi Sahit Sabha, New Delhi and editor of *Samkali Sahit*, a quarterly a publication of Sabha.

Balbir Madiopuri has received many prestigious awards including Kav Purskar (1994), Translation Award (2000) from Punjabi Akademi, Delhi; Best Book Award (2003) for his autobiography from Punjab Languages Department, Govt. of Punjab and many more. Apart from it, he has been honoured by the Department of Punjabi, Kurukshetra University and Department of Hindi, the University of Ranchi for his contribution in Punjabi Literature.

His parents were not much aware about his birth and thus, no any horoscope was prepared and even there is no any record of his date of birth. Before the Indian Independence, there was no any particular identity of the people of his caste in Madhopur. There were separate *gurudwaras* for the Dalits and the Jat Sikhs in the villages of Punjab. The low caste people were not allowed to enter gurudwaras built by the upper caste to pay their obeisance before the Sri Guru Granth Sahib or getting *prasad*. The Dalit destitute children would go to get *prasad* at some special occasions like Sangrand or Gurpurab. Their condition was not much better than the dogs because the people used to throw *prasad* upwards towards them so that their hands may not get polluted by the touch of the untouchables. They would even abuse the children and the latter had to sit where shoes were kept.

Madhopuri's classmates also did not behave with him properly and that also kept remoteness from them when they went to take water from the well. They would wash away the pot first and only then they would drink water and if this water was come from a tap, they would wash the tap and only after that they would drink water. Such kind of untouchability was prevailing in his village. Dalit students had to feed and wash the cattle of their teacher Mr Khatri but they were not allowed to touch the water tap to drink water from the house however thirsty they were. It was all this because they were Dalit children. They had to deliver the letters of the post office in the scorching heat with the bare feet.

Poverty makes Balbir Madhopuri's condition very miser. There was an acute dearth of food at home that's why they would go to the jagerry machine holding buckets in their hands to collect sugarcane juice dirt. When the people threw juice dirt, they would collect it and sometime the dogs would also hover around them. If he was not able to go there, his brother had to go because there was nothing much to eat in their homes.

When cattle would die, his family members and relatives would carry them either on their shoulders or on the carts. Balbir also would help them in these woks. He sometimes felt shame to work these kinds of menial works but the circumstances have made him helpless. Their funeral palaces were also different from Jats in their village. He would go for the child labour and the Jat women would throw the bread-crumbs to him like they did to a dog. Even the children of the upper castes would call his father by his name. They had no land and they lived in mud houses. He had to do many jobs in order to run their family. He had to shake off the paddy, harvesting of the wheat and maize in the wee hours. They would kill the snakes also when they came under their feet.

Madhopuri's experience outside his village was also not good. He joins Government College, Tanda in district Hoshiarpur in 1972 after passing his tenth class. He met there Professor Didar Singh who was a Punjabi poet and writer. When there were annual examinations of twelfth standard and eight boys of his caste were travelling in the bus. They bullied her and one of them. One of these boys put his feet over the feet of a beautiful girl who was sitting there and teased her by pushing three or four time. She started shouting in Punjabi and English and asked the bus conductor to take the bus directly to the police station. She became very furious. When the bus reached at the Tanda bus stop, they fled from the bus stop and he could not sleep well at night and kept thinking about that girl. This incidence came as a turning point in his life and he wrote lengthy lines in the praise of that girl. he wrote his poems about the social discrimination in the society.

He became a member of the Communist Party in 1972. He worked for the farmers and the labourers. When he was working in the Food Corporation of India, he saw that the upper caste people would cut jokes at the Dalit women who worked there.

Balbir had come to know about everything by this time. He knew about the cruelty of the caste discrimination and that's why he thought to write his autobiography and he penned down one chapter of his autobiography and got it published. This chapter gave him very good response and he started receiving phone calls from established Punjabi writers within a week. He got published two more chapters of his autobiography in the next two years. He got an overwhelming response from different people and he thought that he should write an autobiography now. In the next four-five months, he completed his autobiography. It was published in Punjabi under the title *Changiya Rukh* in 2002. This autobiography describes the accounts of his life up to forty-five years. It was published in Hindi in 2007 and its English translation came in 2010. Since then it has become a matter of international importance. The Punjabi Department of Delhi University has prescribed it in its syllabus.

So far as the agonies of the caste people are concerned, the chamars of his village had to see this discriminatory attitude in their village. Balbir Madhopuri becomes a voice for it and he brings their pain to the common public. Dr Ravi Bhushan writes in this context, "*Changiya Rukh* is a powerful testimony to the suffering, angst and attempt at rebellion of the Dalit community of *chamars* in Punjab but it is something more....It is a lively chronicle of a host of people, each significant and memorable, not as a representative of a caste in one part of the country but as an individual" (Bhushan 3). Madhopuri writes about his village in his autobiography, "Actually, Madhopur in district Jalandhar is one of the villages located in the *mand* – the land where the river Beas once flowed" (Madhopuri 1). It was a very small villages and its population was only twelve hundred. The upper caste Punjabi Jats enjoyed a good status but the condition of the chamars or leather workers was not good. They had to strive even for their food. They were discriminated in the village because they were not allowed to pull water from the well. They were fully depended on a well that was dug for the low caste people.

The discriminatory attitude was prevalent in the society to the extent that the Dalit people were the sole sufferers of the system. They were not considered the part of the social system. Outwardly, it seemed a single village but the roots of untouchability and discrimination were very deep in the village. He writes, "The village appeared to be one, but every group had its own drinking well. Later some Muslims also settled in the village and bought land for themselves. They did not practice untouchability against the Dalits, but this could be because many of them had once belonged to the untouchable and artisan castes" (Madhopuri 2). The high caste people were not happy to see the Dalit students wearing good clothes that are why they would beat them or throw mud at them. There was no any chance of protest because they knew that if they opposed it, they are sure to be beaten up. Balbir Madhopuri writes:

> If an untouchable appeared in the village dressed in the new clothes, he was certain to be given a beating on the pretext that the low castes were trying to become the equals of the higher castes; no one knew or could predict when such an incident would occur and where. (Madhopuri 02)

This discrimination on the basis of caste or class is prevalent since ancient time. The Shudra people were treated badly and they also had to do menial works. They were humiliated, terrorized and suppressed in the society and they had not any right of education. Sutputra Karna is its burning example who could not get education from Dronacharya just because he was not Kashatria and belonged to a low caste. The chamars of his caste were also treated very badly by the upper caste Jats. They had to be depended on the Jats because they were rich and dominant in the society. The low caste children had to be depended on the *prasad* of the Gurudwara and the upper caste people would look down upon and showered humiliation on them through their words. Thus, they had to be depended upon their fate. Madhopuri writes about hunger, "The crux of the matter is that no one can fight fate. Faminine has reduced many to penury" (Madhopuri 102). Dalits were suppressed at every occasion. Balbir Madhopuri writes that they were not allowed to put names at their own choice. He writes about an incidence:

> Names like the ones used by Thakurs or Rajputs! Names of gods! ... My parents named by younger brother Udai Singh, and all the Thakurs came with sticks to beat us up for using their father's name! They said that we were trying to become their fathers! What right did we have – how dare we take name like theirs! They threatened us saying that for our own good, we should not use such name,' said the Purbia bhaiya sadly. (Madhopuri 72)

Madhopuri has described in this autobiography how Dalit boys were treated very inhumanly by the upper caste boys. They abused Dalit boys just because they were poor and from a low caste. They remained anxious for any morsel of food which maddened them. Balbir narrates how Dalit boys were being treated in his village, "You can't control this litter. I myself will drive them away, the mother's ...' and he would jump up mouthing an obscenity, which we all completed in our minds" (Madhopuri 12).

Dalits had to do all sort of works in their village and he wages of these people were decided by the zamindars. Apart from that, they had to do the sort of works which could not be done by the upper caste people, instead they hated those Dalits. Madhopuri describes that the Chamars of his village had to carry the carcasses. He narrates, "They tied the hooves of the dead animal together and passed a hold through them, which they then carried across their shoulders, so that they could walk easily and comfortably. The animal hung upside down, and swung from side to side, its ears and neck shaking with every step" (Madhopuri 25). Sheoraj Singh Bechain's father and his relatives also did the same work and Sheoraj also helped his father in this work because his father's one of the legs was broken and he faced difficulty in his work. He had also seen many difficulties in his life like Madhopuri. Omprakash Valmiki describes how they were forced to eat the left-over food. Laxman Gaikwad describes how his tribe was branded as the thief by the police. The autobiographies of these people have created milestones in the Dalit Literature.

Caste has become a very serious issue these days. Politicians also grab good votes at the name of caste discrimination and the poor public easily comes in their oily words. Dalits have been humiliated badly and Madhopuri has frankly described how Dalit children were treated by the upper caste people, "Which bitch gave birth to you? Stop, or I'll cut you into pieces!" (Madhopuri 41). Madhipuri's grandmother also kept reprimanding him. She considered him a fool. She would tell him about the bad days she had seen in her life. Madhopuri has written about this incidence in the chapter "Daadi's Saga". She was a dominant woman who ordered everybody in the house. She did not allow her to boil water for taking bath. Balbir writes in this context, "Daadi would scold and taunt my mother whenever she bathed us with hot water during winter. She would say, 'Don't use all the wood to heat the water! Couldn't you put it in the sun for some time?" (Madhopuri 127)

Balbir Madhopur had to face many difficulties in Delhi also when he lives at a rented house. People were not ready to keep him on rent due to his low caste. They did not like his large family. When he was looking for a house on rent, a person from Himachal Pradesh comments after knowing about him and his job, "You have been living in Delhi for so many years and are still looking for rented accommodation! Do you have any bad habits ... drinking or ...?" (Madhopuri 207-08)

Conclusively, it can be said that Balbir Madhopuri has combated with so many problems of his life. His autobiography has brought his pain to the world. Other Dalit autobiographies also have paved way to open new avenues for many people. Dr Sadhana Agrawal holds the view, "The grim pictures of penury can easily be seen in Dalit narratives" (Agrawal 99). These autobiographies have revolt and resistance as a strong theme in them. Balbir Madhopuri has remained successful in depicting the pain of his caste in his autobiography. Dipak Shivaji Jamdhade also comments in this context:

> Differentness and revolt are the special qualities of Dalit literature. In comparison to the mainstream literature, Dalit literature is different in case of language, experience, and hero. While the mainstream literature is merely for entertainment, Dalit literature puts the heart- rending stories of Dalit life. Dalit hero suffers too much in life and fights to get his inborn right to live, and social justice. (Jamdhade 86)

Works Cited

Agrawal, Sadhana. "Exploitation of Leather-Workers in Balbir Madhopuri's *Changiya Rukh: Against the Night.*" *Dalit Men's Autobiographies: A Critical Appraisal.* Ed. Bijender Singh. New Delhi: Kalpaz, 2017. 95-102. Print.

Bhushan, Ravi. "Balbir Madhopuri's *Changiya Rukh* - A Critique of Dalit Identity and Politics." Ed. M.S. Thirumalai. 11.3. (2011): 1-8. Web.

Jamdhade, Dipak Shivaji. "The Subaltern Writings in India: An Overview of Dalit Literature." The Criterion An International Journal in English. 5.3 (June 2014): 86-89. Web.

Radhakisan, Yeshwant Madhav. "The Dalit and Non-Dalit Women Autobiographies." 2.3. (Sept. 2011): 1-5. Web.

Sharma, Himanshu. "Prejudicial Caste Hegemony in Balbir Madhopuri's *Changiya Rukh: Against the Night.*" *Indian Dalit Autobiographies: Marginalised Voices*. Ed. Bijender Singh. Authorspress, New Delhi, (2015): 219-225. Print.

Singh, Shweta. "Representation of Dalit Women in Dalit Men's and Women's Autobiographies." *SubVersions: A Journal of Engineering Research in Media and Cultural Studies*. 2.1 (2014): 48- 66.

25

The Hunted Body and the Haunting Retaliation in Mahasweta Devi's *Draupadi*

— *Dr Sakunthala A.I.*

Since time immemorial, women have always remained the underdogs and have been made the victims of humiliation, torture and exploitation. Condition of women from the marginalised section of the society need to be closely analysed as there is no real independence for them. Tribal and lower caste women stand at the lowest end of the hierarchy of women. Even after more than seventy years of Independence, India's rural poor and tribals are lamenting under the curbing effects of destitution, unemployment, illiteracy and human trafficking. For these people, notions of liberty, equality and democracy have no meaning at all. However, partly because of their biological, sexual difference and the socio-cultural surroundings to which they belong, the consequences of these above said social evils are much more on women, especially subaltern women. Giving voice to such oppressed subalterns, gendered subalterns and Indian women in general, Gayatri Chakravorty Spivak says, "For if, in the context of colonial production, the subaltern has no history and cannot speak, the subaltern as female is even more deeply in shadow" (Bill 218-19) and she concludes with the declaration that the subaltern cannot speak.

The worst among all tortures was the establishment of his control over her body that would ensure her subordination as long as he wanted. Mahasweta Devi, the renowned Bengali writer, was disgusted by the modes of humiliation that the lower castes, especially, the womenfolk are subjected to, and the dirty game of politics that tries to break the spirit of men and women who fight for emancipation from slavery on behalf of their class and clan. Hence she embarks on a project of presenting the shocking realities that happen behind the socio-economic and political iron curtains, through her most powerful work, *Draupadi*.

Mahasweta Devi presents the politics of domination, caste oppression, material violence, inhuman torture, repressive discourse, historical marginalisation and engineered exclusion and liberates conventional epistemological bind. But surprisingly, now the woman, the so-called 'subaltern' can ultimately resist and speak when pushed to the ultimate margin. In this story her aim is to focus on the strength of women who walked shoulder to shoulder in the insurgencies. The tribals have lost their land and their identity is trodden over, likewise their women are raped and humiliated. At the end of the story, the protagonist Dopdi emerges as empowered; who can challenge her assailants even when unarmed. The corporal torture this tribal woman underwent is metamorphosed into a tool for asserting her femininity.

"Literature is, by its very nature, intensely allusive: its classics or models once recognised as such, echo and re-echo through all subsequent ages" (Northrope Frye 41). In her short-story *Draupadi* (first appeared in *Agni Garbha* or *Womb of Fire*, a collection of loosely connected short narratives) Mahasweta Devi ventured to write an episode from the great epic, *Mahabharata* and as a feminist response to the myth of Draupadi, she reinvented cultural history that deconstructs the representation of women, cultures, images, stereotypes and archetypes. The characters of Draupadi in the *Mahabharata* and Dopdi of Mahasweta Devi's *Draupadi* are so different, yet there is a meeting point where both try to fight against the injustice meted out to them in their own manner. The revenge motif in both the cases is very much prevalent; however, there is some kind of difference. The revenge of Draupadi is one reason behind the great war of *Mahabharata*. In Mahasweta Devi's *Draupadi* there is no revenge taken for her humiliation, but she decides her own method. By using her mutilated, bruised body as a weapon for counter-offense and counter-resistance, she emerges as a new female.

The story has at its backdrop the Naxalbari Movement of Bengal which started as a rural revolt of landless workers and tribal people against landlords and money lenders. Dopdi Mejhen, a Naxalite informer-activist, along with her husband Dulna Majhi, had rebelled against the oppressive state-feudal nexus. In the time of drought, Surha Sahu refused to let the tribals share their unlimited water resources. This instigated the rage of the suffering tribals and led them to join the Naxalite group and culminated in the revenge killing of Surja Sahu and his sons. In the aftermath of this killing, and consequent upon the brutal and indiscriminate man hunt launched by the state, Dopdi and Dulna were forced to flee and live the life of fugitives. They kept on informing their comrades about the movement of the army. In order to suppress the Naxalite movement and contain the deviance inherent in it, the state launches 'Operation Jharkani,' initially under Arjan Singh and then under Senanayak, "a specialist in combat and extreme left politics" (Spivak 393).

After escaping from Bakuli, Dopdi and Dulna have worked at the house of virtually every landowner and hence they can inform their comrades about their targets. In their movement, they too are soldiers, for they too are fighting for their rights. But Senanayak and other soldiers act like hunters and the tribals are the hunted. The wild animal can easily be located and hunted down near a water hole, so the soldiers in hiding guard the falls and springs that are the only source of drinking water. Finally, with the help of army informant Dukhiram Gharari, the soldiers succeeded in locating and killing Dulna when he was drinking water lying on his stomach. But the search for Dopdi continues. All measures are taken for her entrapment. Senanayak uses the body of Dulna as bait thinking that Dopdi will definitely come to take the body, but she doesn't fall prey to this trap. Since then, Dopdi Mejhen is on the 'most wanted' list of the police and is living life anonymously. It is at this stage that the story opens.

Dopdi is introduced to the readers between two versions of her name, Dopdi and Draupadi. Named after *Mahabharata*'s heroine Draupadi, Devi's lower-caste protagonist is given the name by her upper-caste mistress. We are told that she can't even pronounce it as Gayatri Chakravorty Spivak explains "the Dalit tongues and dialects simply don't form those syllables, and she is called Dopdi, instead." The story opens with the discussion between two liveried uniforms, "What is this, a tribal called Dopdi? The list of names I brought has nothing like it! How can anyone have an unlisted name?" (Spivak 392). Dopdi is on the list of wanted persons, yet her name is not on the list of appropriate names for the tribal woman.

A reward of two hundred rupees is announced for her head. Mr Senanayak, the official, moves with the tribals as their friend and successfully corners Dopdi in the evening. "Draupadi Mejhen was apprehended at 6.53 P.M. It took an hour to get her to camp, questioning another hour exactly. No one touched her and she was allowed to sit on a canvas camp stool. At 8.57 P.M. Senanayak's dinner hour approached and saying, "Make her. Do the needful," he disappeared. "She turns her eyes and sees something white. Her own cloth, Noth-ing else. Suddenly she hopes against hope. Perhaps they have abandoned her. For the foxes to devour. But she hears the scrape of feet. She turns her head, the guard leans on his bayonet and leers at her. Draupadi closes her eyes. She doesn't have to wait long. Again the process of making her begins. Goes on. The moon vomits a bit of light and goes to sleep. Only the dark remains. A compelled spread-eagled still body. Active pistons of flesh rise and fall, rise and fall over it" (401).

What follows is a horrible description of the ordeal Dopdi underwent. "Opening her eyes after a million light years, Draupadi, strangely enough, sees sky and moon. Slowly the bloodied nail heads shifts from her brain. Trying to move she feels her arms and legs till tied to four posts. Something sticky under her ass and waist. Her own blood. Only the gag has been removed. Incredible thirst. In case she says 'water' she catches her lower lip in her teeth. She senses that her vagina is bleeding. How many came to make her? ...then Draupadi Mejhen is brought to the tent and thrown on the straw. Her piece of cloth is thrown over her body" (401).

In the morning, the time comes for Dopdi to be taken to Burra Sahib. But in a flash the whole scene shifts. We suddenly come across a completely transformed Dopdi. At first, it is a sense of shame that pervades her. But soon, her tough spirits make her realise that her body is her weapon and her voice. Deprived of everything in life, she has to hold on to her physical self, which alone is her sole possession in this inhumane world. When struck with this comprehension, she realises that there is nothing for her to be ashamed about because it is an immoral act practised on her by men who profess to be the guardians of women's chastity. Like Draupadi of *Mahabharata*, Devi's Dopdi also refuses to abide by conventions after being humiliated and mutilated. She changes her nakedness into a powerful weapon. Refusing to cover herself in front of Senanayak, Dopdi tears away the sari and throws the water on the ground in a symbolic gesture. She then walks towards Senanayak with her head held high, full of anger, disdain and defiance. Senanayak is bewildered to see her naked walking towards him in the bright sunlight with her head held high. "What is this? He is about to bark, but stops" (402). The reader, along with Senanayak is taken aback when Dopdi bursts out "The object of your search, Dopdi Mejhen. You asked them to make me up, don't you want to see how they made me?" (402) Dopdi wipes the blood on her palm and says in a voice that is terrifying, sky splitting, and sharp, "What's the use of clothes? You can strip me, but how can you clothe me again? Are you a man?" (402)

Mahasweta Devi makes it very explicit through Dopdi's reaction that the physical body that experiences torture and humiliation is in fact a weapon in the hands of a woman, to be brandished boldly against all forces of oppression that seek to subdue her personality and her status. Her reaction is an effective mode of resistance and transference of the guilt on to the shoulders of the perpetrator himself. The irony lies in the fact that the patriarchal hegemonistic societies, which weave myths and legends about protecting the honour of women at any costs, at a given opportunity, make all attempts to violate it, exposing the hypocrisy behind all such ideals. All activists are subjected to inhuman and brutal punishment and women activists especially are intimidated which inevitably culminates in sexual exploitation. Looking at *Draupadi* from this point of view, one can understand that the rape of Dopdi is an act by the chauvinistic men whose main aim is to subdue femininity.

Mahasweta Devi who is famous for reinventing epics and mythologies has wonderfully woven a story of exploitation round the ancient epic Mahabharata to suit the modern industrial age. The resistance of Dopdi definitely brings to mind how Draupadi, wife of Pandavas, was publicly humiliated when her husband Yudhishtira loses her in the game of chess to Kauravas. Draupadi was in a state of seclusion and insists that she should not be taken away, but is dragged to the assembly hall by her loose hair which is tantamount to rape in symbolic terms. Dushasana further goes on and attempts to strip her publicly by pulling her sari, but fails to do so as the sari continues to lengthen endlessly due to the divine intervention of Lord Krishna. Draupadi vows that she will not do her hair till the time she washes her hair with the blood of Dushasana, and thus, she avenges the violation of her dignity. She exhibits her violated condition by displaying the unbraided hair that was an instrument of her violation. Draupadi plays a pivotal role in the epic as she is the one who was responsible for the great battle in Mahabharata between Pandavas and Kauravas.

Devi reconstructs the myth of subaltern woman as her protagonist breaks away from the shackles of false notions of shame. The ancient Draupadi is rescued by divine intervention but the modern Draupadi i.e. Dopdi in contrast does not even appeal to the humanitarian considerations of her captors since she is sure that no help will arrive from any quarter. Unlike the mythical Draupadi, she does not entreat for divine benignity too. She is positively definite that since all morality and humanity has vanished, no redeemer will save her from harassment; instead there are only predators all around waiting to attack and denude her. Hence she takes her own decision to boldly confront her offenders. Just as her ancient counterpart swears not to tie up her hair that was dishevelled until Bhima smears it with the blood of Dushasana, so Dopdi too refuses to wear the clothes that were forcibly removed from her body by Senanayak's men.

With her unconquerable will, she gives Senanayak a challenge to counter her. Turning the bleeding dreadful wounds of her breasts into defensive attack, she pushes Senanayak with her mangled breasts and "for the first time he is afraid to stand before an unarmed target, terribly afraid" (402). It is ironical to know that Senanayak who at the beginning of the story gave order to make up Dopdi, finds himself badly afraid at the sight of her crude female sexuality. This is how Draupadi, a subaltern and exploited tribal woman represents her class.

Rajeswary Sunder Rajan notes that when Dopdi is asked to come to Senanayak's tent for further questioning, she refuses to wash herself and erase the sight of night's brutality, thereby she challenges and derides their masculinity, "It is simultaneously a deliberate refusal of a shared sign-system (the meanings assigned to nakedness, and rape: shame, fear and loss) and an ironic deployment of the same semiotics to create disconcerting counter effects of shame and confusion and terror in the enemy" (Rajan 352-3).

Mahasweta Devi insists and emphasises that at this point of the story the male leadership fails and Dopdi ceases to exist as a subaltern. It seems as if Dopdi dies in her and a new Dopdi is born out of the ashes. When she protests against the entire hungry phallus society and contemptuously asks "what more can you do? Come on, counter me – come on counter me" (402). Here she challenges the entire politico-sexual enemies to encounter her. Gayatri Spivak writes that the illiterate and low-born woman teaches the male officials a shocking lesson that they are unable to face 'the unarmed target.' It is when she crosses the sexual differential into the field of what could only happen to a woman that she emerges as the most powerful 'subject', who still using the language of sexual honour, can derisively calls herself 'the object of your search,' whom the author can describe as a terrifying super object – 'an unarmed object.'

The term empowerment refers to a range of activities from individual self-assertion to collective resistance, protest and mobilisation that challenge basic power relation. For individuals and groups where class, caste, ethnicity and gender determine their access to resource and power, their empowerment begins when they recognise the systematic forces that oppress them, but act to change existing power relationships. Empowerment, therefore, is a process aimed at changing the nature and direction of systematic force that marginalise women and other disadvantaged sectors in a given context" (Miller 53).

Draupadi depicts how a marginalised tribal woman derives strength from her body and her inner feminine core to fight against her marginality. Here, the woman's body becomes an instrument of vicious denunciation of patriarchy and hegemony which are ironical, counter-canonical, anti-literary and contradictory. Draupadi embodies hegemonic masculinity, female emancipation, double colonisation, centre-periphery articulation, master-slave dialectics and gender-bender dynamics. Here the erotic object transforms into an object of torture and revenge, where the line between hetero-sexuality and gender-violence conjures.

Mahasweta Devi does not romanticise the tribal woman, rather her writing is so realistic that it shakes each reader out of his slumber and asks for renewed understanding with regard to tribal identity and their rights. A constant supporter of the marginalised, she tells through Dopdi that women who endure physical abuse and sexual assault need not suffer from distress or resort to suicide. Their victimised physical body that has been misused and regimented by power wielding men can itself be transcribed to become an autonomous voice of fierce protest. In this context, Dopdi's act can be seen as an act that subverts the exploitative system and it empowers her. Beauvoir says, "If the respect or fear inspired by woman prevents the use of violence towards her, then the muscular superiority of the male is no source of power" (Beauvoir 212). Empowerment makes the two ladies, Draupadi and Dopdi, question the members of the society of their roles that pulls up the unmitigated hidden power in them that simply jolts the patriarchal authority.

Dopdi is the new woman born and even if she is not able to bring some magical change, which is not possible, it is predictable that she is going to usher a new outlook of woman. This new woman has challenged the age old patriarchy without any movement and without any sound. She begins another war in her own silent manner. This questioning or rather this challenge on the part of a subaltern certainly causes discomfort to the authorities or to the community, but it is a definite therapy to effect healing operations to the long-drawn infections inherent in the society. Thus, Mahasweta Devi's *Draupadi* reveals a new true face of feminist assertion where the protagonist uses her wholeness of mind and body to fight against her marginalised identity.

Works Cited

Frye, Northrope. "The Developing Imagination." *Learning in Language and Literature.* Cambridge: Harvard U P, 1963. Print.

Miller, Lisa Valerie. *A New Wave of Power and Politics: The Action Guide for Advocacy and Citizen Participation*. Aurora: Just Associates, 2007. Print.

Rajan, Rajeswary Sundar. *Real and Imagined Women*. London: Routledge, 1993. Print.

Simon, Beauvoir. *The Second Sex*. London: Vintage, 1997. Print.

Spivak, Gayatri Chakravorty. Trans. "Draupadi" by Mahasweta Devi. Kolkata: Seagull, 1988. Print.

26

Hunger, Thievery and Resistance in Laxman Gaikwad's *Uchalya: The Branded*

— Dr Sadhana Agrawal

Dalits are the marginalised and underprivileged populace found almost in every state of India. They were known as Shudras or untouchables by the society. But time has undergone a change now and these days their position has been gradually improving since the last two centuries. They were considered callous and many people looked down upon them due to their low living status and awkward eating habits which all stem from their penury. Vinayraj writes about them, "If God is immaterial, God doesn't matter for Dalits" (Vinayaraj 7). In fact, they were bound to live a degraded life because they were deprived of their education and the fundamental rights. Now they are achieving status and reputation because many Dalit activists and writers such as Dr B.R. Ambedkar, Baburao Bagul, Jyotirao Phule, Savitribai Phule, Namdev Dhasal etc worked for the upliftment of Dalits. Many writers created Dalit consciousness through their works; they shared their agonies with other people and took the path of resistance which opened the way of liberation and equality for them. Among such Dalit writers and activists, Laxman Gaikwad's name can be taken at the topmost level because his social and literary contribution is very remarkable.

Laxman Maruti Gaikwad is a Marathi Dalit literary figure born in a small village Dhanegaon in Latur District of Maharashtra state on July 23, 1956. He had been a convener in the Sahitya Akademi, New Delhi. He had been a member in Maharashtra State Commission for Backward Classes and the president for All India De-notified Nomadic Tribes Association. This organisation works for the liberation and welfare of the tribal people who are at the fringe level in the society and have to live their life from hand to mouth. He had also worked for the labour class, slum dwellers, farmers, and the have-nots. He has dedicated his life to the economically disadvantaged people whose life is not much better than the animals. He has won many prestigious awards such as Sahitya Akademi Award in 1988, Sahitya Ratna Anna Bhau Sathe Puraskar in 2000, SAARC Literary Award in 2001, Gunther Sontheimer Memorial Award in 2005 and Maharashtra Gourav Puraskar etc. He is a social activist also and he has been working for the upliftment of the Dalit and tribal people. He had been the president of the Jankalyan Vikas Sanstha from 1986 to 1990. He has written his novels in Marathi. His first published book was 'Uchalya'. Before that had had written poems. His novels are *Dubhanga, Chinimaatitildiwas, Wadarvedaana, Uthao, Wakil Pardi*; and his critical works are *Samaj Sahitya aur Swatantrya, Vimuktbhatkyacheswatantrya, Dr Baba Saheb Ambedkar Chajeevanaurkarya* (edited), *Buddha ki Viapaasana* etc.

The autobiography *Uchalya: The Branded* is a realistic portrayal of hunger, poverty, starvation, odium and resistance. The people of this community were branded as thieves and in fact, their main occupation was also petty thievery. Hunger was their major problem and these people were forced to take the path of crime so that they may be able to fill their empty stomachs, "Due to the same reason, the life of tribal has been reduced to inhuman level where there is no option left for them but to steal and live" (Deshmukh 2).

The people of these nomadic tribes had no any other option except petty professions which yielded meagre income to them. They had to either beg or steal failing which they had to remain hungry. Hunger turns a man into a criminal. The people of this community were not given any work for their livelihood lest they should commit a crime at their working place. Moreover, these people were ostracised from the main locality and had no any place to live in. The people of their community were considered wretched and impure and they had no identity of their own. Laxman Gaikwad depicts the social stratification and its subsequent consequences in an interview with Dr Bijender Singh:

> The social system of my village was under the dominance of Varna-Vyavastha and caste system. Because of this, there was no respect for us in the village. We were not even the permanent residents of the village. We were residing outside the village in tiny huts. We belong to a tribe which was branded as a criminal tribe and the people were considered as criminals by birth. I was the first kid from this community who went to school. (Singh 350).

Even the women of the family had to work so that they may help fill the empty stomachs of their family. Gaikwad's mother Dhondabai had to go in the search of some work but she was not offered any kind of work at the farmhand. His grandmother Narasabai had to go to fairs and markets to pick pockets or steal something. Her targets remained particularly the children. She used to remove gold lockets and earrings from their necks. She used to steal ears trinkets and necklaces from women's necks. The hunger was prevalent in the houses of Uchalya community to the extent that if the people had returned empty handed, the children at home had to sleep without food. Sometimes their family would have nothing to eat for four five days and in that condition the people would beat the stolen ears of corn, winnowed the grain, grinded the grain coarse and put it on the fire to boil so that they may satisfy their hunger. There were big families and many mouths were in a single family and it was impossible for a single person, without job, to fill the stomach of all these people without any permanent source of income. There was no any attention on cleanliness in this community. Gaikwad writes about it, "I did not take a bath for months. Nobody from the household ever told me to take a bath. Washing clothes was not even thought of" (Gaikwad 12).

The hunger had made these people selfish and tyrannous to the extent that they had to eat the animals they picked up such as rats, rabbits, deer, sheep, doves, mongoose, goats, peacocks, partridges, ducks, cranes, tortoises etc. The hunger makes a person degraded also. Whenever Gaikwad's hunger was not properly satiated and his brother also would not give him any share of his food, Gaikwad would lick his hands to show his hunger. He had to beg to fill his stomach and he did not hesitate in begging. He would sometimes go with his sister-in-law. She would plead to give some food telling that the poor child was hungry. She would ask for a few stale pieces of leftover Bhakar. In this way, he would live his life. He showed childish habit of licking the plate with his tongue when he would not get the sufficient food to eat. He would look at other family members and he would start scrapping whatever was struck at the bottom of the pot. Even the food was a major problem for these people. Gaikwad also had to see very bad days in his life. He writes about his temptation of food:

> I used to set out with this food to the farm where father worked. From the vegetable in the bowl came an enticing smell. When I saw those white Jowar Bhakar and buttermilk, my mouth would water. My conscience told me that the Bhakar given was just enough for my father. My belly, on the other hand, was all afire with hunger; moreover, never did we get such delicious bhakar and vegetable at home. (Gaikwad 38-39)

Gaikwad and his family faced many problems in their lives. They had to go to remote places so that they may get any farm from where they could steal full ears of wheat, jawar, bajra and ground-nuts. They removed all the evidences after stealing these corn ears. Thus, even after many efforts they were not able to eat to their fill. Gaikwad narrates about his hunger, "But my hunger was even then not fully satisfied. So I would get up in the morning and pick and eat the particles that had popped out of the pot while the grain was being boiled, and eat those caked-with-mud morsels" (Gaikwad 42).

The Ucahlya people had to take the biggest risks in their lives just to fill the empty stomachs of their family members. Gaikwad narrates a very terrible incident of his life. One day, his elder brother Dada had plucked the ears of the grain-crop. The farmers noticed the thieves and all the people of Uchalya community fled after throwing down the plucked ears. But Gaikwad's elder brother Dada took the risk and he ran carrying the plucked ears with him. He lagged behind from the other members of his gang. The farmer threw a stone at him and it hit him badly at his head. Dada did not pay attention to his deep wound and he kept on running so that his family members may get something to eat. Thus, these people take the risk of their lives in order to fill their stomachs.

The people of this community always remained in the lookout of some marriage feasts, funeral feasts and village feasts so that they may satisfy their hunger. They remained so anxious to eat at those occasions that they did not drink water before eating because they would not be able to eat well if they drink water. It was a common advice to the children of Uchalya community, "Children, don't drink water. If you drink water, you cannot eat well" (Gaikwad 44). The people of this community showed dishonesty also so that they might fill their empty stomachs. Gaikwad gives a description of the wedding of the Patil's son of Bhuani. Bundi was being served to the people who were invited to the feast from different villages. The people of Uchalya community also reached at this feast without any invitation and they got their share of bundi in the first round. They sat at the second and subsequent rounds also and filled their pockets with bundi. They finished the bundi in few minutes. Such occasions remained rare for them but they never missed such occasions and they would even put their honour and dignity at stake for a morsel of food. Gaikwad depicts it in his autobiography, "Eating such food that we rarely got; I began to crave for it. I did not care if I was cursed, beaten and thrown out; I ceased to feel ashamed of such humiliation. I would do anything to get even a little tidbit" (Gaikwad 46). They formed their gangs and reached at the ritual meals. When the guests had been taken their meals, they kept on looking at them greedily like dogs. Not only this, they started wailing loudly so that the people inside the house may hear their wails and give them some food to eat.

These people had no contribution in the social and cultural activities. They were given inhuman treatment and there was no place for them in any village activity because they were not considered the part of the mainstream society:

> Dogs barked and we wailed. Dogs also crowded with us for food to lick the left over from the thrown-out Patravali when the dinners had their food and left the hall, someone from among them would say, 'Oh there, throw these Pathruts some food'. Then we used to get half a roti and some vegetable in a bowl. Something they would throw at us the leftovers from the Patravalis of the dinners. We collected the Patravali and ate there right on the street (Gaikwad 46).

Gaikwad's school experience was also not much better than his time spent in his village. He had to face many difficulties in his admission to a school. He is refused to give admission in many schools. Omprakash Valmiki also had to face the same problem because he is not admitted in the primacy school so easily. Valmiki writes about his problems in getting admission in his autobiography *Joothan: A Dalit's Life*. Sharan Kumar Limbale faces problem in the school regarding the name of his father. Kumud Pawde describes her struggle to get her higher education in Sanskrit in his autobiography *Antaspot*. The essay "The Story of My Sanskrit" depicts her hindrances how her teachers were against choosing Sanskrit as a subject by her. All the Dalit writers had to face many problems in getting education, status and equality. Likewise Laxman Gaikwad remained firm at his decision of getting education. Ultimately, he got his admission in Songaon Residential School. It was a residential school and the students were given only two rotis and a piece of bread in their meal. It was not a strange thing for him because he had seen even the worst condition in his village. He did not complain to anybody regarding lack of his food. Instead his words reflect a ray of optimism, "Let it be, we are at least certain of getting daily meals. That is enough for me" (Gaikwad 72). He had to go to school without taking meals and he had to go outside the school in the search of food during interval. He writes his pain in these words:

> On occasions I had to go to school without eating Bhakar; and felt hunger gnawing in my belly; on such occasions Dagadya and I skipped school during the short recess and escaped through

> the window. We searched for beehives in the woods, looked on trees for the nests of pigeons. If we came across an egg, we would smear it with cow dung, boil it and eat it. We always kept a catapult and a match-box in our school bags. We killed pigeons and khaduls with the catapult, roasted them and ate them without Bhakar. (Gaikwad 74)

Gaikwad had to remain hungry during the harvesting season because all the men and women of his family would go to the fields and there was nothing to eat at home. When he was terribly hungry at him home, he would dig out and eat the roots of the Takali plant that grew by the Babhalgaon road. The taste of these roots was like coconut-kernel. When he went to school without eating any meal, his friend Ankush Mekle requested other friends to give some share of their food and then they gave him Bakhar.

Hunger and crime have been depicted as a main motif in this autobiography. The lower status of the people became the cause of social discrimination in the mainstream. The Uchalya people were ready to do anything to get food. Gaikwad also decided to learn magic so that he may be able to fight with his hunger. He thinks that after learning the skill of sorcery he would get some money but he hesitates in this act after much contemplating, "Whenever I felt hungry, I thought of asking Anjalibai to initiate me into the craft of sorcery and of eating human excreta on five Saturdays, so that I would never have to starve. Should people from good families practice sorcery? If I did not acquire the craft even after eating human excreta, what then. These questions deterred me from asking Anjalibai anything" (Gaikwad 85). Thus, hunger and penury were the unsolved problems for these people. They had no place which they can call their own. Laxman Gaikwad narrates about his life in an interview:

> The people of my community were leading a life worse than animals. I saw people in the religion, in which I was born developing intimacy with animals and keeping them along with them, but they despise human beings like us and they do not allow us to go near them. They pour food for the stones and other such statues to eat in the name of religion but they do not

give any food to the starving human beings. My community did not have any place to live (Singh 352).

Once Gaikwad's own household items were stolen and he had to eat at Shobha's house. His elder brother was suffering from epilepsy and there was neither money at his home nor a good medical facility nearby. These people had nothing to eat in their homes and whatever they had, there were chances that they might lose that also. Gaikwad's grandfather Lingappa was a state informer and he provided all the information of thievery to the police. The people of the Uchalya community were against him. They held a panchayat and they decided in their meeting that his murder could be the only solution of their problem otherwise they and their family-members were doomed to be hungry. They murdered him mercilessly and Gaikwad's grandfather was cremated secretly and the criminal activities of the Uchalya people resumed.

Police also enhanced the problems of the Uchalya community. The policemen were not the honest people and they misused their power. People of Gaikwad's community were treated inhumanly by the police. Some of the people were beaten to death even at the ground of suspicion in the criminal activities. Police never spared even the pregnant women, children and the old members of the Uchalya community. The backbones of many people were fractured by the police due to the barbarous thumping of the policemen's boots on their backs. Gaikwad's grandmother was barbarously hung upside down by the leg and the police thrushed burning cigarette-butts into her anus. Gaikwad's elder brother Anna was caught from the market when he was trying to steal an oil-tin. The police did not spare him and they thrust chilli powder in Anna's rectum, eyes and beat him black and blue.

Beating was a common practice in this community. It was one kind of training for them. The people were trained by beating so that they may not reveal the names of their crime partners if they get arrested. Thus these people were made so strong that they might not reveal the names of the other people of their gang even after the tyranny by the police. There was total chaos at the name of law and order. Whenever there had been the raid of the police, all the people of this community started trembling with fear because police did not spare anybody. Police whipped everybody whether the person is a thief or not. The police also involved in the criminal activities and they themselves took the valuable articles from the homes. If good things are found in their house, the police took them in their charge and later they distributed these things among them. Gaikwad writes in this context, "Dhondamai never knew stealing. She never went that way. Yet they pressed and squeezed her breasts and grilled her: Tell us where yours sons have hidden the stolen goods? She only wept bitterly. There was nothing in the hut, what could the poor mother show? They snatched away her Manglasutra and another cheap necklace" (Gaikwad 15). The police put false charges on the people so that they might extract money from them. The life of these people was much disturbed as they were not allowed to go outside from their village without getting a pass. This pass was like a God to them otherwise they were not allowed to leave their area. Dr Bijender Singh writes in his article, "These tribal people were not allowed to travel without the permission of the police. They had to seek permission if they went out of their territory. They were allowed to go at other place only for three days. They were not allowed to stay anywhere more than that period. Laxman called these people equal to animals as both need a certificate for carrying from one place to another" (Singh 52)

The Uchalya people were exploited from everybody. Upper caste people did not spare the women and the rich people charged high rate of interest from them. If the debtor is not able to pay the loan on time, he is captured, tied and kept in the house. Poverty had made these people criminal. The people failed to bring the material to cook food at their homes and thus, they became malnutritioned and weak. Laxman Gaikwad writes about his father, "My father was a tall man with a good bone-structure. Now he looked only a skeleton" (Gaikwad 171). There was lack of education and other faculties in their village and people lived at the mercy of their destiny alone. Gaikwad's autobiography depicts the life of people when India was still fighting with many more challenges but now the position of Dalits has improved a lot. S.M. Michael observes in this context:

The aspirations of contemporary Dalits are completely different from those of Dalits in traditional India. This change is due to the difference in the vision perceived by the Untouchables of the past and of today. Visions set the agenda for both thought and action; philosophical, political, or social theories are built on them. Believers in one vision will view themselves in a very different moral role from the followers of another (Michael 14).

Works Cited

Deshmukh, Suresh B. "The Upheaval of Tribal Women in Laxman Gaikwad's *The Branded*." *Epitome Journals*. 1.1 (May 2015): 1-8. Web.

Gaikwad, Laxman. *Uchalya*: *The Branded* (1998). Trans. P.A. Kolharkar. Delhi: Sahitya Akademi, 2009. Print.

Michael, S.M. (ed.) *Dalits in Modern India: Vision and Values* (1999). 2nd ed. Delhi: Sage, 2007. Print.

Singh, Bijender and Laxman Gaikwad. "Marginal Roots and Writings: A Conversation with Laxman Gaikwad." *The Expression: An International Multidisciplinary e-Journal*. 3.3. (June 2017): 349-355.

Singh, Bijender. "Dalit Resurrection in Laxman Gaikwad's *The Branded*." *Indian Scholar: An International Multidisciplinary Research e-Journal*. 1.1 (Sept. 2014): 50-56. Web.

Vinayaraj, Y.T. *Postcolonialism and Religions: Dalit Theology after Continental Philosophy*. New Delhi: Palgrave Macmillan, 2016. Print.

Index

C

D